Praise for *Women of Divorce*

"*Women of Divorce* is an authoritative, disciplined and illuminating work—equally fair to divorced wives, stepmothers and the daughters they share. Susan Shapiro Barash has given voice to the new millennium concept of co-mothering, and it is an empathetic voice. I suspect that women going through this painful time will find these pages comforting and supportive."

> – Sherry Suib Cohen, contributing editor of *Rosie* magazine and author of 18 books including *Hot Buttons: How to Resolve Conflict and Cool Everyone Down*

"In Susan Shapiro Barash's breakthrough book on the issues between mothers, daughters and stepmothers, the strains of failure are discussed and the opportunity for open communication is explored. Finally, there is a hopeful book on the subject of women in stepfamilies."

> – Susan Wilson Solovic, author of *The Girls' Guide to Power and Success*

"This is the book that will dispel myths and stereotypes that have plagued stepmothers since the beginning."

> – Susan Wilkins-Hubley, founder, secondwivesclub.com

"Divorce and remarriage can be emotional and frustrating. Thank you, Susan, for offering an insightful look at the intricate relationships between mother, stepmother and daughter. The heartfelt words of the women interviewed certainly put us on the right road."

> – Jann Blackstone-Ford, director of Bonus Families, a non-profit organization offering support and counsel to stepfamilies around the world

"In her groundbreaking book, Susan Shapiro Barash covers the territory of mothers, daughters and stepmothers, exploring each female's point of view. *Women of Divorce* offers encouragement for the millions of women in this triangle."

> – Nechama Tec, author of *Defiance* and *Dry Tears*

Praise for Susan Shapiro Barash's *Mothers-in-law and Daughters-in-law* and *Second Wives*

"Very candid. Readers will feel as if they know the women in this book personally. Beneficial for a mother-in-law, a daughter-in-law and even the son/husband."

   – *Bride Again*

"A fresh look at in-laws...provides hopeful advice for all parties, making this a valuable tool for newlyweds as well as those who have been experiencing in-law problems for years."

   – *Beach Haven Times*

"Barash reminds readers...even the worst relationship can be healed."

   – *Newsday*

"Help[s] women create solid bonds with their husbands and avoid feeling second-rate as Wife No. 2. [Barash's] helpful book...offers solid strategies for beating the statistics."

   – *Publishers Weekly*

"The book is for women thinking about becoming a second wife and those who have already taken the plunge."

   – *Tulsa World*

"Women will find Barash's voice comforting."

   – *Library Journal*

"A thoughtful account...Barash does a commendable job of presenting an objective view. Readers are given the tools to make the marriage successful."

   – *Today's Librarian*

"If you or someone you know is a second wife, don't hesitate to get or give this book."

   – *Bookviews*

"If there's anything wrong with this book, it's the title. First wives, second wives...and men would benefit from the insights and wise counsel."

   – *Stepfamilies* (Publication of the Stepfamily Association of America)

"Susan Shapiro Barash knows whereof she speaks—or in this case, writes. She's been there."

   – *Palm Beach Daily News*

"The author's lucid reasoning and logical advice are a boon."

   – *ForeWord Magazine*

"Fascinating, informative reading...for any woman anticipating marriage...as well as second wives who have already taken the plunge."

   – *The Midwest Book Review*

Women of Divorce

Women of Divorce

Mothers, Daughters, Stepmothers –
The New Triangle

Susan Shapiro Barash

New Horizon Press
Far Hills, New Jersey

Books by Susan Shapiro Barash

Mothers-in-Law and Daughters-in-Law:
Love, Hate, Rivalry and Reconciliation

Second Wives:
The Pitfalls and Rewards of Marrying Widowers and Divorced
Men

Sisters:
Devoted or Divided

A Passion for More:
Wives Reveal the Affairs that Make or Break Their Marriages

The Men Out There:
A Woman's Little Black Book

Inventing Savannah

Reclaiming Ourselves:
How Women Dispel a Legacy of Bad Choices

New Horizon Press
P.O. Box 669
Far Hills, NJ 07931

Susan Shapiro Barash
        Women of Divorce: Mothers, Daughters, Stepmothers –
        The New Triangle

Cover Design: Robert Aulicino
Interior Design: Susan M. Sanderson

Library of Congress Control Number: 2002101394

ISBN: 0-88282-222-5
New Horizon Press

Manufactured in the U.S.A.

2007   2006   2005   2004   2003   /   5   4   3   2   1

For my children, Jennie, Michael and Elizabeth Ripps

Author's Note

This book is based on extensive personal interviews of mothers, daughters, stepmothers and experts in the fields of matrimonial law, psychology, sociology, family therapy and counseling. Names have been changed and recognizable characteristics disguised of all people in this book except the contributing experts in order to protect privacy. Some characters are composites.

Table of Contents

Acknowledgments

I am deeply grateful to many people. Above all, I thank my husband, Gary Barash, for his understanding and unconditional love. I thank my parents, Selma and Herbert L. Shapiro, for their support. My father, as always, is an amazing researcher. I thank my in-laws, Helene and Theodore Barash, for their continual support, and I thank my dear friends and family members who are constant and patient. The impressive team at New Horizon Press, Joan Dunphy, Joseph Marron, Lynda Hatch, JoAnne Thomas and Rebecca Sheil, have been faithful and share my vision. I thank Suzanne Murphy at Sarah Lawrence College and Lewis Burke Frumkes and Carol Camper at Marymount Manhattan College. In publishing, I thank Cynthia Vartan, Lori Ames, Sarah Gallick, and Debra Sloan. I thank Robert Marcus, my attorney, for his guidance. Emilie Domer and Lillian Thairu, my student assistants, and Karen Wilder, my computer expert, have been terrific.

The professionals who contributed their thoughts to this book deserve acknowledgment: Brondi Borer, New York City divorce attorney, specializing in mediation and nontraditional family law; Dr. Ronnie Burak, clinical psychologist in private practice in Jacksonville, Florida; Dr. Donald Cohen, certified marriage and family therapist practicing in Weston, Connecticut, and co-author of *My Father, My Son*; Dr. Margorie Engel, President and CEO of the Stepfamily Association of America; Dr. Michele Kasson, psychologist practicing in New York and Long Island and staff member of the Lifeline Center for Child Development; Alice Michaeli, sociologist specializing in marriage and the family; Antoinette Michaels, ACSW, founder and director of the Hope Counseling Center in Sayville, New York; Claire Owen, psychologist and professor of psychology at Marymount Manhattan College; Amy Reisen, matrimonial lawyer practicing in Milburn, New Jersey; Brenda Szulman, CSW, therapist certified in marital counseling and specializing in Anxiety and Depressive Disorders; and Dr. Nechama

Tec, sociology professor at the University of Connecticut in Stamford, and author of *Defiance: The Bielski Partisan*.

To the hundreds of mothers, daughters and stepmothers who have revealed their heartfelt experiences, I am deeply indebted. These women cannot be thanked by name in order to preserve their anonymity and privacy. To each and every one and to the readers who share in their pain and joy, failures and successes, I am thankful—you are the reason for this book.

Foreword: Banishing the Evil Stepmother
by
Ronnie L. Burak, Ph.D.

One day long ago when we were small children, my sister and I were picking on each other as we often did. Our argument finally escalated to the point that my mother had enough and said in her stern drill-sergeant voice, "Both of you go to your rooms NOW." My sister, who must have been about four or five at the time, innocently turned to me and asked, "Is she our stepmother?" The myth of the wicked, cruel stepmother is longstanding.

We all grew up reading fairy tales written long ago that describe the plight of children whose mothers die, leaving them to the cruel fate of being raised by evil stepmothers. The story of *Hansel and Gretel* describes a poor family that was on the verge of starvation. The stepmother in the story is so mean that she tells her husband to send Hansel and Gretel out into the forest, so they will get lost and never return. In *Snow White* the stepmother's jealousy of her stepdaughter goes so far that she plans to kill poor Snow White by feeding her a poisoned apple. *Cinderella* depicts a wicked stepmother who treats her stepdaughter as a lowly servant forcing her to clean and tend the hearth, while her own daughters are pampered and spoiled. Both Snow White and Cinderella are portrayed, in direct contrast to their villainous stepmothers, as noble, all-giving and of course, extremely beautiful. The father in each story is noticeably absent, leaving the young maiden to fend for herself until she is rescued by a handsome prince.

Bruno Bettelheim, in his book, *The Uses of Enchantment*, writes about the role fairy tales play in child development: "The more I try to understand why these stories are so successful in enriching the inner life of a child, the more I realize that these tales in a much deeper way than any other reading material, start where the child really is, in his psychological and emotional being. They speak about his severe inner pressures in a way that the child unconsciously understands and without belittling the most serious inner struggles which growing up entails they offer examples of both temporary and permanent solutions to pressing difficulties."

Although Bettleheim uses the masculine example, many fairy tales reveal how painful it is for a female child to lose the safety, security, and love of a mother who provides the foundation for her emotional well-being. They convey how difficult it must be when a father remarries to positively attach to someone who appears to have moved into the place once occupied by the mother. After the original family unit is dissolved a young girl needs her father more than ever and now she must compete for his love with the new woman in his life. The situation is often made more difficult when the new wife brings along her children who are dealing with their own emotional needs. In this newly termed "blended family," parents are often blinded by their love for each other and naively imagine that the children will be as happy about this union of two families as they are. Many times this is not the case.

In this book, Susan Barash concentrates on the women of divorce. How well the relationship between stepmother and stepdaughter develops depends on many factors, the most important being the ability of father, mother and stepmother to be sensitive to the daughter and any of the daughters' needs and put them ahead of their own. This is often difficult to do when hurt feelings and anger get in the way. Sometimes these bad feelings can go on for years and fill two households with tension that affects all children and especially daughters.

Another major factor affecting the relationship between stepmother and stepdaughter is timing. Divorce is traumatic for any child. Adding a stepparent very soon can be an overwhelming experience that is just too much for a child to handle. A daughter needs to solidly establish her new relationship with her divorced or widowed dad and feel secure in it. This is especially important in the case of divorce if the daughter is not living with her father. It is equally important that mother and daughter have time to recover from the divorce and fortify their relationship before a new woman comes into the father's life.

Conversely, if the daughter has a strong relationship with her dad and he remains single for a long time, a daughter can feel abandoned when he does begin a serious relationship with someone. He will need to go out of his way to help his daughter through this difficult time or she will most likely be very resentful of his new wife. If the new wife has children of her own, the couple must be extremely sensitive to the difficulties that inevitably will arise around sharing rooms, toys, parents, time, money and love. As the story of Cinderella demonstrates, issues of favoritism and jealousy can go very deep. Blended families often come to see me for family therapy when the bitterness has gone too far, making it difficult to repair the damage. I strongly suggest that when a couple with children from previous marriages plans to marry, they consider counseling as soon as possible to talk about the potential problems that could arise before resentment develops.

The arrival of a newborn into the blended family often brings further complications. It is understandable that a daughter from the first marriage would feel that the father and stepmother will love the new baby more. It will take a lot of work on the stepmother's part to make sure that her stepdaughter feels included and has a special role in the baby's life. If every effort is made to help the stepdaughter feel comfortable, she can form a very close relationship with her new sibling.

One of the most important factors which determines how well the relationship between stepmother and stepdaughter will go is how well the stepmother and biological mother get along. Both women must be mature, and sensitive to the needs of the child. The child's biological mother needs to put away hurt, jealousy, and anger toward her ex-husband. When a daughter's divorced father remarries, the situation creates a tremendous amount of stress on the child and can lead to behavior problems, and depression. If the daughter can see that her mother has positive feelings about her ex-husband's remarriage and can get along with the stepmother, the daughter feels relieved and can stop worrying about how her relationship with her stepmother will affect her biological mother. Once the daughter recognizes that her biological mother can move on and find a new life for herself with work, friends, and possibly her own new relationship, the daughter can feel more at peace and allow herself to have a positive relationship with her father's second wife.

Money is a large issue in many second marriages and is something about which most mothers, daughters and stepmothers have strong feelings. Having money translates into maintaining a certain lifestyle and everyone in the triangle suffers because the money is divided into thirds. There is money that is allocated to the mother, money that is allocated to the daughter above and beyond child support, and money to support the new marriage. When the new marriage suffers financially, as it often may, this brings up many antagonistic feelings in the stepmother who may have to work very hard to help her husband support his first family. She must remember that this is part of the deal and that she is married to someone who still has obligations to his first family. The stepmother has to enter the marriage with her eyes wide open in terms of financial support and time that her husband should give his children from his first marriage. She has to be prepared to accept his obligations and make the best of them. Sometimes the biological mother watches as her children get less than they would have because her ex-husband has a new wife to support, and the mother feels that her family's quality of life is altered because of the divorce. All around, money evokes strong reactions. In some instances, the daughter observes that her father and his new wife live better than she and her mother live and, even though she may be fond of her stepmother, the daughter can not help but compare their lifestyles.

In a society where divorce is so frequent, remarriages will become more and more commonplace. In this atmosphere, many children are forced to adjust to new structures of parenting. In the case of daughters whose father remarry, stepmothers will play an increasingly important role in the young girls' lives. When a woman falls in love with a man who has children from a former marriage, she has to be willing to manage the responsibility of stepmothering. She must recognize that her husband's daughter is an innocent victim in the divorce and needs her father. Making the relationship between a stepmother and her stepdaughter work well takes an enormous amount of patience on the stepmother's part and the ability to greatly compromise her own needs.

Although there are now more triangles composed of stepmothers, daughters and mothers than there have ever been, guidelines on how to make the relationship work well are still in the process of being formulated. Because of this, it is especially important that women share their experiences with each other. Mothers, daughters and stepmothers need role models. They also need to know that they are not alone and that their feelings are shared by others in the same situations. They need to know that what may feel like a very uncomfortable relationship in the beginning can, with nurturing and work, one day turn into a very positive one.

Introduction

From the start, divorce casts its male and female participants into an unknown life of scheduling time with the children, battling over expenses, and being forced to choose sides. Despite all civility, it often seems to either parent that whenever a child is with the other parent, she is on that parent's side, while the absent parent is the odd one out. This sensation might prevail, whether intentional or not, for many years to come, perhaps a life time. Thus is the divided world of divorce and children.

After the divorce, new concerns arise, other problems occur and everyone regroups. Life as it was once known—the house, the car, the morning routines, feeding the dogs, the smallest rituals, all of it—is forever erased or changed. Initially the old life often is replaced with a new, transient life: a new apartment or home, a new route to school, a steady confusion. That is the first stage after divorce, when it becomes obvious that daughters, in particular, will never be the same. Since fathers are many times idealized by their daughters, it is often their mothers that daughters blame the most. The mother has made a major mistake in her life—a failed marriage— and asks her daughter to join her in paying dearly for it. Of course, fathers pay too, since in divorce, no one escapes, no one remains the same as before it happened. In time, however, with shaky faith, the participants reemerge to build again. This is true for the children and the adults. But it is an especially difficult realization for daughters of divorce.

It is with good reason that our daughters, as they step into the changing tide brought on by divorce, view their mothers with mixed emotions. The mother who could no longer tolerate an unhappy marriage and leaves or one who has been left, shatters many daughters' conceptions about family and marriage. The daughters learn that their mothers' roles, as divorced women, are not easy and that our society is not kind to single women, especially those who have had husbands and children. In their own pain, daughters often both resent and respect their mothers. Just as mothers must regroup, walk rocky roads toward second chances and heal their bruised souls, children also need to heal and form new lives. Although most wish the divorce never happened, once reality sets in, daughters must brace themselves for a long journey. When there are several daughters in the family, one common by-product of their parents' divorce is a fierce loyalty among the daughters which often sustains them.

Because second marriages, especially of divorced men, are common, daughters often find themselves sharing dinners with their fathers and their fathers' future partners. Daughters notice these women's style of dress and listen closely to their conversations, comparing these women to their mothers. When these daughters tell their mothers about these new women, it has to hurt the mothers. Some of these new women, undoubtedly, have their own daughters at home, kindred souls, also daughters of divorce. And in these cases, what do both sets of daughters wonder about this potential relationship? How can a daughter of divorce trust another man or another woman after what has occurred between her parents? How could a daughter possibly reconcile her mother's inability to live with her father with another woman's desire for him or another man's desire for her mother?

The year which follows the divorce is in many ways the most difficult period. By then the divorce status is recognized and people treat the splintered family accordingly. If the family lives in a small, conservative town where few marriages fall apart—visibly, at least—the new family unit is the cause of great gossip. Ironically, stepfamilies may be readily tolerated, while a single mother or father with children is scrutinized. Homes are often sold and smaller properties are either rented or bought as substitutes. Coupled with the knowledge that the original family will never be a whole unit again, children often begin to experience a lesser quality of life which is endemic in divorce. Daughters may begin to pity their fathers especially if the fathers were the one who had not wanted the marriages to end. Daughters pity themselves as well, because their hopes and dreams of a future with an intact family have been taken away.

Many mothers I interviewed described their sons as more settled (at least on the surface) than their daughters, post-divorce. Some sons appear to take their parents' divorces in stride and accept that life will be different. Many daughters, on the other hand, feel an overwhelming loneliness after the divorce; raised in a society that looks to women to nurture and care for families, to keep relatives in touch, the absence of a whole family resonates in every corner of their lives. As much as most mothers try to hold it together for their children, it usually becomes apparent that there are too many moving parts. It is during this period of divorce and immediately afterward that the family unit often erodes.

While research of the past ten years is mixed on how gender plays out for children of divorce, it has been noted that those children living with same sex single parents usually do better. According to Genevieve Clapp., Ph.D., in her book, *Divorce and New Beginnings*, single divorced mothers do better parenting their daughters but have less impact with their sons. Sons typically do better in an all-male environment. Experts agree that many boys act out immediately following the divorce while the majority of girls do not. According to M.J. Zaslow's report, "Sex Differences in Children's Response to Parent Divorce," boys often externalize their issues with their parents' divorce, thus adjusting more poorly to divorce than do girls at the outset. Because girls internalize these feelings, their reactions are less extreme in the beginning, but their distress lasts longer. While these findings do not assuage a mother's guilt, they do make a daughter's behavior and feelings more comprehensible.

There are newly single mothers who keenly remember, as do their children, that they were once a united family, and while damaged on the inside, they were whole to the outside world. In retrospect, a great many mothers realize that, despite the rewards of having had this image, the energy required to sustain it was not worth the effort.

In the years following a divorce, many sons mature quickly out of necessity. They are forced to meet their own needs and they come to accept life as it is offered. The daughters' approach does not seem comparable, nor does the result. Despite great efforts and the old adage that time heals all wounds, underneath, many daughters appear frail and disappointed. Contrary to the old myths about stepmothers, what often improves daughters' lives is the arrival of their father's new partner and the fact that she becomes a part of the fabric of their lives.

Out of my own experience when I divorced, the idea of this book was born. For me it is a very personal quest, and most compelling. As a professor of gender studies and as a remarried mother with two daughters and one son, I am acutely aware of how difficult it is to be female in modern society with the stigma of divorce only complicating this state further. Despite the plethora of books on divorce and children, there are none that explore the relationship between mothers, daughters and stepmothers. There is no literature which specifically addresses the post-divorce triangle that forms between mother, daughter and stepmother. It is because of my own daughters, and the healing process we each endured following my divorce, as well as the relationship that developed between myself, my daughters and their stepmother, that gave this project so much significance for me. It has become more important with the passage of time and as events unfolded.

I have studied daughters of divorce and their relationships with their mothers and stepmothers in an evolving process. Some daughters' lives are enriched by the double mothering of a mother and stepmother and others find their lives complicated without much reward. Between these stories are a myriad of possibilities for daughters of divorce. While there is the substance that two mother figures offer, it remains doubtful that there will ever be a time in their daughters' futures when being a daughter of divorce—with all the concomitant emotions—won't be a key part of them, of who they are and who they become.

Women of Divorce is the result of years of devoted research. I have spoken with psychologists, psychiatrists, social workers and divorce attorneys and I have read broadly on the topic. Most importantly, I have interviewed women and listened closely to hundreds of personal stories of mothers, daughters and stepmothers of all ages, walks of life and ethnicities. I have learned that most mothers, even angry ones whose ex-husbands left them for others, usually get on with their lives. The majority of stepmothers with whom I've spoken, many with their own tales of divorce and loss before their new marriages, become reconciled to whatever bond they can create with stepdaughters, despite what their initial dreams might have been. But I also found it is the daughters who years later are still affected by their parents' divorces: socially, emotionally, in relationships and in how they view the world and men. Whatever the future holds for them—marriage, divorce, marriage to divorced men with children, having daughters of their own—one thing is certain: their parents' divorces will influence their lives forever.

In 2000 the National Center for Health Statistics reported that half of all marriages for those between the ages of thirty-five and forty-five last an average of eleven years before ending in divorce. In every one thousand divorces, one thousand one hundred seventy-five children are affected. That leaves a lot of daughters struggling to make sense of their parents' divorces. Yet divorce isn't the only change in life with which these girls and young women must contend. Within five years, sixty percent of the divorced population will remarry. And while the other forty percent remains unattached, the Census reports that among the four million unmarried couples in the nation, half of these individuals have children of divorce. On top of their parents' split, daughters of divorce must deal with living in two homes, custody arrangements and not long after, parents' boyfriends and girlfriends, stepparents and stepsiblings. With men remarrying at a greater rate than women, often within three years of their divorces, the likelihood of having a stepmother in a daughter's life is great.

In the last fifteen years, over four million women in the United States have become stepmothers to eighteen million stepchildren. Thus daughters are not only more likely to have stepmothers but also to have to deal with stepfathers. These stepmothers will become integral parts of the daughters' lives, depending on the ages of the daughters. For instance, if a daughter is under ten years old, she will likely view her stepmother as another mother figure since her allotted time with her father will be shared with this woman for many years to come. For a daughter who is in her teens or older, the impact of the stepmother is diminished, because the daughter is more independent, more grown-up and has a life of her own.

With stepfamilies accounting for sixty-five percent of the population, the hope for most families is that the father's new marriage will be complication-free, without any competition between daughters and the new wife and with little impact on the mother/ex-wife. However, even in the best of circumstances, there are new schedules, new personalities and a restructuring of roles for everyone involved: the daughters, mother, stepmother and father. In reality, the beginning can be tenuous, evoking feelings of despondency and anguish for the daughters. This is further complicated with stepsiblings and, eventually for the forty percent of second wives who have not had children who will have babies within the first two years of their new marriages, half siblings. A stepfamily with stepsiblings and half siblings introduces new realities such as sharing rooms, stretching money and facing the end of fantasies about parents' reconciliations. While the stepfamily may one day become strong and solid, a great deal depends upon the stepmother's and the mother's attitudes toward each other.

The mother's position toward the stepmother is pivotal in terms of the success of the daughter of divorce/stepmother bond. Most daughters take their cues from their mothers. If their mothers accept the second marriages, the daughters may as well. Nevertheless, the stepmothers bring unknown qualities into the new marriages/new families and into the stepdaughters' lives. Only if the daughters are responsive to their stepmothers will they benefit. In fact, I found that the distress over the loss of the original intact family is eased if the father's new marriage provides a successful stepmother relationship and if the mother has successfully reinvented her own life. If both parents remarry, the daughter becomes a part of two stepfamilies; a challenge even in the best of circumstances.

I have listened closely to stories told by female friends, students and strangers in this new triangle from every point of view as each person explained her position and her place in the entangled realm of mothers, daughters and stepmothers. This population of girls and women to whom I spoke represent diverse socioeconomic boundaries and ages. The daughters who came forth to share their stories are between the ages of sixteen and thirty. The ages of the mothers and stepmothers who I interviewed range from twenty-five to sixty. It is notable that, regardless of how disparate the backgrounds, there is a great fund of common experience.

Often the daughters to whom I spoke had stepmothers that were substantially younger than their mothers, sometimes midway between the age of the adolescent or college-age daughter and the ex-wife. This was at times disturbing to the daughters who felt competitive. In other cases, it could be beneficial, with the stepmother giving insight in areas where the mother does not. As one nineteen-year-old stepdaughter explained, "My stepmother is the one I confide in when it comes to boys and clothes. My mother guides me about school and friendships and having a career."

Nevertheless, the loyalty of the daughters is divided and the dissolution of the original family haunts them. For these daughters, there is a certain consolation to be found in their friends who are in similar positions. When they gather with these friends, they often compare notes on topics like finances and custody, and they share their hopes and fears, especially about their fathers' dating patterns or new wives—topics that often bring about the most anxiety.

Of the daughters interviewed for this project, sixty percent revealed they experienced reduced self-esteem and senses of insignificance when their fathers remarried. Almost all desire the validation of both their fathers and their stepmothers. For the forty percent of those interviewed who felt sure of themselves despite their parents' divorces and their fathers' remarriages, there was stability found in the co-parenting of the divorced mothers and fathers. The daughters in the forty percent group revealed that their stepmothers are available emotionally but do not try to replace the mothers. Furthermore, they reported that affirmation from the father, particularly for adolescent girls, is evident.

How daughters relate to their stepmothers and what they expect of them and wish for themselves becomes a personal odyssey, one that takes on many characteristics which are unique to the individual stepmothers and daughters, yet remains influenced by the mothers. Undeniably, I found that even in the smoothest of transitions, there is enormous upheaval in the daughters' lives. Until a divorce occurs, daughters believe that they exist in realms where parents stay married, whether they are happy or not. When this fantasy is destroyed, the daughters' lives are no longer the same.

For those raised in conventional families, divorce continues to carry a stigma and a sense of dread. In the optimal scenario for daughters of divorce, inner strength is discovered and endures. The confusion and sadness occasioned by the early experience of parents' divorcing become distant memories and in their place, hopefully, comes resiliency.

In a divorce, no one dies, yet there is mourning, unrelenting grief and wounded survivors. Of these survivors, daughters seem the most vulnerable and fragile of all. The emotional baggage is everywhere, even as the sheer hope of future happiness, of a fresh start, propels us forward. I view myself and my daughters as a part of this group. I have confided to my friends that at times, I feel a failure. I have failed my daughters who will not grow up in the stable, intact family that enveloped me. There is no doubt we have each paid dearly for the divorce. However, the good news is that I and my daughters have slowly but surely recovered and are building new, enriching lives. I know too, from the stories shared with me by mothers, stepmothers and daughters, that most of the women of the triangle are able to move past the pain and anguish of the divorce, adjust to their new lives and build satisfying, even rewarding relationships with one another.

CHAPTER 1

Daughters: Forever Triangled/Forever Hopeful

"Although my parents fought constantly, I never expected them to divorce," admits Bethany, who at twenty has been a daughter of divorce for six years. "I always had this sick feeling in the pit of my stomach when friends told me that their parents were divorced. I couldn't imagine how they got through it, having to pick one parent over the other and living in two houses. Then my parents got divorced and my father moved out, taking my older brother with him. Our family dissolved before my eyes. My mother spent all of her waking hours on the telephone. She cried constantly. We began to eat cereal for dinner every night.

"During the divorce period, unforgettable things were said and done. I saw our house, which had once represented such stability, as a prison. My mother and I were left there to rot. When my father came by to pick me up, he and my mother had these horrifying scenes. I couldn't wait for the nightmare to end. I decided that one of two things would happen: my parents would get back together or my father would remarry, like all my friends' fathers. I don't remember how long it took before I gave up hoping for my parent's reconciliation."

We expect our mothers and fathers to be there for us, a united front against the world. The image of the picture-perfect family is held up to daughters, reinforcing that illusion. From a very early age, daughters feel responsible for this myth. The image of the harmony of family life—dinners, outings, holidays, vacations—is set before us on a regular basis. Beyond these seemingly essential ingredients in the fast moving, superficial profile of the ideal American family is a sense of completion, of oneness. Nothing can be more harmful than to rend this fabric. In every stage, be it childhood, adolescence or adulthood-we would do anything to hold it together, to perpetuate the fiction that all families live in a state of constant bliss.

Brenda Szulman, a clinical social worker, notes that most daughters would prefer to see their parents remain together despite the level of strife in the marriage. "Even if the marriage was fragmented, daughters can stand conflict if the parents still stay together. In fact, there may be a good result from living in a contentious atmosphere. If daughters see marriages can withstand this contention, then the daughters learn how to negotiate the world of ambivalence. It is when the marriage cannot withstand the conflict that a divorce ensues."

The Stepfamily Foundation reports that in the United States one out of two marriages ends in divorce and that over sixty million American children under the age of thirteen are living with one biological parent and that parent's partner. Almost half of the female population who are not mothers, are likely to live in stepfamily relationships, including cohabiting arrangements. The United States Census Bureau reports that sixty-five percent of remarriages involve children from prior marriages and that fifty percent of children will have parents who divorce before the children are eighteen years old. Regardless of daughters' hopes, statistics tell us that the chances of remaining in an intact family are one in two.

The Disintegrating Family

When the seemingly "flawless" family crumbles, often daughters are crushed. Hopeful and idealistic, these girls had banked on the concept of cohesive families. The daughters might blame themselves or blame one of the parents, usually the one who has initiated the divorce. When a parent moves out of the house and the acrimony between the two adults begins, many children still dream that one day their parents will reconcile; one day this terrible wrong will be righted. Because most daughters are raised to please others, they will struggle to be on the good side of both parents, even if they secretly sympathize with one, usually the parent who did not want the divorce. Daughters are often pushed and pulled in both directions in a frantic search for solid ground.

Regardless of their ages when the divorce of their parents is announced, the event pushes them into an alien world. Their identity is irreversibly altered; no longer will they be a part of a conventional nuclear family, but instead they are one of the pieces of a splintered family. Their social conditioning, steeped in patriarchy, encourages them to compromise and to accept. Whatever such daughters see and sense, they are customarily taught to be silent and to swallow their pride.

For Vanessa, the eldest of three daughters, her parents' divorce, which happened when she was twelve, tore apart her family. "My mother was a wreck after my parents split. Living with her was hell and I really resented her. So, when my dad started dating a nice woman, I really liked her. Despite his good relationship with her, Dad always talked about wanting to lead a single life. That was very hurtful for us kids. We all liked his girlfriend and we hoped he'd settle down with her so we could have a family again. Instead, he dumped his girlfriend and focused more on his career, becoming head of his department at the hospital. This was a leap forward for him financially, but my sisters and I didn't care about the money. All the while, our parents were so unpleasant to each other and so embroiled in the divorce proceedings that I ended up raising my sisters, especially the youngest who was only three when it all began. I felt like Cinderella. I did all the chores, because our mother worked full-time and when she wasn't at work she was taking pills and threatening to commit suicide. I became tired of their fighting, trying to keep my mom from being depressed and taking care of my sisters as if they were my own children. When I turned eighteen, I left home and never went back. The divorce was a nightmare and no one in our family ever really recovered."

According to Dr. Michele Kasson, psychologist, most daughters push their mothers away in adolescence whether their parents are divorced or not. "Girls have to separate from their mothers in order to come back to them in adulthood. This is one step in the process of evolution into female adulthood. The female teen is trying to develop her own identity and this is difficult to do in the shadow of an adult female. Often a female teenager will seek out her father in an effort to gain distance from her mother, another female with an already established identity. She also does this to gain more experience and practice the role of an independent adult female." This is a normal and healthy process, but it can be unhealthy and dangerous to the mother-daughter relationship when accelerated and accentuated by a contentious divorce.

Those of us raised in the fifties and sixties were taught that divorce was taboo, a shameful event that forever tainted every member of the family. After a divorce occurred, families fell from grace, neighbors whispered, children were scorned. Daughters who were particularly wounded became lost souls. Eventually, in the decades to follow, divorce became a common occurrence. Not only is over half the married population destined to divorce at some point, but these people are destined to remarry at the rate of seventy-five percent. After the original family has disintegrated, a new one is created. If one or both parents remarry, the stepfamily evolves. A new nuclear family could consist of the divorced family, with each parent remarried, forming two new families. They become recognized as "blended families" or "stepfamilies." For daughters of divorce, these are enormous transitions and forever alter their lives.

The Slow Recovery

In the extensive research conducted for their book, *Surviving the Breakup*, authors Judith S. Wallerstein and Joan B. Kelly discovered that daughters who comprehend the end of their parents' marriages are better able to recognize what divorce entails. For them what follows is the knowledge that divorce can be healthy and is the opportunity for another life for each parent. A mature daughter, adolescent or older, realizes that she has little say in her parents' lives and yet there usually is shock and fear, followed by grief, when divorce takes place. The sense of relief that often transpires once the divorce is announced might be directly related to the amount of bitterness which existed in an unhappy household. Nevertheless, when the family structure unravels, daughters worry about where they will live and who will care for them. If parents look to daughters for support, they cannot reveal their real feelings and fears. It is now the daughters' responsibility to be there for their psychologically-impaired parents.

After the trauma of divorce, most experts agree it takes one to five years to recover and to rebuild the family. "The 'psychic divorce' is a two-to-five-year healing process," says Dr. Ronnie Burak, a psychologist whose practice concentrates on family issues. "I view age as an important factor in the daughters' reactions to divorces. If mothers and fathers separate when their daughters are under eight years of age, the girls will not know father-loss. Rather they will be offered a solid life without the father."

A single mother of young daughters who is bonded closely to these girls has a much easier time of it than when the daughters are adolescent, rebellious and uncooperative. Nonetheless, in many cases she suddenly comprehends that she is all alone, that there is not even the facade of a marriage to insulate her. This mother's loneliness and desolation can be heightened when her daughter is self-absorbed as in the teenage years.

"At the time, I only wanted to talk about boys or be with my friends," said Alice, thirty, who was fifteen when her parents announced their divorce. "My youngest sister, who was eight, was weepy and frail and needed my mother. I felt that between my mother being all alone and my sister crying all the time, I had no place to be myself. I began to spend more and more time on the phone with my friends and out of the house on weekends. I didn't know how else to escape my mother and her emotions."

Despite her disappointment, Alice realized after several months that her mother was better off without her father. "I saw that my father's absence actually caused an improvement in our home life. And when my father saw me, which was regularly, he paid more attention to me and to my sisters than before the split. What bothered us the most was that when he came around, there was so much tension. My parents fought about the same things as when they had been married. My mother played this weepy role; she would always fall apart and I couldn't respect her. My little sister clung to my mother and refused to leave the house when my father came to pick us up. He always became furious and impatient.

"Our father wanted to be reconciled and our mother was convinced that divorce was the only answer. It took a long time for my father to accept this. I began to see that I could have a relationship with both my parents and that they needed to be divorced. I know that my mother wanted me to side with her, although she never said anything. My father said too much; he said our mother had broken up the family. I began to understand, reluctantly, that my mother felt she had to be free. I couldn't hold it against her that she wasn't in love with him anymore. I wanted a loving family, but it wasn't that way. Really, it had never been that way."

Social worker Brenda Szulman remarks about the seriousness of how a divorce can unfold: "If the parents communicate to their daughters that this divorce is for the best and there are no tugs-of-war, the daughters do better in the long run. If we are talking about a daughter who is five versus twelve or fourteen or sixteen, each daughter's reaction is different. For a daughter over the age of thirteen whether her parents' marriage was happy or not, there was a certain stability of living in an intact family. She remembers that for a long time."

A question of loyalty often plagues daughters of divorce. That Alice was able to recognize her mother's needs although she resented the result, is notable. Although a father may leave a marriage, the daughter will sometimes still sympathize with him. The daughter is in a powerless position—yearning for her father and the illusion of the perfect family without hostility. The best that the daughter can expect at this time is that her father will love her. To this end, the daughter cannot risk being angry with her father and pushing him away. She only requires that he be a good parent. At the same time, what the daughter asks of her mother is much greater. Why did her mother fail her? Why wasn't she her protector? The majority of daughters want their mothers to hold their marriages together. When this doesn't happen, they feel that their mothers have abandoned their families.

Adolescent Daughters and Their Mothers

Peer pressure is unavoidable for adolescent daughters of divorce. Many teenage daughters have been embarrassed by their parents' breakup and are reluctant to tell their classmates. To worsen the matter, when parents are too preoccupied and overwhelmed with the machinations of divorce, they are not aware of their daughters' misery. In direct response to this, as my research confirmed, daughters may resent the parent who instigated the divorce. While both parents, mothers and fathers, have to reestablish themselves, they also have to be acutely aware of their daughters' problems surrounding their divorces and the peer pressure specific to every age.

Marie, thirty-eight, has been divorced for two years and separated for three. She decided that she could not stay married despite her fears of what divorce would do to her daughter. "My marriage to Jeremy was such an unhappy time for me. We were never on the same team. It was a hierarchical relationship and my ex-husband always had to be in charge. I didn't think it was a mistake to marry this man, because we found in each other what we lacked in ourselves. At the same time, once we knew each other well, I realized I had to leave.

"To my daughter, who is very bitter, I say, you have two parents who love you. Divorce is not the worst thing that could happen and you should not make our divorce the ruination of your life. I'm sorry that my daughter has suffered, particularly the first year of the separation when she was seven. There were times when she refused to go with her father and I felt caught in the middle. But I told her that she had to go, she had to observe the custody arrangement. How my ex-husband treats her now that she is an adolescent reminds me of how he treated me. Again, there is that hierarchy. And as it hindered me, it hinders her."

In some situations, adolescent daughters' rates of development are directly related to the divorce. Some might mature faster and others might fall behind. What is least healthy for daughters is when residual anger in a divorce situation is played out by both parents. The mother might use the children's erratic behavior after visitation with the father to prove that the set-up is not successful or vice versa. Such friction between the parents spills over to the daughters, building tension and driving wedges between the children and the parents. This is particularly difficult for adolescent daughters, already caught in the mire of poor self-esteem and socialization difficulties and precarious friendships. Dawn Bradley Berry, author of *The Divorce Recovery Source Book*, reminds us that the aftermath of divorce produces conflicting feelings of pain, anger, guilt, fear and anxiety for children and adults alike. It is only when the adults are able to face the changes and losses and take control of their own lives that they can move forward. Berry believes that a significant part of the recovery process depends upon who asked for the divorce.

This theory is given credibility by the case of Helena. At the age of forty-nine, she is the mother of three daughters who were seven, nine, and twelve when she was divorced. "It has taken me many years to get over this divorce. My husband was cheating and I was very angry and lost all trust. I hated him. I have eventually gotten over it and I feel better toward him and his new wife now. But it was very difficult for me to get where I am today.

"My daughters see their father and they still love him, but they resent him for what he did. At first I didn't like the girls to visit him and, since he lived several states away, it didn't happen often. If my husband had simply divorced me and met someone else it would have been a different circumstance. I never told the girls not to like his new wife and I am in touch with him because of them. Now that my daughters are in their twenties it doesn't matter to me if they interact with their father or not. The most difficult part after the divorce was getting my life in order and getting over my anger."

In her book, *Divorce and New Beginnings*, Genevieve Clapp, Ph.D. observes that once children feel rejected by divorce, abandonment issues appear. In the California Children of Divorce Study, Wallerstein and Kelly discovered that the majority of children between the age of three and adolescence were worried about being abandoned by their fathers and, to a lesser degree, by their mothers. For daughters, divorce does not represent the hope and second chance at happiness that it can for one or both parents.

Victoria, thirty-one and presently attending law school, lived through her parents' divorce at the age of twelve. "I felt guilty. I wanted to fix the marriage. I felt like I was being disloyal to my father if I went somewhere with my mother. I felt disloyal to my mother if I enjoyed time spent alone with my father. My little sister longed for our parents to get back together. I understood, having witnessed the dysfunction of their marriage, that despite my sister's and my pain and bitterness, divorce was necessary. My parents were not a happy couple, but the divorce was so difficult anyway.

"My sister and I worried about where we would live and who would take care of us. I look just like my father and I think for a time that really bothered my mother. I had this horrible sense that she didn't want to be near me. I had nowhere to go. Also, my mother began to act very single. She threw away all of her 'married clothes' and laughed with her single friends over her dates. This was during the divorce and it frightened me. I didn't really consider whether my mother should have a life or not. I just worried about myself and my little sister. One positive that came out of their divorce was that they finally stopped fighting. I am someone who knows the benefits of a quiet, if divorced, household. I was actually luckier than a few of my friends whose parents made it very hard on their daughters by fighting after their divorces and undermining each other."

Many parents do not recognize how upsetting the ordeal of divorce is to their daughters. When parents drag their children into this drama, it will become more difficult for the children to heal. The adolescent daughter is often hardest hit by the divorce. Frequently a girl will have problems in school or with her peers several years after the divorce is over. In many instances, when a daughter exhibits behavioral problems, it can be a cry for help. This is particularly true since she harbors a great deal of residual anger and disappointment.

Daughters Who Parent

Most daughters I found are hyper-aware, at every stage, of the growing distance between their parents as the couple moves from separation to divorce. Many daughters, burdened by their own concern and guilt for their parents' failed marriages, feel compelled to care for whichever parent seems neediest at the time.

"In the beginning," Opal, forty, recalls, "I watched my daughters' wistfulness when they greeted their father at the door. They looked back at me longingly as he embraced them both. They said softly in his ear, 'I love you, Daddy, I missed you.' He raised them over his shoulder and they checked me out, naively believing in my approval, and somehow anticipating my sadness. My heart ached. There we were, my ex and I vying for our daughters' attention, wondering who the better parent was, who the winner would be in the long run. It was a stage, I knew, and we would get beyond it. However, during the hellish year which began when I served my husband the legal papers and ended with the finality of divorce, the competition persisted."

Eventually divorce becomes a reality and a mother's focus may shift. If the mother doesn't remarry immediately, she has to concentrate on the daunting task of single parenting, must closely watch how her daughters choreograph their lives to accommodate their divorced parents, taking on roles that are not necessarily obligatory or fair. Brenda Szulman, a clinical social worker, believes that in the healthiest of break-ups, the parents properly communicate their decision to divorce to their daughters. In this situation, both parents are open and stay involved in their daughters' lives. "Everyone regroups after divorce; it is simply a matter of time. However, what the father tells the kids and what the mother tells them is another component of how they deal with the break-up," says Szulman. Both parents want to look like the good person in a divorce and look to their daughters for some kind of affirmation that they aren't failing. "For the daughters there are issues of abandonment, betrayal, boundaries and trust."

As the original family structure dissolves, parents may lean on their daughters for support. No longer committed to each other, these adults cannot always offer a united front to their daughters. Therefore, daughters of divorce are in continual search of foundations, many of which have disappeared. I found those instances, however, when daughters would rather live through their parents' unhappy union than watch them divorce. If the father was absent during the marriage and is now absent as a single father, his daughter knows the difference. Early studies by the well-respected divorce expert E. Mavis Hetherington indicate that when fathers are not in the home, daughters suffer long-term effects. In adulthood, these daughters may feel less easy with men and may become more sexually active. This has been confirmed in a study by David Popenoe, author of *Life Without Father: Compelling New Evidence that Fatherhood and Marriage are Indispensable for the Good of Children and Society*. Popenoe notes that over forty percent of children in the United States live without their fathers and the chances of them having their own marital problems in adulthood are increased by their fatherless homes.

"I was sure it was a rejection of us the day that my parents announced their divorce and my father left home. My two younger sisters and I huddled together and cried," admits Janet, age thirty-three. "I was sixteen at the time. I'd seen the ups and downs but I wanted to have my parents married to each other, regardless of their misery. Now that I have some maturity and all these years have passed, I understand that people really cannot stay in a marriage for the sake of their children. At the same time, what happens to the children is a serious matter. My middle sister didn't do well. After a while, her grades went down and she had trouble concentrating. But my little sister really got lost in the process. At first, she was quiet and almost obedient. After all, she was only six. But about three years after the divorce, she really fell apart. She had to repeat a grade and had behavioral problems. I would have to say both sisters seemed less affected immediately and more affected in the long-term. During that time, I was trying to be mature, because my parents were not. And when my mother moved us back to her hometown, away from our father, it was worse than ever."

Janet's first major problem was that she felt left on her own and responsible for her siblings. "I saw myself as the parent throughout the ordeal. I made sure that my younger sisters were doing their homework and getting picked up from school. I wasn't sure who I was pleasing, my mother or my father. I was confused, but basically, in retrospect, I did it for myself. Leaving for college was a huge relief for me."

For daughters, a reliable mother during the period immediately following divorce is critical; it is she who can provide constancy. Daughters recover from the trauma of divorce sooner if the mother is secure and content. A mother, who is depleted emotionally and physically after a divorce, causes stress and obligates her child to take on an adult role. Authors Wallerstein and Blakelee refer to the daughter who takes care of her mother as the "overburdened child." Eventually, most of these daughters come to resent the feeling that they had to be the adults, not children, during their childhood. They may be hostile toward the stronger parent who left the weaker parent. "A mother," says Dr. Michele Kasson, "who is getting divorced could be frightened by her daughter's behavior rather than understanding it as typical. Gradually, as the mother makes a life for herself, an opportunity for an improved relationship between the two can exist."

Divorce appears as a large, dark force in the lives of daughters of divorce during the transition. If parents do not recognize how their daughters are impacted by the divorce, it often is because they are too wound up in the process themselves. No matter how many efforts are made to provide their daughters protection against heartache during this period, most daughters can't help but fear for their own well-being. A younger daughter may feel even more forsaken in the midst of divorce if an older sister leaves for college or boarding school. Responsibilities ease for most of these daughters once their mothers get their emotions and lives back on track and the daughters' senses of urgency abate as their new lives take hold.

Abandonment and Loss for Daughters

When researchers Paul Amato and B. Keith conducted a study which involved thirteen thousand families of children of divorce, from preschool to young adulthood, they found that these children have more problems at school, with friends and with self-confidence than do children whose parents remain married. These children may not get along as well with their parents as do children in intact families. However, E. Mavis Hetherington conducted a study in 1993 and found a discrepancy in the behavior of daughters and sons, with sixty-six percent of daughters of divorce falling into what Hetherington describes as "a normal range" compared to seventy-four percent of sons, in cases of divorce. She concluded that daughters have more difficulty adjusting to divorce than do sons.

These are the kinds of issues that haunt daughters of divorce, young, adolescent and adult alike. For most daughters the burning question is, what did I do wrong? How could I have prevented this from happening, prevented being left alone? Daughters of divorce are reluctant to face the acute problems that caused the breakup in the marriage and are eager to idealize what was good. Verbal or physical abuse is often repressed and the divorce itself is often denied. Because divorce causes anxiety in daughters, and their own identities are forever altered, they may forget that they were relieved initially when their parents' divorces began. What matters most to them is how their interactions with each parent and how their lives are affected after their parents' divorces. How the parents treat each other is critical to the well-being of daughters. If there are unresolved issues between the parents, even after the divorce and they are openly hostile and divisive, the daughters will have difficulty feeling comforted and secure.

Jenna, at the age of thirty-five, is a daughter of divorce and a mother of a daughter of divorce. Looking back on her parents' divorce, she confesses to lapses of memory. "My parents came from very different cultures and never got along. There was screaming and fighting, even physical violence. My older sister tried to shelter me, but I saw it all and I felt out of control. I was only five when they divorced, but when I became a teenager I still felt ashamed and sorry for myself. My father had left our house and that is what frightened me the most. Really, he not only left the house but he left our lives. We were without a father. He would come by on occasion, but my sister and I were cool to him. I know how much the divorce has affected me. I am recently divorced myself and have my own little girl, who is only four. I resisted this divorce for a long time because I knew what divorce does to children. My mother was so lonely. My sister and I missed our father. No one was divorced in our town. It had a terrible stigma and it harmed me. Now I have similarly hurt my own daughter."

Mandy, now thirty-two, watched her father leave her mother for another woman when she was six years old. "It was hard for my mom. She was very angry and bitter for a while. But she actually put her anger aside pretty quickly and focused on me and my little sister. It wasn't easy, but as we grew up, the three of us became very close. It was an all-female household and we really worked together as a team. My mom leaned on us sometimes, but she also encouraged us to do our best in school and to go out in the world on our own. She didn't hold us back or try to keep us at home with her for company. Today both my parents are remarried. My sister, who is twenty-nine, isn't married and neither am I. Some of my failed relationships with men are definitely a result of the negative impact of my parent's divorce, but I also learned a lot growing up in that environment. When I talk to some of my female friends, I see how unrealistic they are about men and relationships and that's why some of them are getting divorced already. I learned at a young age about the realities of the ups and downs of life, love and marriage. As a result, I am stronger and more resilient. I'm also hopeful; I believe there's a man out there for me with whom I could have a successful marriage."

Diane Fassell, author of *Growing Up Divorced: A Road To Healing For Adult Children Of Divorced Parents*, describes some of the positive results divorce can have for children. She asserts that the divorce can foster resiliency and a sense of independence for daughters. Despite this possible positive outcome, many daughters sense a loss of their parents as a unit long before the divorce has transpired. When marriages are held together for the daughters' sakes, the daughters often know it and are quite uneasy with the decisions their parents have made.

Now that she is thirty-six, Beth has had twenty years to reflect upon her parents' divorce. "I saw," Beth admits, "the demands of a poor marriage and then the demands of the divorce as keeping my parents away from me. They were each too preoccupied with getting it right to pay me any attention. My sister, brother and I were left to wander. I was the middle child and became a buffer for the others. It was a burden and very frightening. The final divorce was actually a break for us. I do not judge when someone tells me she is divorced or that her parents are divorced. Rather, I know what it takes to get there.

"Although I know that my parents' divorce has had a huge impact on my life, so did their horrible marriage. I believe that both my mother and my father lamented their lost youth. Before they split up, I saw my mother looking in the mirror, checking for wrinkles and to see if she still looked good. I was only five at the time. She cried all the time, whether she was driving us in the car or cooking hamburgers for dinner. She was so unhappy. And there were fights because my parents could not agree about anything. My siblings and I were praying they'd get divorced. My parents fought a lot both during and after the divorce and it took years for us kids to regain our equilibrium. But the divorce was a good idea. I look back on it as a positive step and I know my mother, in particular, would agree."

Relocation and Cooperation After Divorce

A team of researchers, Janet R. Johnston, Marsha Kline and Jeanne M. Tshann, reported that when children have divorced parents who are combative instead of cooperative, they become disturbed emotionally and behaviorally. Published in the *Journal of Family Issues*, Paul Amato's research suggests that the causes of difficulties for children of divorce are parental loss, economic loss, increased life stress, poor parental adjustment, lack of parental competence and the exposure to inter-parental conflict. What can help daughters of divorce is when mothers, fathers and stepmothers co-parent effectively and when the mother keeps in touch during the father's visitation by phone, without interfering with the daughter's relationship with her father and vice versa.

Ten years ago, Dana's father moved several hours away from her mother. Visitations for Dana and her sister, then twelve and eight, were scheduled for every other weekend. As Dana recalls, the trips were hard on her, her sister and her mother. "The trip there and back was long and boring. Mom drove halfway and dad met us on the side of the road. Katie and I hated the arrangement. We complained constantly about the drive. What made things worse was dad's unreliability. Sometimes he arrived late; other times he didn't show up at all. It upset my mom and our complaining didn't help.

"On top of all that, we didn't like being at his house. We hated being so far away from our friends and the places we knew. Plus my dad didn't do anything with us when we got to his house. He just expected us to amuse ourselves. I often asked myself, what is the point of visiting him if he doesn't want to do anything with us? Then my dad met and married Liz. I could tell my mom wanted to hate her and pretend she didn't exist but Liz soon took over picking us up when we visited our dad. So my mom had to acknowledge her. Katie and I wanted to hate Liz too but she was so nice and took us places and paid attention to us when we visited. We couldn't help but like her. Before long, Katie and I stopped complaining about the drive and visiting my dad. We actually enjoyed going there. We even made a few friends. My mom came around and seemed to appreciate Liz. We could tell she trusted Liz to take care of us. Life became more stable and Katie and I were happy for the first time in a long time."

The sense of being grounded is an important goal both for the mothers and for the daughters as well. Any disappointment during and after the divorce may be magnified because the daughter's sense of loss is already so acute. "I couldn't face any rejection," said Celia, a medical school student who was eighteen when her parents divorced. "If my friends canceled plans, I took it to heart. I was depressed. It all had to do with my parents' split. And I kept siding with my mother, because she did not want to be divorced. As an only child, I really felt I had to support her, but she would have none of it. What I appreciated about her was that she refused to let me stop my life because she didn't have one. And I believe that she was right, because it forced us both to do what was age-appropriate for each of us.

"My mother urged me to go away to school and to leave the mess behind. I did, although I worried about her constantly. Then the divorce came through and she focused on her own interests and needs. She has a good job and close friends. Recently she met a man who is quite nice. And my father remarried a woman who I really do like. I appreciate how unlike my mom she is, and I try not to compare them. Instead, I get along with everyone. I know how much going to college helped me through this bad period."

Since mothers learn quickly that everything, including their social lives and relationships, changes after their divorces. Since most of the friendships she and her husband shared were originally based on mutual experiences, particularly married life, once the dust settles after the divorce, some friends will break away citing a lack of common interests. In other words, the newly single mother's life is not simpatico with theirs. Many single mothers will then make new friends who have more in common with them. For daughters, friendships are of extreme importance and give comfort in a changed universe.

Antonia, at the age of thirteen, was relieved when her mother moved, taking her and two older sisters back to Boston after the divorce. "My mother had this job in advertising and she worked long hours. When my parents were married, her career was something people talked about because most mothers didn't work where we lived. Everyone was picked up by their moms after school and taken on errands. My mom would do it two days a week, and the other days, a baby-sitter picked us up. I felt like my friends talked about me because of the baby-sitter. Then my parents got divorced and it was horrible. Then I thought that the kids were talking about me at school because of the divorce. It was much worse. I heard my mother on the phone with her mother one night and she was saying that this wasn't the right environment for us, because we were no longer a family.

"We moved and our father was angry at first. Then he decided it was better for us. He and my mother began to make joint decisions about us and there was less tension. My sisters were happy. Although at first I didn't want to leave my friends, I was happy afterward. In Boston, there are more divorced people than in a small town. It makes life easier and I know a few girls in my class who also live with just their mothers."

Aftermath for Daughters

Our society continues to hold up a picture-perfect ideal of family. When divorce shatters this picture, there usually is no shelter for daughters who are impacted, no escaping the angst. Often a young child will feel responsible for the divorce whereas an older daughter tries to fathom her mother's and father's needs, despite the disturbances this causes. For sixty-six percent of daughters of divorce between the ages of nineteen and twenty-three, according to authors Wallerstein and Blakeslee, the repercussions of the divorce may involve a fear of intimacy with a man, a fear of betrayal and a fear of losing love. Adult daughters of divorce sense the despair of their parents' divorce more than do adult sons of divorce.

Hillary, now twenty-two, saw her parents' divorce unfold when she was sixteen. Her younger sister, Lisa, who is now eighteen, was only twelve at the time and her brother, Alec, was fourteen. "While my sister couldn't believe that the divorce was happening, I knew that my parents did not get along and that our household was peaceful only when one of them was out of town. I dreaded their getting a divorce, but I knew that it was for the best. Nevertheless it was a terrible time for everyone, because my parents were so preoccupied and acted infantile. My little sister couldn't face it. She cried every night and moved into my bedroom to be with me. She kept hoping our parents would get back together, which I knew was impossibile. We were able to see our father frequently, because it was a joint custody arrangement. When we were with him, Lisa called our mother constantly. When she was with our mother, she missed our father. As my sister grew up, she became reclusive and would not go out with her friends. She had a boyfriend for almost three years who was a rock for her and whom she depended upon. Recently, she blew him off because the thought of making any kind of commitment to him was frightening to her.

"I saw the divorce differently. I saw it as a liberation and a chance to start again. And the fact that there would be no more arguing in our house was very appealing to me. I felt sadly about the breakup of our family, but my hope was that everyone would be better off. So while my sister is still in anguish, I became more independent and more mature. I suppose I was like my brother in this way. Though I cried and he never shed a tear."

There is a mourning period accompanied by anger and resentment when most parents put themselves ahead of their children. Divorce is testimony to both the mother's and father's needs. The child comes second and this is very unsettling. For daughters in adolescence, the absence of a role model is traumatic. The parents are admitting a mistake, one of the biggest mistakes of their lives. The other side is that the daughters cannot assess their parents realistically. This elicits an earnestness and concern on the part of the daughter. If the parents are not there for their children during and after the divorce, as their resource for emotional support and for the day-to-day demands of life, then the daughters are not anchored. Researcher Paul Amato views this as similar to when a parent dies, but it is compounded because the parent is not dead, but has gone on without her/his child.

"One must be very careful about repetitions," says Brenda Szulman, psychotherapist. "If the daughter is forgotten and left behind by her mother because of the divorce, she could do the same to her own daughter or husband. Boundaries and trust are big issues after divorce for these daughters. They will reenact what has happened to them unless they can work through it, and in many cases this requires professional help and some kind of counseling." The danger is that the daughter might mimic what happened to her in the divorce once she is an adult. Her experience is the only one she knows, and even if she hopes for a successful marriage and to raise her children in a nuclear family, there is no positive role model for the daughter.

Daughters ought to be assured that they are not a part of the divorce decision and that the divorce exists between the parents only. Utilizing the daughter as savior is a common and unfortunate scenario. In these circumstances, as the parents place unfair burdens on the daughter, she may come to believe that her parents will not be there for her, and yet she knows she cannot interfere with the course of action. This can cause both young and adolescent daughters alike to feel impotent and fear the unknown. Experts agree that even in the best of circumstances, divorce causes destruction and bereavement for children. The hope is that parents will emerge with fresh attitudes and less quarreling between them than in the past, thus empowering their daughters and not hindering them.

Elaine, who is thirty and divorced with one young daughter, was thirteen when her parents announced their divorce. While she had expected that this would happen, the event hit her hard. "My brother, who is two years older, used to whisper that our parents would be divorced one day. He said this from the time we were really little. And I always knew he was right. The divorce was not a surprise, but it was a nightmare. I was more attached to my father than to my mother when he left the house. He seemed more available to my brother and would come over to take him to soccer practice and to go bowling.

"This made it worse. I struggled to become close to my mother. I knew I needed to become close to her in a way that I hadn't been before. But I would not give up on my father. He was the one who had historically taken me places and had spent hours listening to my anxieties. I kept calling him and asking him to do things with me. My mother never objected, although she seemed lonely and lost.

"Then my friends learned about the divorce, because we lived in a gossipy suburb. I wasn't ready to tell anyone and they learned about it too soon. That seemed worse than all the adjustments I had to make with my parents. I couldn't stand the way people looked at me at school. Still, my parents' divorce forced me to build character and it also taught me to try to avoid a bad marriage. Nevertheless, I repeated their mistakes, but I was strong enough to get out while I was young and have a chance to start again. As for my daughter, who is only three, her childhood will have no resemblance to mine. My parents operated as a unit, whether it was a healthy unit or not, until I was in eighth grade. This will not be the case for my daughter; instead she will have divorced parents for her entire childhood. But her friends won't be saying nasty things about her parents' divorce; it will be accepted as a part of her life."

Slow Acceptance

The quicker that parents can accept and adjust to their divorce, the more secure daughters will feel. The benefits of divorce eventually surface: parent/child relationships might improve during and after the crisis of divorce. In many cases, a daughter finds herself solidly connected with both parents or with one in particular. For instance, a daughter who might have been estranged from her father before the separation because he was absent may attempt to fix the relationship because of the divorce. And while the father/daughter bonding which may occur after divorce is significant, it often is the strong identity with the mother which if it prevails helps the daughters to recover from the divorce and to move onward.

Amy Reisen, matrimonial lawyer, has witnessed successful remarriages for both parents after divorces. "In my practice, where most divorce judgments are reached by settlement, children can profit from additional caring adults, those of stepmother and stepfather. Ever-changing patterns of child custody and visitation arrangements do not allow for generalizations. However, a daughter in a divorced family usually retains a healthy relationship with her mother and more and more often with her father as well." The latest Gallup Poll substantiates the new world of divorce which Reisen describes when it reveals that eighty-two percent of the divorced population believes that divorcing was the right decision. Despite the financial, logistical and emotional restructuring that divorce demands, especially for couples with children, there is the hope that each member of the family will find her/his equilibrium and emerge the wiser.

"All children feel caught between a mother and father because they do not want to split their loyalties," says Dr. Ronnie Burak, psychologist. "Initially the divorce exacerbates an adolescent daughter's dilemma. If the teenage rebellion is in full swing then the divorce provides the crisis that makes it so prominent. Only time will take care of this. The daughters grow up, and the aftermath of the divorce can become somewhat routine."

The recurrent theme of daughters hoping for their parents' reconciliation which I heard so many times may shift their thinking. Gradually they may see divorce as a positive for both parents. And while the interviewees give testimony to the imprint of divorce, at every stage of their lives, as mothers and daughters, this constant awareness is a form of both fragility and strength. In my research, I came to see that what works best for daughters of divorce is when the parents, despite their desire to be divorced, stay consistent in their parenting and remain sensitive to their daughters' needs. In many situations, it takes time and great maturity on the parents' parts to reach this objective.

When the concept of being a daughter of divorce begins to register for daughters, they may come to realize the unique strengths of both parents. It is optimal for mothers and fathers to attend to the needs of their daughters in the traumatic post-divorce stage, before parents embark on their next marriages. However, in looking at the remarriages of fathers for this book, I found that this new stage of transition calls for sensitivity on the part of each adult family member. This is especially true for the mother and stepmother who are so crucial to the daughter's adjustment and making the new triangle, with all its conflicts, function effectively.

CHAPTER 2

Mothers: Redefining Their Roles

"I doubt that I ever considered the idea of a stepmother for my girls or thought seriously about my ex-husband's remarriage," sighs Joelle, forty-two. "I was very relieved to be divorced and I expected that Art, my ex-husband, would date, because he was still relatively young and attractive. I had no emotional connection to him and I was the one who wanted to divorce. So I can't explain why I was so taken back by his quick remarriage to Lucy. It was as if the girls, who were only ten and twelve at the time, had no chance to adjust to their parents' status as single parents when suddenly Art and Lucy were planning a wedding. The girls became really involved with this wedding—they picked out the dresses they would wear and they were the ring bearers. This was all very dreamy, but afterward the reality of having a stepmother hit them and it hit me. I felt defensive for them, as if I had to protect them from any further confusion in their lives caused by Lucy's presence. Not that she wasn't nice to the girls or that she didn't try her best.

"I had nothing against her personally; it was her position in their lives that bothered me, once it really happened. I think the most amazing part of Art's remarriage is that it is now a permanent part of the girls' lives and my life as well. When the girls are with her, I am conscious of my daughters being in the care of another woman. I have this urge to shout, 'I'm their mother, I'm the mother!'"

Motherhood is a complex role for women; divorce only complicates that role further. Since most mothers are extremely attached to their daughters and this female bond is usually a lifelong connection, mothers need to remind themselves of this when their daughters find themselves with stepmothers. The idea of other women attempting to mother their daughters is disconcerting and can be threatening. There is a population of divorced mothers who do not anticipate sharing their daughters with stepmothers. Some of these mothers are simply short-sighted when it comes to the realities of divorce and remarriage and they have not imagined that stepmothers might actually materialize or that they will resent these women.

Divorced mothers confront many issues and often I found in my interviews these women view the obstacles of being single mothers as challenging, and at the same time as wake-up calls. There are those mothers who may have been the initiators of divorce who now say that, had they anticipated how the world would be afterward, they might not have chosen this road. These second thoughts usually occur, in my findings, when divorced women realize they have lost their identities through their divorces. To these women, the status of wife and mother is now reduced to just mother and much of society values less a woman who is a single mother rather than a married mother. From many of the mothers' viewpoints, stepmothers step into these mothers' shoes, without the daily grind and responsibilities of motherhood. For many of these women, the stepmothers' existences remind them of their old lives with their ex-husbands and the shattered dreams of ever after. Some mothers, even if they do not want to be married to their exes anymore, still feel cheated and jealous.

Once there are stepmothers, the mothers have a variety of responses. Some feel relieved to share responsibility for their daughters with other women while others may feel threatened. This depends greatly on the mindset of the mother and the kind of stepmother who materializes. Some of the mothers imagine that they will feel okay sharing their daughters with stepmothers, only to find that it isn't acceptable and raises many issues for them. Nevertheless, since according to the Commerce Department's Census Bureau men now account for one-sixth of the nation's 11.9 million single parents and the majority remarry, most mothers will end up interacting with stepmothers whether they would prefer to or not.

Altered Mothers

John Tierney reported in the July 11, 2000 issue of *New York Times*, "at least two-thirds of divorce suits [in America] are filed by women." However, this is sometimes perfunctory and does not mean that two-thirds of women initiate or want divorce. Furthermore, since more divorced men than divorced women remarry, many mothers must adjust to their ex-husbands' new wives. Whether or not a mother seriously considers the arrival of a stepmother on the scene when she divorces depends on the individual. Yet the reality is that most daughters of divorce will have stepmothers, since the United States Census Bureau reports that, within three years of divorce, three-quarters of men remarry.

When the stepmother appears on the scene too quickly it is often the timing rather than the remarriage itself that rankles many of the mothers with whom I've spoken. For the mother, a stepmother can be either good news or intrusive. Much of the mother's reaction depends upon how territorial she is as a mother and what her situation is at the time that the stepmother appears. The mother also has to deal with her daughter's take on the stepmother. As the daughter sorts out her relationship with her father, in some cases there are repercussions as the daughters adjust to their stepmothers. Usually it can take from four to seven years for the stepfamily to become a unit, as reported by Patricia Papernow in her book, *Becoming a Stepfamily*. This could be a long ordeal. If the stepmother indulges her stepdaughter and becomes close to her, this may cause the girl's mother to become resentful. "I doubt that I've been fair about Tina, the girls' stepmother," admits Maureen, "because I did nothing to prepare them for her. For my younger daughter, Bethany, who is only five, there is an advantage to having Tina in her life. She bakes cookies with my daughter and takes her to the book store. They play board games. I should be happy that Bethany has this kind of attention from a mother figure. Instead I resent it and this has made me a different kind of mother. I find myself stricter with Bethany and more of a drill sergeant, because I know how spoiled she is by Tina. My older daughter, who is thirteen, doesn't fall for any of it, and so I am not as hard on her. Then I think about Tina's efforts and how my older kid pushes her away, like she pushes me away and I feel sorry for her."

There is a gender spin to the mother/daughter/stepmother triangle, of course, since it is comprised of three females, each affected by divorce. However, the trickiest part for the mother can be working the triangle out with the stepmother. Both mother and stepmother are adult women, although in many cases I found there may be a discrepancy in age, with the stepmother usually being younger than the mother. In addition, the two women's sensibilities, despite the gender affiliation, can be worlds apart. Some of the stepmothers I interviewed did not share the mothers' maternal instincts, and the idea of caring for their husbands' daughters from first marriages is not always desirable to them. In these cases, some mothers become defensive for their daughters and have expectations of the stepmothers. These expectations are often met and stepmothers react warmly and considerately toward the daughters of divorce.

Thus many mothers can be conflicted about the stepmothers. On the one hand, many want to work out these relationships for their daughters' sakes and they know intellectually that there is enough caring and love to go around. Emotionally, however, some mothers claim their daughters for themselves. Sometimes they do not feel competitive with the fathers when it comes to the daughters' affections, but when stepmothers are in the picture they provoke feelings of competition. Motherhood is about nurturing and self-sacrifice, and many of the mothers with whom I spoke, upon seeing stepmothers in this role with their daughters feel that this is their turf; they are the only mothers and they become territorial. "When the stepmother takes the place of the mother," explains Nechama Tec, sociologist, "the mother feels that she is not important anymore and that she has been supplanted, which creates jealousy." If the mother feels guilty about the divorce and its aftermath, and then her daughter enjoys spending time with her stepmother, the mother may fear that she has lost her daughter. Since the mother's identity is tied up in motherhood, this is quite disconcerting and not about the stepmother per se but the role she fills. "Women as mothers make the best of motherhood," writes Jeffner Allen in her essay *Motherhood: The Annihilation of Women*. "Without the institution of motherhood women could and would live otherwise." The investment is obvious, time-wise and in terms of emotional toil—and, my research indicates, many divorced mothers are protective when stepmothers begin to spend time with their daughters.

"Mother-love," criticized, honored and desired, becomes highly scrutinized by certain stepmothers. Some mothers I interviewed reported that they sense how carefully they are being watched by the stepmothers, and after these two women interact out of necessity, the mother may feel betrayed despite a supposedly civil display of feelings. Our culture emphasizes the extraordinary strength of mothers as well as the limitations. I found that for the mother of a daughter of divorce, who now works full-time and is less available to her daughter, there often is a heightened awareness of the stepmother's life and her role in the daughter's life. This plays out in several ways. If the stepmother does not work she might become the one to take over some parental duties for her busy husband, the father. In this case it is the stepmother who picks up and drops off young daughters and checks schedules with the mother. Then there is the stepmother who does not work but does not offer her services and keeps her distance. In some cases a mother is fine with this arrangement and prefers to deal only with her ex-husband and not his new wife. A mother who sees the stepmother living a more luxurious life with her husband may be bothered by the stepmother's disinterest in parenting duties. After all, the mother thinks, the stepmother enjoys a fine life because of her husband and she ought to pitch in when it comes to his children. Also, there are those mothers and stepmothers with whom I spoke who both work full or part-time yet still share the responsibilities for the daughters.

It is often difficult for mothers to imagine how stepmothers will affect their lives until they become part of the family. There are those mothers who are determined to keep their distance from the step-mothers. They don't want any interaction "as long as she (the step-mother) is good to my daughters" is what this type of mother will say to her friends. Yet my research bears out that it is rarely this simple and a mother who begins with an open mind toward the stepmother in time may find there are benefits in having a relationship with the other woman. Unfortunately, despite the high rate of divorce and remar-riage, our social construct has not encouraged mothers and stepmoth-ers to forge relationships, and the triangle of mother/stepmother/ daughter is fraught with unrealistic expectations and misunderstand-ings. Ideally, a mother would establish a civil, respectful relationship with her daughter's stepmother. But a mother, whether she is remarried or not, often has her own issues to deal with regarding her past marriage and her children's care. Her emotions and experiences often spill over into the relationship with the stepmother. What I have seen in my pool of interviewees is that there is a variety of ways in which the mothers begin their relationships with stepmothers, yet in many cases, over time, the mothers' and stepmothers' interactions change as the daughters grow up and their needs change. For instance, some mothers I interviewed who at first accepted the stepmothers so long as they were kind to their daughters, later came to feel that this was not enough. In other cases, mothers who first viewed the stepmothers as necessary evils, eventually welcomed the stepmothers' input regarding the daughters because this joint-parenting approach benefited their daughters in the long run.

"I thought that as long as Maria was good to my daughter, I didn't care that her style was so unlike mine," recalls Rosanna, a forty-four-year-old single mother. "My daughter Gabby was only nine when she met Maria, and I was very hopeful. The two of them went food shopping together and they spent time knitting and doing things that I didn't normally do with Gabby. I thought it was fine that Gabby was doing things with Maria, since my ex-husband was rarely around. But after a while, it became a kind of tug-of-war and I felt that Maria was intruding on my relationship with my daughter. She picked up Gabby after school and she took her to places that I had planned to take her. One day Gabby and I were planning to see a movie together that Sunday and Maria called and told Gabby she was taking her on that day.

"Instead of being happy about Maria's involvement in Gabby's life, it bothered me. I felt that we were no longer sharing Gabby but instead we were fighting for her attention. I called my husband and told him that Maria was trying to ruin my relationship with Gabby. I think that if I had been happier in my own life, I might have liked the fact that Gabby had a stepmother who wanted to spend time with her. Today, I'm a different person and I look at the situation with Maria in another way. Now everyone has been in each other's lives for a while and now Gabby's a teenager. She's becoming independent and wants more time to herself. Now that I am living with someone, I am pleased that Maria has some time for Gabby so I can work on my own adult relationship. I see that life as a single mother is a slippery slope. I needed to be there for my daughter but let her have relationships with her father and stepmother. I had to find common ground with Maria and get over my own issues."

What many of these mothers forget in the midst of their turmoil is how complex the mother/daughter bond is, how closely daughters observe their mothers and how meaningful most of their mothers are to them. "Our daughters evaluate us everyday," sociologist Alice Michaeli remarks. "They see how complicated marriage is, yet the mother/daughter bond is so strong that our lives may become cautionary tales for our daughters." If mothers are to set an example for their daughters, then it would be meaningful and productive for them to remain open toward their daughters' stepmothers.

Territorial Rights

In my interviews I found that some mothers are quite threatened by the idea of joint custody and the concept of their daughters no longer living under their roof every night. Some mothers imagine evils inherent in the fathers' homes. According to the United States Census Bureau, three-quarters of men remarry within a few short years of divorce. It is little wonder that many mothers are suspicious of the strangers now involved with their daughters. Whether the mother expects that this woman will 'mother' her children appears to depend upon the personality of the mother, the circumstances of the divorce and the type of woman the stepmother is. "The mother has to consider if the stepmother has children of her own and what her experience with children has been," remarks Antoinette Michaels, relationship expert. "The mother also has to think about what she wants for her children—a hands-on stepmother or someone in the background."

An ex-husband may be quick to criticize his ex-wife's methods, especially if he is bitter or angry over the divorce. It has been documented that mothers are often interpreted as the ones to blame in a divorce. This bias against mothers in divorce stem in large part from the traditional view of women as mothers and homemakers. A woman who initiates the separation represents someone who has turned her back on her motherly and wifely duties by precipitating a divorce. Even if the mother is not the one who wanted to be divorced, her new status as a single, divorced mother is proof of her failure at her primary job—that of mother, wife and homemaker.

For mothers who have dedicated themselves to their daughters and devoted their lives to the challenges of parenting and have in many instances compromised their careers to become mothers, it is a cruel blow to be thought of as inadequate and selfish. Motherhood has long been underrated, as noted by Ann Crittenden in her book, *The Price of Motherhood: Why the Most Important Job In the World Is Still Least Valued*. In the case of divorced mothers, this point of view is especially pervasive. With a stepmother firmly planted in her daughter's life, a mother may question her role in this new dual-family dynamic. This is especially true for a mother who is single and remains distraught over the divorce. The fact that an ex-husband has created a new family life in some cases causes mothers to unravel further.

"I wanted to be divorced," explains Betsy, who at forty-five has been single for seven years. "I could not stand my marriage another minute. But I have paid dearly for wanting to be unmarried, and when my two girls, who are now sixteen and nineteen, were younger, it was worse. They visited their father and stepmother, who had this 'normal' life, and I felt that I had taken all of that from them. Letitia, the girls' stepmother, is a 'perfect person,' and runs a tight ship. There is always a plan for when the girls visit; the house is quite lovely. The girls first brought over their friends and now they bring boyfriends. Letitia and I are always polite to each other and she definitely would be more open toward me if I didn't seem so icy. I'm like that because she reminds me of what I didn't do right. She is so pleasant to my daughters that I worry sometimes they'll want to live there permanently.

"My daughters are probably ashamed of the way we live and that I am always working late and not running our home better. It is hard for them to understand that I gave up life with their father gladly because it just didn't work for me. Letitia may fill my place as wife but she doesn't replace me as mother. She has been their stepmother for four years and she has made every effort on their behalf. I cannot begrudge her anything. So why is it that when I drop my daughters off there on Friday afternoons, after school, I feel slightly ill when I see her come to the door?"

Even for mothers who want to be single, who are compelled to change their lives, the consequences of divorce and their ex-husbands' remarriages are vast and unrelenting. The stress that these mothers endure, I found, can be heightened by the mother/stepmother interactions, whether positive or negative. If the mother believes that the stepmother has had her own sadness and losses, it can be easier to accept her than if she is unscathed by the results of divorce. Anna, who is a divorced mother and stepmother, had a very similar trajectory to her stepdaughter's mother, in her first marriage.

"I was raised to be a good wife and mother," says Anna, a thirty-nine-year-old stepmother to a nine-year-old stepdaughter and eleven-year-old stepson. "And I did a good job because I was trained for success. I gave up my big job as an accountant and became a part-time accountant to accommodate my son's schedule. My husband had an affair and after two years of it, I asked for a divorce. My son was only eight at the time. When I married Luther, I was determined to make it work. He told me that he had cheated on his first wife, Miranda, and that was why she divorced him. Luther and I met when we were both divorced, although I doubt Miranda believes that.

"Miranda and I are the same age and we both have graduate degrees. We both worked part-time to be available to our kids and husbands. We both asked for divorces and we both suffered financially afterward. The difference is that I have remarried. Maybe it isn't fair, but the world treats divorced mothers horribly. Since Miranda is still in that place and it is her ex-husband who is now my husband, taking me out of that role, she seems threatened by me. She resents me, no matter how nice I am to her children and how many times I have reached out to her. If this wasn't my personal story, I would have total sympathy for her. I wish that she would meet someone and that we could be friends. I do believe we have a lot in common, and I love her children."

Mothers who do not remarry suffer a seventy-three percent decline in their standard of living after divorce, according to Lenore Weitzman in *The Divorce Revolution: The Unexpected Social and Economic Consequences for Women and Children In America*. The forty-three percent increase in the quality of living for fathers after the divorce substantiates why divorced mothers who remarry are able to live better than unmarried moms. In my research I found when the stepmother comes from the same world as the mother, there can be solidarity or there can be envy, shame and a sense of territorial rights concerning the daughters. Some mothers who choose to be single still feel themselves needing to protect their boundaries with stepmothers and are not in the emotional frame of mind to be open to the stepmothers. "Over time," Dr. Michele Kasson remarks, "the mother and stepmother can find ways to get along, even when the history of the first marriage haunts the mother. In time, she will make a new life for herself and this can ease the tension between the mother and stepmother."

Mothers of Young Daughters

Among my interviewees I found that when a stepmother enters picture, the experience for a mother of very young daughters is quite different from a mother whose daughters are adolescent or older. If the father and stepmother live nearby and the father regularly sees his young (under age ten) daughters, the mother and stepmother often find themselves planning for the girls together. Flexibility in scheduling children under the age of three or four who aren't in school all day is imperative and both the mother and stepmother have to be attuned to this. While a father might become frustrated with his screaming three-year-old daughter, a stepmother who cares can ease the situation. Although the mother is not there when such behavior transpires, she sometimes gets word of it, usually through her ex-husband or her daughter. Some mothers who want to dislike the stepmothers find themselves grateful because of the kindness the stepmothers have shown to the daughters.

"I did not welcome Chuck's new young wife," Deandra, thirty-seven and a mother of two daughters, ages three and five, confides. "But I knew that she was good to my two little girls from the start. I tried to keep my distance, and in the beginning I would make all arrangements through Chuck, my ex-husband. Why, I would joke with my girlfriends, would I want to deal with Chuck's twenty-four-year-old squeeze? Then they became engaged and Jennifer was brave enough to bring the girls back to me without Chuck one time. She explained that he had a meeting and had to dash off. At first I was livid, because I hadn't given permission for her to drive my girls and

I thought I should have been asked about it. But when the girls walked up the path with Jennifer and they were each holding her hand and smiling, I felt they had been well cared for.

"The proof for me will be how Jennifer deals with them once she's been at it for a while. I think that for some people who haven't chosen to be mothers, the novelty of children eventually wears thin and these are not her girls. Right now it is like playing house, having a husband of a few months and his little girls to practice with. And Chuck loves her more for loving his girls, so it works for Jennifer all around. Then I tell myself not to be so critical, she really does care for them. One night my older daughter had a high fever and Jennifer was the one to call to let me know what was happening and ask if she should bring her home. I told her it was fine, that she'd be okay until the morning since they were giving her Tylenol. Since then I've been won over, even though I wanted to hate her."

Unlike Deandra, Kathleen has gotten the opposite feeling about her daughter's stepmother. In her zealousness for everyone to get along, Kathleen invited Faith, her ex-husband's new wife and her ex-husband to dinner. "I thought that Joy, my daughter, would feel secure if everyone sat around the same table," Kathleen begins. "I was so wrong. Joy was only six, but I think she felt the awkwardness of the situation and I'm sure she didn't quite get why we were altogether. Maybe I should have made arrangements for lunch with just Faith instead of including Rick, my ex-husband. The night was so uneasy and I never had the chance to talk to Faith about anything meaningful. Even though the evening wasn't a great success, I thought that my gesture would somehow bring us together to some understanding. Wow, was I wrong. Faith has always felt burdened by my daughter and Joy has sensed it. I have found that Faith is not kind toward Joy and she only acts like she cares when Rick is around.

"I have mentioned this to Rick over the past two years and he really doesn't see it. Not only does he defend Faith, but he goes out of his way to make arrangements for them to be together. While I would have welcomed a connection to my daughter's stepmother, it has never been available to me. When I call the house to make an arrangement or to talk to Joy and Faith answers the phone, she gets off so fast she isn't even polite. I wouldn't care for myself, but for my daughter I really wanted something more. This woman is a part of Joy's life and Joy will always remember the way she was treated by her. I don't understand why Faith is so distant and disinterested."

When the mother reaches out to the stepmother and finds the stepmother's response to be icy, their relationship becomes rocky. "A mother can afford to be confident," explains Dr. Michele Kasson, "because in this world, there is only one mother and that bond to the child is a given. Some stepmothers are wise enough to know they cannot take on the roles of mothers to their husbands' children, but feel they have roles to play as well and that is to be concerned and caring adults. Unfortunately, many other stepmothers do not see it this way and may instead maintain their distance from their husbands' children." There are a number of reasons a stepmother is distant and inattentive to her stepdaughter. For example, many stepmothers feel uneasy with their roles initially and are reluctant to make gestures toward even young stepdaughters for fear that they will be shut out. Many mothers don't like this reason and don't care to hear other excuses. Mothers, most of whom are seasoned at their job of parenting, are not always forgiving of a stepmother's reticence. There is no guide book for divorced mothers when it comes to establishing rapport with stepmothers, and my pool of interviewees had diverse reactions. There are those mothers who truly believe that another mother figure in their daughters' lives is beneficial and welcome the stepmother. There are those mothers who feel, all biases aside, especially when their daughters are young, that it is better for their daughters to have women who watch over them on weekends when they visit their fathers. This group of mothers is quite irked when stepmothers separate themselves from the daughters and treat the girls coolly. This makes many mothers feel doubly wounded, for the repercussions of divorce play out both in the family lives offered to the daughters post-divorce, and in the discrepancies between their statuses in their father's lives and that of their stepmothers.

Juliette, at thirty-five, is a mother of three daughters, between the ages of five and nine. Two years ago her ex-husband remarried Augusta, who has had little energy for her stepdaughters. "What I imagine," begins Juliette, "is that Augusta married Judson and expected that he'd take his girls to dinner once in a while. She must have thought that she'd have this great life with him and that he'd see his daughters on the side. But that isn't what is happening here. In fact, the reason that Augusta is so confused is because during their courtship, Judson gave up some of his nights with the girls to see her. And he kept the girls very separate until they were engaged. While I respect that, I can't understand why he doesn't explain to Augusta that it matters that she is nice to the girls. I want them to have a happy home with their father. I'm not competing; I'm just hoping for the best circumstances for my daughters no matter which parent they are with.

"If my girls were in high school or college, I wouldn't care so much. But they need to feel wanted. They pack up their bags and take their stuffed animals and leave every Saturday for Judson's, filled with joy to see their dad. Then Tammy, my oldest, comes home and tells me that Augusta sat and read magazines and refused to play Monopoly with them when Jud asked her. I say to the girls that Augusta doesn't know how to treat children; she's only twenty-five and that she'll learn. On the surface, I try to make light of her actions. Meanwhile, it makes me furious underneath. She has every luxury and could treat my girls better."

The extended blended family exists whether the mother and stepmother interact or not. My findings indicate that the intensity of the triangle between the mother, daughter and stepmother depends upon many circumstances, as does the relationship between the mother, daughter and father. Studies by Abelsohn and Saayman report that the psycho-social adjustment of children in divorced families "is related to dimensions of family-systems functioning, including cohesion and adaptability." However, there are mothers who simply cannot consider the implications for their daughters when there is a hostile relationship between the parents. "Small children sense what is going on," Antoinette Michaels, relationship expert, observes, "and they react to the parents' relationship. The daughters feel insecure because their parents provide no stability if they quarrel or refuse to speak."

Whatever experience has brought the mother to her life as a divorced woman, as an enlightened single mother who deals with a stepmother on a continual basis, the realities are there. Some mothers with small children feel jealous of the stepmother's input, yet at the same time they need them to help care for their daughters. I observed that there is, often times, a struggle for what is best for the daughters and what kind of loyalty the mother imagines that she deserves. With young daughters, the requirements are specific; scheduling, bedtime, playtime, special treats. Usually mothers reported that after they sorted out their feelings, they were able to recognize that reaching common ground with the stepmother would yield the most rewards for all involved.

Communication between Women

At the other end of the spectrum, I interviewed mothers who do not readily acknowledge stepmothers and refuse or strongly prefer to communicate only with their husbands about their daughters' schedules and purposely leave stepmothers out of the loop. These mothers decide to operate only through their ex-husbands. Such mothers want little to do with the stepmothers because it aids their denial of the stepmothers' existences. This denial is so deep-seated that mothers will explain this behavior as "more efficient." This seems a weak explanation since most single mothers find it exasperating to make plans with their ex-husbands for their daughters' visitation.

In many cases there is an eventual break down in this kind of thinking on the mothers' parts, as exhibited in Debra's experience. "I wanted nothing to do with Sara, Kurt's new wife, initially," Debra, a thirty-four-year-old mother of one daughter, begins. "Sara and Kurt were married for two years before I even spoke to her. Then, one day, my daughter, Kendra, who was eight at the time, was hurt in the school yard. I called all over the place looking for Kurt but I never found him. Finally, with no one else to call, I contacted Sara. Despite my earlier feelings toward her, I was relieved and grateful when Sara rushed to the school to meet me. Together we went to the hospital for Kendra's x-ray and stitches. Ever since then, our relationship has gotten better and better. Sara is so attached to Kendra that I can't help but appreciate her for it. Now, we have a lot to say to each other. And it makes it special for Kendra, because she truly does have two mother figures in her life."

Another category of communication addresses the expediency of the mother making plans with the stepmother simply because she is another woman and the same caretaking and planning skills seem to be ingrained in both. I found that the mothers who choose this route feel that their ex-husbands are not "Mr. Moms" and can be careless or forgetful when it comes to details and so they entrust this duty to stepmothers whom they perceive as more responsible. In these instances, the mother is not only counting on the stepmother, but views her as a stabilizing factor. If the stepmother has children of her own, the mother's confidence in her is often heightened. Both women are mothers, both share that unique gift of "motherlove."

"I have always wanted Charlene to watch the girls when they visit their dad," begins Donna, who at forty-eight has been a single mother for five years. "She has been their stepmother for four years, but she's been a part of our family for ten years. Some of my friends think I'm crazy since Charlene was the girls' baby-sitter when they were small. Fred, my ex-husband, used to take her home, and I guess one thing led to another. My girls have always loved Charlene, so I've let go of my anger for their sake. I don't want them to suffer anymore, especially after the divorce. Charlene is their stepmother now and a part of their lives and that's it. At times, it is very hard for me to bite my tongue, but I know Charlene watches my daughters closely and she cares very much for them. My only real concern is that when Charlene starts having babies of her own babies, will she still be nice to my girls? Will she still be involved in their lives as they get older? I hope so, because they will still need her then."

As I studied the triangle of mothers, daughters and stepmothers, it became clear in many instances that the history of the divorce and the timing of the remarriage play parts in the mother's reaction to the stepmother. Donna's story is clearly filled with pain and deceit; still, her pragmatism is impressive. She keeps her eye on the bigger picture, which is that everyone should get along for the sake of the daughters. Her concern is not about her husband, but that Charlene, the stepmother, remains involved with her daughters' lives.

Some mothers are wise enough to communicate with stepmothers despite their bitterness. I found that when the mother wants the stepmother to treat her daughters fairly, she overlooks a tremendous amount. If the mother wanted the divorce, at any cost, then there rarely is second guessing about the decision. Several wives reported that though their lives as single mothers or as remarried mothers are less than optimal, it was worth everything just to get out of failing marriages. However, almost all of the mothers whom I interviewed expressed displeasure at the idea of joint custody once stepmothers materialized. While joint custody was acceptable before the stepmother came about, her presence changed the dynamic between the co-parenting divorced parents. And almost half of the mothers I interviewed felt that a stepmother's influence had obscured theirs at some point in the mother/daughter/stepmother triangle. As Dr. Ronnie Burak points out, a stepmother can encourage her stepdaughter in ways the mother might not like. "Maybe the stepmother smokes, or drinks, or isn't serious about her stepdaughter's education," comments Dr. Burak. "Or the stepmother thinks that the mother is too strict and when the daughter is at her father's house, the father and stepmother are much more lenient. This undermines the mother's intentions and isn't healthy for the daughter. Then there has to be some communication between the two families."

"There were times when I spoke to my daughters' stepmother, Elyssa, and I felt confident that she and I were on the same page," begins Shannon, a single mother of four years, with two teen age daughters. "Lately, I don't think we have as much in common when it comes to the girls. I thought that she was looser about letting the girls go to parties and drive in cars with kids on weekend. And I thought that she was encouraging Will, my ex-husband, to allow this. The girls go there every Saturday night until Sunday evening, so I was pretty worried. I think now that Elyssa has another way of dealing with it altogether, and that is she expresses her concern and then tells Will that it's really up to him and me. But Will is thinking the way that Elyssa thinks because he's married to her and in her thrall. I can't seem to be heard anymore, by either of them.

"I don't leave the girls there every weekend anymore. Will called me a few months ago and said he wanted to change the visitation. I am now living with someone and we are accustomed to the girls being at my ex-husband's house on Saturday night. Besides that, they are with us every other night. I think that whatever Elyssa and I used to agree upon has changed and she is angling for what's best for her. I wish I could call her up and say, *Isn't it hard with these teenage girls?* And we would agree, and try to figure out what is best for the girls. But that isn't happening these days. A year ago I could have done that, but not anymore."

Regardless of the status quo between mothers and stepmothers as they navigate the world of co-parenting and attempt to forge a relationship of their own at the same time, the dynamic keeps changing. Some mothers begin on good terms with stepmothers and then find issues arising because the two women do not share the same values or point of view after all. If the mother and stepmother have established a connection and the daughters have become accustomed to it as well as to the mother, stepmother and father, it would be wise to hold on, even if there are reasons that the mother feels entitled to let go. There are those situations where the mother and ex-husband simply do not speak and harbor negative feelings toward each other. This is fundamentally unhealthy for the daughters, and the younger they are, the more impact such predicaments have. As Jeannette Lofas points out in her book, *Step Parenting*, a mother who 'badmouths' her ex-husband contributes to a low sense of self-esteem in the children. Lofas also encourages a single mother to have a rapport with the stepmother because it is better for everyone—mother, stepmother and children. When the mother realizes that the stepmother is willing to act as a referee, or a go-between, she is grateful and both women benefit from her efforts.

"I think of myself as mediator or peacemaker," explains Glory, who has been a stepmother to a six-year-old stepdaughter and an eight-year-old stepson for the past year. "I try to believe that things will improve but nothing gets better. Whatever went on in the past, I see it must have been very ugly. I don't want to be in this position, but at least on a weekly basis it is effective and I am able to pick up the kids from their mother's apartment and I bring them home. Already I do projects with my stepdaughter and try to make her feel at home. I see that she misses her mother when she is with us, so I make time for her.

"Lee, my husband, won't talk to his ex-wife, Bett. In fact, the vacation schedules are drawn up by the lawyers and sent by mail. Any communication between the two of them is done through me. Nevertheless Bett and I are starting to have a relationship; we laugh about the kids and worry about their dates with their friends. Lee did not tell me much about what went on in his first marriage and how he feels about his ex-wife, but I like Bett. I know that with such young children, the only thing that matters is that everyone makes an effort to get along."

Distant Fathers/Joined Mothers

In my book *Second Wives*, I caution second wives or those embarking on this mission to beware of men who have not evolved and thus repeat the patterns of their first marriages. In a situation with mothers and stepmothers, this warning is applicable to how the fathers parent their daughters and how this positions the mothers and stepmothers. While a divorced mother might sound bitter and like she has a case of sour grapes when she predicts that her ex-husband will leave his new wife to care for his children while he goes to a ballgame or to the office on a Saturday, she may be right. The disturbing part for some of the mothers I talked to, especially when their daughters are young, is that they are handing their children over to fathers who are absent during visitation. In these cases mothers report the fathers will give their daughters to their wives, who may be eager to please or resentful of being positioned as baby-sitters. If the daughters are very young, some mothers and stepmothers end up leading parallel existences when their time is spent with the daughters. The irony is that these absent fathers also spend their time in much the same way as they did in their first marriages when it comes to their daughters, and so for their purposes, mothers and stepmothers are interchangeable. Many of these mothers wonder why the stepmothers want to take on the responsibilities of parenting someone else's daughters alone. In her research, "Stepfamily as Project," Irene Levin points out, "Whether mothers or stepmothers... the women's roles are very similar. Irrespectively, they take care of children and housework."

"Being a stepmother to my daughters wasn't the best job in the world," begins Juanita, who at thirty-seven, has been a single mother for five years. "The girls, who are now twelve and fourteen, were demanding and any mother figure would do. I knew that when I sent Marilyn and Lisa to Mina's, their stepmother, she was stuck. There have been so many divorces in our family and so many aunts helping me with my girls that Mina just seemed like another caretaker in the family. As for their dad, who knows where he disappears to on the weekends. He wasn't there for me and I knew he wasn't going to be there for Mina.

"At first Mina was shocked by their visits, because they looked like young, frail things in the beginning, but they weren't. My girls really fill a room. She was desperately tired by the time I picked them up on Sunday night. I never asked where their dad was. Mina got her mother to help too, and that was something I used to do. I never blamed her for anything, I blamed him for not showing up for her, for the girls. I even gave her a few tips, since he was far away and not able to help her. I said, rent movies, because the girls love that. And when they got older, she and I agreed on curfew times and how to deal with them. It's like Mina and I are in it together."

Those mothers and stepmothers who become teams for the sake of the daughters reported they did so because the fathers had distanced themselves from their parental roles. The gender expectation—that women are the nurturers—seems to take over and if this works for the mother and she accepts the stepmother, in many cases it is a successful endeavor. If the mother feels that the father is letting his daughters down or if she resents the stepmother who fills in for her as custody dictates, it gets more complicated. "Mothers are expected to take care of their children," comments Dr. Ronnie Burak, "while stepmothers are placed in an entirely different position. Usually they take their cues from the father and that can cause confusion if the father has not really considered what is expected of him as a single father and how it will affect the mother and stepmother."

When mothers witness stepmothers taking on fathers' responsibilities, such as shopping, giving daughters spending money, giving advice, making rules for daughters on weekends as it applies to their social life, this often is disturbing. Many mothers, who feel lonely and don't have significant others or new husbands, report suffering when their daughters are out of their houses anyway. When the children's visits to their fathers are compounded by the fact that the fathers are not accessible, this is very distressing to some mothers with whom I spoke. Many divorced mothers find themselves diminished by the divorce and custody, particularly if they remain in the proximity of their ex-husband for the sake of the daughters. This can be very painful for these women.

"I knew exactly what Linda was getting into when she married Frank," Gerry, a single mother at fifty, says sadly. "She was quite confident that because Frank seemed so smitten with her that he would be around on weekends, that he would quit his card games. But I knew he wouldn't. And I felt sorry for her, because Linda is a nice woman and she's been very kind to my girls. She tried to win them over when they were small, ten years ago, when she and Frank were first together. All of my friends asked me if I minded, and I said that it was fine, that if Linda wanted to offer something to the girls, why not? I knew that it wouldn't be between me and her, but she'd be saddled with them while he did his own thing. That was how it was with me when the girls were little. But then they grew up and now their father's absence is felt in another way. The truth is, Linda and I are on the phone all the time worrying about my older daughter. We don't even bother consulting Frank for his opinion because he never seems to be available.

"Recently Linda and I disagreed on how to deal with my younger daughter's boyfriend, who we both dislike. At that point, I thought we should call Frank and ask him, but Linda was the one who dismissed the idea, saying we could ask, but the decision was ours. I used to be sorry that Frank wasn't more involved with his daughters' lives and that he dumped so much of it on us, the mother and stepmother. The truth is, had I stayed with him it would have been a lousy life for me and I still would have raised the girls alone. This way, at least my girls and I have had Linda there too, for all our sakes."

In this type of situation, I found that after years of mothering and carving out comfortable position with stepmothers, some of the daughters begin to grow up and move away from both mother figures, and from distant fathers as well. Mothers and stepmothers who have formed solid relationships report they commiserate over the extreme behavior of their adolescent daughters/stepdaughters. Neither woman is exempt from daughters' new methods and manners of operating in the world. These daughters become quite independent. Yet the mother's responsibility doesn't disappear and the belief that older children bring more problems than do younger children seems more applicable today than ever before. Therefore, I found that the 'distant father' who has not been involved and has allowed the mother and stepmother to care for the daughter, has less input and understanding

now than ever before. As Alice Michaeli, sociologist, observes, co-parenting is essential for the mothers, fathers and stepmothers. "The
stepmother has the skills to be the negotiator," comments Michaeli,
"when the mother and daughter are too close. It is the stepmother
who is better positioned and this helps the mother and daughter. The
daughter comes out the winner in these situations."

Tug-of-War: Mothers versus Stepmothers

Sometimes when there is a sense of rivalry between mothers and stepmothers, the two women engage in unrelenting competition. In some
instances, mothers who hold tightly to their daughters after divorces
and who lean on them for their social lives—which works until a certain point and then the daughters grow up and become independent—are threatened by stepmothers' presences in their daughters'
lives. If the mother and stepmother have disparate views of the
world, these mothers feel that the stepmothers are not entitled to any
influence.

If there is acrimony and contention between mothers and
fathers, and the stepmothers sympathize with the fathers, the mothers often are well aware of this. Whatever tactics are used by these
fathers to lure the daughters to their sides, the stepmothers often
implement these techniques as well, leading mothers to view the stepmothers as enemies. Fathers often blame ex-wives who initiate
divorces, even after the fathers are remarried, of 'breaking up' the
families by asking for divorces. What is curious is that even those
stepmothers who had similar experiences in their own previous marriages, may still be judgmental toward the mothers and not as accepting as they could be about the mothers' decisions. As Sheila Ellison
writes in her article, "My Life Didn't End After Divorce," which
appeared in *Oprah Magazine*, "There must be more to our waking
moments than feeding children, caring for a house, playing taxi driver
and meeting financial obligations. We are complete human beings who
need to have places and times in our lives that make us laugh, that
make us feel good and that help us to grow." This sentiment is very
valuable for women, who as mothers and wives reinvent themselves
through divorce and remarriage. Both the mother and stepmother
should try to recognize this wisdom.

"My daughters' affections were bought by Roberta, their step-mother," laments Diana, a forty-two year old single mother. "I saw it from the start and since it was their father's way of operating, she just kept it going. Instead of Erik taking them to the mall, Roberta began to do it. Instead of Erik booking lavish vacations, Roberta did it. I am not only objecting to this materialism, but the entire value system which Roberta and Erik share. It isn't good for my daughters and I am unhappy every Sunday evening when they return from a weekend with their father and stepmother. I would have thought that Roberta would be different because she actually was a friend of mine and had suffered through her own divorce. We were once at the same place but I have come to learn her true values are like Erik's. She had to tighten her belt while she was getting divorced but once she got her settle-ment, she began to spend freely, living as she's always lived.

"This isn't easy for me, because I feel that my way of looking at life is negated by Roberta's. And I'm conflicted, because I appreci-ate how good she is to my girls, who are nine and fourteen, but I also dislike her message to them. They never go to a diner or a simple restaurant, and they never stay at home to cook. They run around constantly; the girls do not get their homework finished before they arrive back on Sunday night. Maybe I'm paranoid, but I believe that this is Roberta's way of showing me that she has the upper hand."

When it seems to the mothers that the stepmothers are show-ing their daughters alien and appealing worlds, mothers sometimes feel quite ineffective and fearful of being relegated to last place in their daughters' lives. As author Shere Hite remarks in *The Hite Report on the Family*, daughters feel pain when they see their mothers as victims of "the second-class status of women within the nuclear family." In some of my interviews, the mother sees herself as that victim, and the step-mother as victorious and trouble free. For these mothers, it seems that the stepmother is 'taking away' or 'buying' their daughters. Yet it is not only in the arena of materialism that some mother view the stepmoth-ers as more powerful. When the mother and stepmother have differ-ing views of the work world and what it means to women, this impacts the daughters. For instance, if the mother has a high-powered position in a company and the stepmother has never worked or vice versa, the daughters are exposed to two ends of the spectrum. While this range of choices for mothers might prove enriching and insightful to the daughters, it is successful lesson only if the mother and stepmother who have opposite approaches to life can be open to one another's choice.

A report of this kind was related to me by Mariel who, at thirty-seven, has a part-time job at a local library. "I understand that Ilene, my daughter's stepmother, has an important job as a physician. My daughter, Tanya, is now nine and she is already looking at the world and wondering where she will fit in. So Ilene's job is a good thing for her to see, and it shows her how far women can go. At the same time, I feel like less of a person because I only have a small part-time job. Tanya looks at me and wonders why I can't be more successful or important. There all these underlying problems as a result. On a school holiday, Ilene took my daughter to her office to show her around and Tanya was quite impressed. At first I felt like Ilene did it to show her the difference between us. Then I thought about it and I decided that I shouldn't be so supersensitive. There have been problems with my ex-husband and me, and Ilene and I have kept our distance. But now that she has given my daughter her time and energy, I have decided to embrace our differences. It does not matter anymore. I don't want to fight for Tanya's attention with her stepmother, I want us both to show her the world as best we can."

Remarried Mothers

The mother represents a side in two different triangles, that of the mother, daughter, stepmother and that of the mother, daughter, father. In both triangles, the mother is up against the incalculable moods of the daughter and the irresolution of the stepmother. The father is influenced by his daughter and his present wife, the stepmother, and less so by his ex-wife, the mother. Everyone in the triangle has his or her own agenda. The mother is struggling to raise her daughter with her beliefs and values. The father is as well, however, he is likely preoccupied with trying to see his daughter as much as possible, jockeying for position even though custody is set. As the daughters grow older and can come and go on their own, some mothers believe that the fathers vie for extra time. The two triangles become complicated by the mother's remarriage, which affects the mother and stepmother, the mother and daughter, and the mother and her ex-husband. As Lamanna and Riedmann write in their text, *Marriages And Families*, "double remarriages involving stepchildren have a very elevated risk of dissolution." The authors also point out that the happiness of the couple is not directly related to the success of the stepparent/child relationship. Thus the mother, though she may remarry happily, still has much with which to contend.

Although Susanna's divorce became final six years ago and she remarried John, her steady boyfriend, three years ago, her daughters and their stepmother have made the new relationship difficult for her. "My girls had a stepmother long before John came into the picture. I purposely didn't marry him for two years because I didn't want to upset the girls, since their father remarried so quickly. I look back and I know that I made every effort to get it right and still it's been so hard. My ex-husband and his wife, Helena, made disparaging comments about John, about his work and the house we had bought. I felt that as the girls' stepmother, Helena could have been more supportive. It was almost like my ex-husband and his wife didn't want me to have a life because I had made it so easy for them. I always bent if they wanted to change a night or needed me to keep the girls on a Saturday. John never minded, but once he became my husband, he cared more because he didn't want me getting pushed around by the other side. It came down to me and Helena, and I knew she wasn't on my side. I felt Helena wanted me to be a pathetic single mother, and once I wasn't, she planted thoughts in the girls' heads about me not being there for them.

"Finally, I decided to get everything out on the table. We were both in our forties and we'd been through a lot. The girls were getting along with everyone and I wasn't going to slip backward. I met with Helena and I told her that my new marriage was very important to me. I told her that the girls were getting older and that both of us would have more freedom and that we had to keep working together. And I explained that I expected support from my ex-husband too. Now I am waiting to see if they can live up to their part of this deal."

My research shows that mothers who truly believe that in caring for their daughters share a bond with the stepmothers, can be quite shaken when their own happiness is undermined by these same stepmothers. Often times the stepmother sides with the father, who can be ambivalent about his ex-wife's remarriage. Other times the stepmother is worried about how the mother's remarriage will affect her own situation. While E. Mavis Hetherington's study indicates that stepfathers usually do not take on as significant a parenting role in their stepchildrens' lives as do stepmothers, the father, nonetheless, is able to subvert his intentions toward his ex-wife's new partner. This can create friction between the mother and her ex-husband, and the stepmother, as well as the mother and daughter.

"When I remarried, things got a little harder for June as a stepmother to my daughter, Cammie," admits Samantha, a thirty-five-year-old remarried mother of one. "Before I met and married Tom, I was available twenty-four hours a day for my twelve-year-old daughter. I made life a breeze for Roy, my ex-husband and his wife, June. But once I met Tom, things changed. I wanted time alone with my new husband, and I wanted to change some visitations to make that happen. I tried to be flexible, but June and Roy resisted. Finally, when I complained, they claimed it was Cammie who didn't want things changed around. Next thing I knew, Roy told me that I was no longer the same mother as before my marriage to Tom. I was outraged. Roy's accusations were extremely unfair. He got off the hook as a father for years; all I wanted was a little time alone with my new husband. I know June told him to say something. I thought since she knows how hard it is to be a mother and a new wife, that she'd be more understanding and helpful. This incident really hurt my relationship with June. Later June apologized, saying she felt Roy was overly harsh and she wanted to work with me. She actually said she was happy for me and Tom."

When a remarrying mother is questioned about her decision by her ex-husband (especially when he claims he is only asking out of concern for the children), she often will suspect the that behind the ex-husband's query is the stepmother pushing him in an effort to stir things up. This is not always the case, and some stepmothers not only see the stratagem of happier ex-wives/mothers but are genuinely pleased for them. "When both parents have created new lives for themselves that are successful," notes Dr. Donald Cohen, "everyone profits. The mother and stepmother need to be tuned into this. What matters is that the adults work together for the daughters' sakes."

Because she was able to work things out with June, Samantha's experience in remarriage differed from that of Sonia's, a single mother who remarried at thirty-nine.

"I was so uninformed when I remarried three years ago," Sonia recalls. "I thought everyone would be happy for me, from my daughters, who were seven and twelve at the time, to my ex-husband and his wife, Emily, whom I had always trusted. Instead I was totally naive, and unprepared. I felt like Emily was watching me like a hawk from then on, just waiting for me to screw up somehow. She insinuated to me that I was too caught up in romance to care for the girls anymore. It simply wasn't right; it was more like I was floundering, trying to please everyone. I felt tugged in every way. In the end I swallowed my pride and spoke with Emily because she was the only one who could make a difference, who mattered to the girls and was in a position to help. I asked her to change the days so that when my husband was traveling for business, the girls would be with me and when he was around, they could be with her and their father. She understood and made it happen—which wasn't so easy. I suppose I was chickening out on the hard work it takes to make a stepfamily, but I needed time, which she understood."

Having spoken with hundreds of mothers whose ex-husbands remarried, I see how difficult it is for these women to meet the demands placed upon them, as single mothers or remarried mothers. In either circumstance, the interaction of the mother and stepmother has a great effect on both women and the daughters as well. If mothers and stepmothers understand each others' needs without envy or resentment, and recognize the complexities of their roles, they can have very productive relationships. Many remarried mothers recognize how hard it is to balance new marriages and children. Some feel fortunate that their daughters have stepmothers who also struggle with this balance and empathize. Both women are facing the challenges of forging lives for themselves without sacrificing their daughters and their roles as good parents in the process.

Mothers must deal with several issues at once if they are going to successfully negotiate the potentially mine-strewn path of divorce, remarriage and stepfamilies and build strong, healthy relationships in the mother-daughter-stepmother triangle. Whether struggling with miscommunications, the fragilities of parenting very young daughters, carving out their own territories or coping with co-mothering in the wake of absentee dads, mothers must put aside their own egos and personal feelings to work with involved stepmothers for the sake of the daughters influenced by both sets of women. Real success comes when the daughters are grown into well-adjusted adults who credit their mothers *and* their stepmothers for their happiness and well-being.

Rx for Mothers
1. Recognize the complexity of motherhood.
2. Realize that divorce further complicates the role of mother.
3. Be consistent in one's mothering after the divorce.
4. Pay attention to your daughter's feelings about the stepmother.
5. Avoid preconceived notions about the stepmother and encourage your daughter to also be open and nonprejudicial.
6. Do not let feelings about your ex-husband influence your feelings about the stepmother.
7. Move slowly and carefully in developing dialogues about your daughter with the stepmother.
8. Do not compete with the stepmother; recognize there is room for her in your daughter's life.
9. Never doubt your unique role as a mother, however, recognize the value and importance the stepmother can have in your daughter's life.
10. Remember the advantages for daughters when the triangle relationship between mother, daughter, stepmother is supportive, nurturing and loving.

CHAPTER 3

Stepmothers: Paving Their Way

"I wanted to be Gregory's wife, but being a stepmother to Jillian, his daughter, and dealing with his ex-wife, Clara, is another story altogether," admits Katrina, forty-three. "Still, because I feel strongly about my commitment to Gregory, I have made an effort to extend myself to both my stepdaughter and her mother. Jillian is an adult and has twins of her own, so I never knew her as a small child and I am closer in age to her than to her mother. I naively believed that she and I would get along. In the beginning, five years ago, I expressed an interest in spending time with Jillian and her children. But Clara controls her daughter and keeps me at a distance from Jillian. I am treated like a trespasser, someone who doesn't know her bounds. At the same time, Clara encourages my husband to spend time with his daughter and grandchildren. In this way, Clara makes my husband choose constantly—should he spend time with his wife or his daughter.

"For me, the hardest part is being on the outside looking in at Clara, Jillian and my husband. There isn't much I can do, but I've never given up the hope that Clara will say the word to Jillian and allow me into their world."

In my interviews I found that when stepmothers feel they are up against the strength of the mother/daughter relationship and the mother's feelings toward the stepmother, which can be hostile, this makes the stepmother's role even more difficult. Even for stepmothers who never assumed they would be closed off from their husbands' daughters or who married men despite unfriendly daughters and mothers, these stepmothers still do not want to feel like interlopers. Just like Katrina's case, in which the mother wields power over other members of the family, so it is for many stepmothers. If the mother approves of the stepmother, the daughter is free to forge a relationship with this woman. If the mother feels negatively about the stepmother, the daughter often follows suit and keeps her distance. If the stepmother reaches out to her stepdaughter despite the mother's negative feelings, the situation becomes complicated for the daughter. Daughters who were living through such situations told me they did not know what to do: reject their stepmothers or accept their appeals and, as a result, betray and upset their mothers. Without the mother encouraging her daughter to have a rapport with the stepmother, the daughter may well never resolve her ambivalence. In the end, this situation makes life difficult and, at times, unpleasant for all three women.

At first a stepmother can feel triumphant in her marriage since she, as the second wife, offers her husband a second chance. While romantic feelings and the happiness of building a future together are positive for the new couple, the stepmother's real obstacle is, many times, the former wife and mother to her stepchildren. As this reality sets in and the stepmother finds herself unable to establish a connection with either her stepdaughter or her husband's ex-wife, the stepmother may become concerned. In my book, *Second Wives*, I note that many stepmothers feel insecurity not about their marriages but about their husbands' first families and ex-wives. Since the interactions between the stepmother and her stepdaughter are influenced by the mother, it is important for the stepmother to establish some kind of positive relationship with the mother. Yet the mother, depending on the history of her first marriage and subsequent divorce, is not always receptive to the stepmother. If the mother is not forgiving of her ex-husband, the mother's anger may now be directed toward the stepmother and she may use her daughter as a pawn in this emotional tug-of-war. In such cases the stepmother not only feels she is on the outside of the family looking in, but her self-esteem is eroded by the mother's hostility. The ways that the mother may manipulate her daughter's behavior toward the stepmother vary, depending on the age of the daughter and the depth of the mother's anger. From the stepmother's point of view, the relationship between herself and the mother changes over time—

improving or worsening, depending on circumstances and the behavior of both women.

Trapped Stepmothers

In some cases, unfair demands are placed upon the stepmother, including the expectation that if she and the mother get along, that she will be the arbitrator for unresolved issues between the mother and her ex-husband. She may also be expected to act as caretaker for her stepdaughters, regardless of their attitude toward her or be viewed as sole chef and housemaid for her husband and his daughters during their visitation. When daunting expectations like these are placed on the stepmother, the results can be quite devastating for her. Santock and Sitterle in their study on stepfamilies found that stepmothers experience more anxiety and depression than do mothers. The uncertainty in the role is paramount, since soon enough the stepmother senses the cultural expectation that she do the necessary "mothering," yet at the same time the stepmother also becomes acutely aware that no matter what her endeavors, she can never be the mother. The stepmother who attempts to establish a bond with her stepchildren can feel shut out by the mother if she does not encourage the stepmother's gestures. Or trickier yet, the mother might be unpredictable in her behaviors and there will be overtures from the stepmother that she accepts and those that she rejects.

"What makes it horrible for me," sighs Nicole, a stepmother of five years, "are the holidays. My husband's three daughters, who are nine, thirteen and eighteen, always come for Christmas Eve, Thanksgiving dinner and Easter dinner. They come to us directly from their mother Gail's house and the girls seem to be pitted against me before I even open the door to welcome them. Every year since Clay, my husband, and I have been married, I have asked their mother, Gail, if they can sleep over. It would please Clay and I if she gave us a little more time with the girls. Maybe they would feel less split down the middle if their time with their father wasn't so short. Gail always quotes the divorce decree which states that five to ten p.m. is the prescribed time for these holidays. I think her inflexibility is a result of anger directed at me and is a way of reminding me that she is the mother and she doesn't want these girls to be too close to me.

"This kind of rigidity colors our weekends as well. Clay has told me that Gail wasn't so strict before I came on the scene. This makes me feel guilty, like I've sabotaged his special times with his girls. Another factor is that my stepdaughters are different ages and have different interests. But Gail instructs them to band together, so we can't even do something one on one, such as Clay taking the older girls somewhere and me taking Lacey, the little one, to a movie or the mall. I am constantly reminded of how hard this job is, being a step-mother, not because of the girls, but because of their mother."

Our culture is invested in the idea of the intact family. There are no guidelines or rules for stepmothers, only a social stigma against their existence. In some stepfamilies every move the stepmother makes is under the scrutiny of the mother and is often criticized. While some mothers complain that stepmothers do not truly care about or have an interest in the well-being of their daughters, the step-mothers complain that they have no chance of forging relationships with their stepdaughters because the mothers won't allow them. Even in those cases where the stepmother and mother have similar sensi-bilities and might have been friends in another life, the chances of these two women bonding, at least in the beginning, are little to none. "The stepmother has to be very patient," explains Dr. Michele Kasson. "There is nothing about her job as a stepmother that solidifies quickly. The mother is watching and waiting to see what will happen next."

Only a few women with whom I spoke came to their marriages looking forward to being stepmothers to stepdaughters. Rather, most stepmothers loved their husbands and vowed to be the best wives possible. If pleasing their husbands meant accepting stepdaughters, some were ready to do so. But it was the husband who came first. The husband is a pivotal component in how the triangle plays out between his ex-wife, the mother, his new wife, the stepmother, and his daugh-ters, as we have seen in previous chapters. In many instances not only are the husbands not equipped for the machinations that ensue between stepmothers and mothers, but these conflicts are more than the men bargained for. Rather than dealing with the mess of interced-ing on his wife's part, the husband may shut off from the drama, keeping his emotions to himself. Many stepmothers sense this and, rather than burden their husbands further, they suffer alone. After all, stepmothers may see it as pointless to attempt to solicit their husbands' help if they suspect the men will not contribute. As Shere Hite writes about wives in *Women and Love: A Cultural Revolution*, "the kind of love they (wives) have in their marriages is not based on in-depth two-way emotional support." The stepmother and mother have much in common; For example, it is in dealing with the mother that the stepmother recognizes the lack of support from her husband; the mother likely divorced her ex-husband for exactly these same emotional deficiencies.

I found similar scenarios among the stepmothers I interviewed. "I think about Renee, my stepdaughter's mother, all the time. It's as if she haunts me," Melissa, a new stepmother at the age of thirty-eight, confides. "I think that Lanie, my seventeen-year-old stepdaughter, is spoiled by Renee. This is a peculiar, I know, since most mothers think that stepmothers and fathers spoil their daughters. I would make more time for Lanie if her mother didn't anticipate her every need and buy her every piece of clothing and every accessory that a teenage girl would want. I can't imagine anything I buy would matter, she has it all. There is no place I could take her that her mother hasn't already shown her. I feel so inadequate. And all the while, Lanie watches me with her father, and reports our every move back to her mother.

"My only hope in this is that Renee will get married or find a job or something, so that her daughter is not her obsession. Then maybe she and I will be on an equal playing field, since we'll both have husbands or jobs. Now Renee has Mitchell's daughter and I have the rest. I feel like a second-class citizen as the stepmother and I am waiting for Renee to get a life of her own, one not completely wrapped up in Lanie, so that things can change."

The role of the mother, her sacrifices and her unconditional love are recognized by the courts as manifested in the majority of mothers being awarded custody. The stepmother often feels she is less, since she is not the real mother. Along with many mixed messages, our culture continues to encourage motherhood as the quintessential role for women. As anthropologist Sarah Blaffer Hrdy remarks in her book, *Mother Nature*, "Mother love could safely be interpreted then as a 'gift' consciously bestowed." The stepmother is labeled a mother of sorts, but not a real mother. And so the stepmother waits for something monumental to happen to her stepdaughters' mother so that the mother will be more accepting of her.

Connections: Forged and Unforged

The history of the divorce and new marriage has a great deal to do with how the stepmother relates to the mother. If the father/husband has confided that his ex-wife acted reprehensibly during the divorce, the stepmother will sympathize with her husband. The stepmother, as the new wife, is invested in this marriage, and wants to believe that her husband has provided for his ex-wife and daughters. A stepmother seeks comfort in believing that her husband has not shirked his responsibilities to his ex-wife and first family. If the husband tells his wife, the stepmother, that his daughters have been prejudiced against him by their mother, she may join in her husband's crusade to win them back and to appease the mother. As the late Emily Vischer stated in her presentation for the Stepfamily Association of America in February of 2001, the couple needs to work together on these family issues, which creates greater depth in the relationship. Some stepmothers believe that they can right any wrong of the past, that they can somehow achieve working relationships with the mothers. While this is the optimal outcome, believing it is possible from the start creates unrealistic expectations. Emily Vischer viewed "unrealistic expectations" as an "undermining dynamic" in the world of stepfamilies, and pointed out that adults are more unrealistic than are children.

One of the stepmothers to whom I spoke who had the problem of unrealistic expectations was Stephanie. "When I found myself a stepmother," begins Stephanie, thirty-six, "I wanted to be close to the kids, especially my ten-year-old stepdaughter, Tamara. I felt that this was my only opportunity to be motherly since my husband, David, had already made it quite clear that he didn't want any more children. I had this vision of a happy family and the mother praising me for taking care of her children. Since I am neither the same race or religion as my stepchildren, I thought they would find me interesting and that the differences would work. But I now know I was being naïve and foolish.

"David's ex-wife tries to keep the kids from developing a relationship with me. I thought it was because of the cultural differences, but

I have come to realize that it is because I am the stepmother, plain and simple. I know now that it has nothing to do with me personally and everything to do with the fact that I married her ex-husband and that her children see me every other weekend. While I am relieved that her bias is for the position of stepmother and not against me personally, I'm also very disappointed. I still hope that one day, even if it takes years, there will be a rapport between us. I know that this can happen with the kids, but I want it with their mother too. I don't want to give up."

Many stepmothers lose their illusions early in their marriages, but the hope might never die. Often there are differences not only of personality but background between the stepmother and mother. A stepmother who is from another race and religion than her stepchildren is not uncommon. According to Lamanna and Riedmann, this is a result of a combination of a smaller pool of eligible mates with a wider range of backgrounds and the fact that "divorced people tend more toward heterogamy." The theory is that homogamy—like attracts like—is more common in first marriages than in second marriages. Such differences make many stepmothers feel even more like outsiders. Yet I found some stepmothers are not dissuaded from trying to make connections by any of this. As Claire Owen, psychologist, believes, the stepmother wants to be liked. "The stepmother is hoping that things will go easily. She wants to be connected to both the mother and the daughters." What the stepmother with an idealistic outlook doesn't see at first is that mothering is complicated for mothers, let alone stepmothers. In her book, *The Enlightened Stepmother*, Perdita Kirkness Norwood writes, "Many [stepmothers] talk[ed] about the fun they expected to have with their husband's children. Only in retrospect do women realize that many of their ideas about stepmotherhood are unfounded, ill-advised, or downright wrong." Often, being a mother before becoming a stepmother makes a big difference in having realistic expectations and dealing with the realities of child rearing.

Gina, a stepmother for almost two years, has two young sons and a stepdaughter. Being a mother prepared Gina to smooth the family blending process for her sons and her stepdaughter, but she still had a thing or two to learn about the delicate balance between mother and stepmother. "I have been lucky because Alicia, my stepdaughter, has a mother who is quite friendly toward me," begins Gina. "The mother even called me once to say that I am the best thing that ever happened to her ex-husband and that I am a good influence over her daughter, who is nine. I want Alicia to do her homework and to lead a good life. I want my boys to get along with her and to play ball in the backyard together. I think this can work because the children are young enough that we can be a family.

"I got a bit of shock on Alicia's birthday when I invited her mother and grandmother. My husband warned me that it was a bad idea but I thought it was the right thing to do. We had family friends and Alicia invited six little girls over, plus my two boys. Everything seemed to be going fine but when I brought the cake out, her mother stormed out. I think she expected me to ask her to carry and cut the cake for her daughter. The next day I called and tried to patch it up. I told her that if I had offended her in anyway, I was sorry. I learned my lesson. I know now that I can't trust the mother to always think of her child first. Even so, I felt I should apologize for Alicia's sake. I want to share Alicia, I want her to be a big sister to my boys and I know that will only be possible if her mother and I continue to get along."

Gina is beginning to see the difficulties of her situation, yet she still believes in the positive aspects of having a stepdaughter and the necessity of trying to create a tie, sometimes unsuccessfully, to the girl's mother. In the case of Maggie, a forty-eight year old stepmother, her determination is beginning to pay off. Her story illustrates how affirming it is for the stepmother to know that she can communicate with the mother and that eventually their concerns for the stepdaughter are paramount.

"I thought that, because I love Mark so much, his daughters would love me and then their mother would appreciate me," sighs Maggie. "And I've been at this for years. I kept waiting for it to change from respect, which I do receive, to something more. Mark has a joint-custody arrangement with his ex-wife, Alice. I have always treated these girls, who are now fifteen and eighteen, like my own. Since I never had daughters, I put up with their messy rooms and their bad habits, but I still felt a bit like an outsider.

"Recently, I have had a glimmer of hope. Alice called me and solicited my opinion. She wanted to know if I thought that my younger stepdaughter was depressed. I said that I thought she was and that I wasn't sure what to do about it. So we had coffee and we decided to speak to Mark together. I am relieved that this happened, because I was worried about my stepdaughter, Sheila, but I was unable to discuss my feelings with anyone. And Alice has made me feel like my thoughts count. I've always believed that our relationship could work out and now it looks like it will."

The Competition

My research indicates that whether stepmothers choose it or not, they often find themselves embroiled in competition with the mothers. This worsens in the case of the stepmother who arrives on the scene soon after the divorce and inherits the negative emotional debris left from the marriage. The stress and confusion which parents suffer, according to the Stepfamily Association of America, is "related to the continuing effect of their prior marriage and the period between marriages." Since this affects both mothers and fathers, the stepmother is positioned in the eye of the storm. Many come to realize that mothers might be competitive with them on any and all issues, ranging from their stepdaughters to their husbands.

Stepmothers in joint-custody arrangements or married to men who are the custodial parent, catch on quickly to the reality that if their husbands have their daughters much of the time, the girls' mothers are angry about it. Whatever the reasons for this arrangement, I found that the stepmother's very existence seems to exacerbate the circumstances. In her new book, *For Better or For Worse*, E. Mavis Hetherington writes, "the competition between noncustodial mothers and stepmothers was remarkably enduring, and youths with close ties to their noncustodial mothers were less likely to be close to their stepmothers."

"I know that I was supposed to disappear at her will," Sally, a relatively new stepmother reveals. "I know that I'm supposed to wither whenever Ginny calls Charlie and complains about something. I've been sucked into their war. Everything I do with Ellie, my seven-year-old stepdaughter, is seen as intrusive and wrong. The way it works is that Ginny calls Charlie at work to complain that I did something like give Ellie an Oreo cookie. Then Charlie has to defend me. After that, Ellie will come over and tell us she is lucky, because ever since I gave her an Oreo cookie, her mother started giving her Oreos. If I buy Ellie a paper doll, she gets one bigger and better from her mother the next week. Ellie reports all this to me with smug satisfaction. One day I was braiding Ellie's hair and I tugged too hard. She said to me, "Mommy's right, you can't do things for little girls. You aren't a mother!"

In the diverse group of stepmothers I interviewed, there was a sense of strong competition with the mothers, particularly in the early stages of stepmothering. Like Maggie of whom I spoke earlier, these women may be aware of the unfairness of their roles and the expectations placed upon them, yet they still hope that the conflicts can be worked out. Yet this is not an easy road. Some stepmothers are able to win the affection of their stepdaughters, only to incur the wrath of the mothers. Other stepmothers find themselves locked in a competition with the mothers when the mothers are going through difficult periods and are having trouble parenting properly. For example, if the stepmother picks up the pieces or notices that her stepdaughter seems depressed, the mother, who has been preoccupied with her own problems, suddenly realizes she has dropped the ball and the stepmother has picked it up. Upset by this, the mother will jump back in to reclaim her daughter and her rightful role as the one-and-only mother. Antoinette Michaels, relationship expert, comments, "Stepmothers focus on their stepdaughters, because this is an important connection for their future. Meanwhile, some mothers lean on the daughter to alleviate being alone and deserted."

Jessica, a single mother, and Nora, the stepmother of Jessica's children, are embroiled in this type of contentious situation. "I will not sit back and watch while Nora takes over my daughter's life," Jessica, forty, told me. "I admit that life has been very hard for me lately and I've been preoccupied, but I am not giving my child up for anything. Recently, when I returned from a business trip and picked up Shawna from Nora and Dick's home, Shawna didn't want to get in my car and come home with me. She refused. I was embarrassed and devastated. Whatever trust I had in Nora vanished. I felt like they somehow convinced Shawna that I wasn't a good mother. I don't mean that Dick and Nora said it blatantly, but I feel undermined. I'm sure they think they are the winners in all of this."

Nora sees it a bit differently. "We never talk about Shawna's mother when she visits. I know Jessica thinks we badmouth her but we don't. The reason Shawna likes being with me and Dick is that we make more of an effort to just have fun when she visits. We go out, we see movies, we go shopping. It's easier for us because we only have Shawna on the weekends so we don't have to deal with the day-to-day stuff like arguing about homework and disciplining her. I'm tired of Jessica's paranoid accusations about Dick and me stealing Shawna away. She thinks we have to compete over Shawna but Dick and I are happy to share her. I'm happy Shawna likes spending time with us. Jessica will just have to learn to deal with it."

Some stepmothers are able to overcome competition with mothers. One example was conveyed to me by Donna, a stepmother of five years who has been cautious about upsetting her stepdaughter's mother along the way. "I would never do anything that would threaten my stepdaughters' mother," Donna explains, referring to her six-year-old twin stepdaughters and their mother, Ruthie. "I know that their mother cherishes these girls and all that I hope to do is add to their lives. I never take them anywhere or do anything with them that would upstage their mother. When they come to visit us on weekends, I call Ruthie ahead of time and describe what Steve and I are planning. I try to not make any grand plans or outdo Ruthie. When we had tickets for the circus, I asked Ruthie if she wanted to join us. I am positive that I can win her over, and that there won't be a sense of competition between us."

By striking a balance between caring for her stepdaughters and avoiding stepping on their mother's toes, Donna provides a fine example from which all stepmothers could learn. Such a balance is not easy and takes effort, but the payoff—a good relationship with the mother and the stepdaughters—seems well worth the effort.

Stepmothers as Interlopers

Stepmothers who imagine that they can become instant mother figures to their stepdaughters and co-mother with the girls' mothers sometimes find themselves at the mercy of the mothers' visions of how stepmothers and mothers should interact. Despite the "sisterhood" of women, many stepmothers told me they are made to feel like intruders. We are warned by Mary Crawford and Rhoda Unger in their text *Women and Gender*, that "stereotypes about women seem to cluster into two groups involving judgments of competency and liability." I found many stepmothers who certainly feel they are being scrutinized by the mothers and this interferes with their efforts to become close to their stepdaughters.

In interviewing stepmothers I heard the same two hopes repeated often: that they will be on good terms with the mother and fill important places in their stepdaughters' lives. When this doesn't happen due to untoward influence by the stepdaughters' mothers, the result can be devastating.

Despite being both a mother to three children and stepmother to two girls herself, Tabitha gave Winnie, her children's stepmother, a hard time from the start. "I divorced in my late thirties and I remarried a year later. My stepdaughters' mother hated me and saw me as an outsider. She never let me forget it. She also did her best to get the children to hate me. It was awful.

"Two years later, when my ex-husband remarried, I had the chance to do the right thing, but I didn't. His new wife Winnie was young and naive. She had no children, no ex-husband, no experience and too much hope. It would have been easy for me influence my kids to like her, but instead I was cold to her and my kids caught on. I knew she was okay, but I let my kids know, without saying it, that she was to remain outside the circle. Maybe I made Winnie suffer, because I had suffered as a stepmother, but I think I also did it to get back at my ex-husband."

Unresolved issues in old marriages spill into the next marriages. Many times new wives are affected by their husbands' behavior or the husbands' inability to break free from first families, including ex-wives. Other times children have more control over their fathers than do their stepmothers. And, as in Tabitha's story, a stepmother can be deliberately sabotaged by the mother. Not all stepmothers can withstand a mother who purposely discourages her from having a chance with the children. I talked to many second wives who crumbled under the pressure of wanting to be close to their husbands' children because of the blatant cruelty of the mothers. Women react differently to similar scenarios. Not only is this evidenced in the stepmother/mother relationship, but within the roles, there are many distinctions in type. Some stepmothers take a long time to realize that they are deliberately being treated disdainfully by mothers, while other stepmothers see it clearly and choose to remain at a distance to avoid any more conflict.

One stepmother who fits in the latter category described her feelings to me. "I am not someone who wants to be in the mix with the girls' mother," sighs Jordan, a stepmother of eighteen months who has just given birth to a daughter. "I have two teenage stepdaughters and their awful mother is in the background at all times. I can't imagine any way that the mother will tone down, so my decision is to focus on the girls, no matter what their mother tells them and encourage them to love their little half sister. If the mother doesn't get that this is my life, then she'll learn in time.

"I never thought I'd be so tough-minded, but this is the result of trying too hard with the girls' mother when I first married Harry. After a while I decided it's better to be on the outside. This way I can't be blamed for everything, because I'm not involved on a day-to-day basis with the mother and her daughters. I like being on the outside of her crazy inner sanctum."

The conventional negative view of the relationship between stepmothers and mothers can certainly erode any attempts to build a relationship with stepdaughters that a stepmother might have. The two women are often seen as being at the opposite ends of the spectrum which negates any easy way to work together. The stepmother is viewed suspiciously by the mother who casts the stepmother as the outsider. Another issue I saw raised many times was the stepmother sensing that she was being ostracized for her role as a stepmother. "Never the real mother, always a step" is what resonates for many childless stepmothers.

Stepdaughters, Young and Old

The stepmother/mother relationship is often greatly affected by the ages of their stepdaughters and the level of interaction between the stepmothers and the mothers. Without a doubt, being a stepmother to an adolescent stepdaughter is the most arduous part of stepparenting. Those stepmothers who have known their stepdaughters since they were young children have another perspective than those who meet their stepdaughters after the girls have entered the adolescent stage.

The population of stepmothers to whom I spoke have found that single mothers to young daughters often look to their daughters for companionship. In these cases the stepmother can be perceived as a threat to the mother. However, some experts view this differently. "The mothers are divided," notes Antoinette Michaels, relationship expert. "I have seen stepmothers who are close with their stepdaughters and the mothers dislike it and I have seen stepmothers who are appreciated by the mother. Small daughters do well with stepmothers who can give them time and energy—the mothers know this, however they react."

One stepmother explained the difficulty of her role. "I know that having three young stepdaughters is a plus, even if their mother thinks I'm some kind of alien," Lauren, a stepmother of one year at the age of thirty-one, tells us. "I don't really know what I can do about Jackie, the children's mother, except to keep being nice to her daughters. I love that the girls are only seven and four, since I have the chance to watch them grow up. At first, when I fell in love with Jim, I was very intimidated, not so much by his girls, as by his ex-wife. I knew that she was not interested in me, but she complained about my inexperience. It is true that I have no children but I have good maternal instincts. I am always doing fun things with the girls and I love them. I take them to the park and the zoo and read to them when I put them to bed at night when they are with us. I tolerate their mother's attitude toward me because I think about the girls and not about her. I imagine that one day she'll be happy that I'm there for them."

Stepmothers who sense biases against them on the part of the mothers say their ages or lack of experience in caring for daughters are usually the stated reasons. The role of a woman in our society is still perceived by many as tied into mothering and mothers consider stepmothers a poor substitute. Many stepmothers with whom I spoke complain that they are not treated with respect. As Carol Tavris writes in her book, *The Mismeasure of Woman*, "Inequities and ambiguities about a 'woman's place' are built into the structure of our lives and society... They will persist as long as women look exclusively inward to their psyches and biology instead of outward to their circumstances..." Thus the stepmother can perceive herself as inadequate because she is a stepmother and not the mother. When the daughters are small and the stepmother is immersed in caring for them, even on a visitation basis, she obviously feels invested in her stepdaughters' well-being. This is true regardless of the mother's perception that the stepmother's gestures are not real or vital.

Some stepmothers I interviewed reported that they struggle to get their stepdaughters' mothers' attention, as if this affirms their roles. Other stepmothers go through the effort of care taking of the daughters (bringing them to school and their play dates, preparing meals for them, shopping for them) and still say they doubt their abilities, because the girls' mothers do not acknowledge the stepmothers' roles. Combined with this lack of self-confidence is a sense of impatience toward the stepmother. Although the development of a stepfamily takes years, as documented by experts including Patricia Papernow, author of *Becoming a Stepfamily*, the stepmother sometimes runs out of steam. Many of the stepmothers reported to me that they feel defeated when they are up against the mothers as well as the problem of winning over their stepdaughters.

"I am always trying to get the girls' mother's attention since I feel I'm such a good stepmother," announces Marylou, a thirty-year-old stepmother. "I have a darling six-year-old stepdaughter, Angie, and I have been there for her. I take her to school on Thursday mornings, because she stays with us on Wednesday nights and her father leaves too early to do it. I have taken off from work on the Saturdays when she is with us because I like to be available to her and to spend time together. But when it comes to her mother, I am *persona non grata*. It's as if I didn't exist. I often call Doreen and report our plans and she would be unreceptive. I used to feel defeated, but now I get on with my day and don't pay much attention to Doreen. I have built my own relationship with Angie and that's what counts, not what her mother tries to do to us.

"Still, my hope is that eventually I will be accepted by Doreen. Now and then, Doreen does make me doubt myself as a stepmother. Then I ask myself how I can be so afraid of Angie's mother. I just hope that things will change when Angie is older. I don't want Doreen to still be trying to sabotage my relationship with Angie then."

It is unfortunate when a stepmother is put on the defensive by the mother of her stepdaughter, as Marylou describes feeling. Marylou's experience also raises the point about what transpires between the step-mother and mother once a stepdaughter is in junior high and high school. As the daughters grow older, the stepmother may offer a view of life and expertise different from the mother's, if the two women are dissimilar in style. Perhaps the stepmother smokes and the mother is adamant about not smoking. Perhaps the stepmother is spiritual and artistic and this is alluring to the daughter, while her mother is serious and business-minded. Though these differences can be threatening to the mother, it is ideal if she can see the value in having her daughter exposed to other ways of life and other ways of thinking. Regardless of how she feels about differences between herself and the stepmother, the mother may appreciate the stepmother's help simply at this point because raising a teenaged daughter isn't easy.

In speaking to women who had spent time and effort trying to be good stepmothers, it became evident that a stepmother considers herself fortunate if she has a healthy rapport with the mother and step-daughter. The concept of being a support system for the stepdaughter is, understandably, a goal for many stepmothers. However, the thought that the stepmother and mother can support each other helps greatly once the daughters have grown. "Any stepmother can be happy with a cute little stepdaughter, unless the mother really has an axe to grind," Rosalita, a stepmother to eight-year-old Mia, remarks. "I'm waiting for Mia's mother to figure out that we'll need each other later on."

As the late Emily Vischer noted when she spoke to the Stepfamily Association of America in February 2001, the expectation by stepmothers of instant love between the stepparent and her stepchild is not only unrealistic, but so is their idea that the develop-ment of a good relationship with their stepdaughters will yield good relationships with the mothers. Eventually many stepmothers dis-cover their expectations are unwelcome. For others who have spent years talking and working with mothers to give their stepchildren the best care, there is surprise and discouragement when they learn the mothers' attitudes and opinions about them have not changed since the beginning. "Adults are more unrealistic than children," Emily Vischer warned. A stepmother who envisions herself as a mentor to her stepdaughter would like some praise from the mother, even if it takes years to get it.

One stepmother who attained that goal told me her story. "By the time that Darcie was nineteen, I felt I was entitled to some praise," recalls Eileen, a stepmother of twelve years. "So I said something to Phyllis, Darcie's mother, and she agreed. The two of us went out for lunch to celebrate having gotten Darcie through high school and into college. Our next project is to see her with a good partner, in a few years. We even laugh about sharing her babies, as co-grandmothers.

"It's been a strange series of events and it took years for me to arrive at this place. At first it was easy, because Darcie was little and she was the only child in both families. Phyllis and I worked on the all the arrangements together, kid birthday parties, movies on week-ends, pickups from school. As Darcie grew up, I had more to do with her life, not less. For some reason, I was able to hang in when she became a horrible teenager. It still mattered that I was available for Darcie. Phyllis has always been full-time working mother while I have a cottage industry and my hours are quite flexible. I have filled in for Phyllis and vice versa. Today Darcie is on her own, and is close to both of us. Being a stepmother feels special to me, not second-best, but something special in its own right."

A stepmother who repeatedly tries to infiltrate the mother's world through the daughter and finds she is unwanted to varying degrees, can become bitter. Yet I have uncovered a pattern of step-mothers who after defining incidents, suddenly become bound to the stepdaughters' mothers. "Stepmother shouldn't count on miracles," Dr. Donald Cohen warns, "but there are times when a poor relation-ship between the mother and stepmother improves and the step-mother finally gets the mother's attention." Such was the case for Eileen, the stepmother who at last felt vindicated. However, by the time that this takes place, many stepmothers blame themselves—was it because they never had their own children that the mothers did not trust them? Was it because of acrimonious divorces? Did their step-daughters complain about them to their mothers? All these questions were voiced during my interviews and I learned that it is only after much soul-searching and a multitude of experiences that many step-mothers stand back and truly accept that it is their role that puts them at such a disadvantage with the mothers. That is why repeated inter-actions between the stepmother and mother can influence the results.

"I have had bad times with Jillian, my thirteen-year-old step-daughter's mother," sighs Emma, a forty-year-old stepmother. "I used to think that it was because I came into the picture late and Jasmine was already eleven. Then I thought it was because I've never had children of my own and the idea of taking care of a stepdaughter was way out of my reach.

"So I did the best that I could until recently when my step-daughter was visiting and we had a crisis. She went out with two friends, saying she'd be back in an hour. She insisted I let her use the subway even though I felt it wasn't safe. At any rate, several hours passed and I began to worry. When I couldn't get a hold of my husband, I really started to panic. I felt I had to call Jillian. I told her as calmly as I could what had happened. She admitted to me that Jasmine had pulled this same stunt with her too! She told me to wait it out and not call the police. She felt sure Jasmine would come home soon. I was so worried, but Jillian assured me that this was just Jasmine's way of torturing us both. Then Jillian came to our house and stayed with me until Jasmine finally returned. Sine then, everything is working out much better with Jillian and with Jasmine. It's like the playing field has been levelled."

Second Mothers

As evidenced in the tales told by the stepmothers, it is no easy feat for stepmothers to achieve good relationships with stepdaughters and their mothers. Stepmothers who accomplish this are praiseworthy. Once this does happen, stepmothers told me they are faced with new sets of issues.

Most stepmothers do want to be liked by the mothers and believe that this is possible. Although they are in the minority, these stepmother interviewees described themselves as "second mothers" to their stepdaughters. I found this often occurs when the stepmother and the mother are able to communicate and is more likely to happen when the daughters are very young at the time of the fathers' and stepmothers' marriage. "The stepmother who begins her role as such when her stepdaughter is adolescent has more difficulties," explains Dr. Ronnie Burak. "A young stepdaughter is more open-minded and available to her stepmother than an independent teenager is. And the mother is more involved with her daughter's life and so this extends to the mother."

"I am in an unusual situation," begins Rachel, a stepmother of nine years. "I have been best friends with my stepdaughter's mother since before I became Tara's stepmother. When Nancy, the mother, divorced Troy, my husband, she was my best friend. I suppose it seemed strange to people that Nancy and Troy's daughter, Tara, was my godchild and then she became my stepdaughter. It has worked out for me, though, since Nancy was the one who wanted the divorce and since Nancy has always trusted me with Tara. Tara was only four when I married Troy and so she has had two mothers for most of her life. Now that she is in the middle of a difficult adolescence, I feel that Nancy and I are so lucky to be able to talk to each other about Tara.

"I know that my experiences wouldn't work for everyone and that plenty of stepmothers get bad raps, but our relationship really works for me. Sometimes Nancy and I go to lunch or to the movies with Tara and sometimes Nancy and I go alone, like the friends we had been before this happened. Tara's mother and I share every step of Tara's life."

Not every stepmother has the ambition of becoming such an integral part of her stepdaughter's lives. However, I found that even for those stepmothers who are committed to this cause, there are obstacles to achieving this goal. Once again, the history of the divorce, the manner in which the mother and father interact and the mother/daughter bond are voiced as the greatest challenges for the stepmother. Some stepmothers simply jump right in, but find that they and their stepdaughters might not be compatible. Sometimes the mother's take on the stepmother's initial gestures toward her daughter prejudice the outcome, as we've seen repeatedly throughout this book. The best outcomes range from either the stepmother and mother tolerating one another but working together or truly joining together as a team to give the daughters the best of both worlds. I found that the mother who becomes the "second mother" to her stepdaughter almost always wins the approval of the mother in time, as well as the approval of the stepdaughter and the father.

Stepmothers who truly accept the fact that their husbands come with ex-wives and children seem to fare better than those who wish the complications of the mother and daughters would disappear. "A stepmother who has her eyes wide open and a good sense of self can benefit from a relationship with both the mother and her daughters," comments Dr. Ronnie Burak. "Such a stepmother will also be welcomed by the mother who has good self-esteem."

While the daughter remains at the center of the stepmother's and mother's exchanges, I found that the two women can end up learning from one another. They can have a working relationship sharing their observations and the trials and triumphs of co-parenting the daughter. Even if the stepmother and mother are quite different, the common bond uniting the two women is always the daughter.

"Betty has told me again and again that she doubts that she could have raised her daughters if it were not for my help as their stepmother," reports Maggie. "She says that raising her daughters has involved me more than it has her husband! When I look back on what Betty and I went through together, as a team, I understand why she feels as she does. Together we raised her daughters to become two stable, productive adults. On top of that, working together gave each of us so much. It wasn't a piece of cake in the beginning, but we both approached each other openly and with the same goal in mind: being good role models and caretakers to these two young girls. I have heard a lot of negative stories about mothers and stepmothers and I just don't get it."

Through the voices of these stepmothers we have come to understand that raising daughters effectively in a stepparenting environment is an arduous task. While holidays and family affairs may be fraught with drama and disappointment, the more that the stepmother hones her mothering skills, the better her future becomes as part of the triangle. It is a fantasy that the mother/daughter/stepmother bond will be successful immediately. However, even a skeptical stepmother can strive for some sort of peaceful co-existence with the mother as well as with the stepdaughter. Although the stepmothers I interviewed felt discouraged at times, a positive learning curve exists for most, and it often is a matter of trial and error for them to learn what works.

The "perfect world" picture of the stepmother and mother would contain two women able to immediately communicate about the daughters at every age and to find solace in the fact that they are not alone, but in fact, have each other to rely on when the going gets tough. Although most of the evidence from my research refutes this kind of bonding between mother and stepmother early on, there is in enough instances a common ground to be established eventually. And for a certain segment of the population of stepmothers, a wonderful, co-parenting relationship develops over time.

Rx for Stepmothers
1. Have realistic expectations.
2. Carefully observe the mother/daughter relationship.
3. Take cues from the husband/father.
4. Be available to your stepdaughter, but do not force a relationship.
5. Disregard negativity from the mother.
6. Avoid getting in the middle of disputes between your husband and his ex-wife/the mother.
7. Do not speak negatively about the mother to your stepdaughter.
8. Be patient with your stepdaughter; give her time to come around.
9. Keep the lines of communication with the mother open.
10. Remember that you are not the mother, but you can be a mother figure.

CHAPTER 4

Parents' Remarriages: A Changing Universe for Daughters

"I find it odd when my father is with this other woman," begins Elizabeth, who is seventeen, "and my father seems different. Claudia is the opposite of my mother in every way. She is not soft or kind. She's very horsey and not delicate and pretty like my mother. She's nice because she has to be nice to me—she's dating my father. When we have dinner together, my sisters and my father and his girlfriend, my father feels like a total stranger. He worships Claudia, and it's hard for me to understand. I do not want a relationship with her, but I do want to have a relationship with my father. I just doubt that I can because of her. But I am very careful of what I say and do, because I want to have my father in my life. I cannot offend Claudia because of that.

"I guess I never saw my parents' divorce coming. They seemed happy together and close right up until the very end. Now my father has changed and he is not very available to me or my sisters. This is very sad for us. He and I were never as close as he is with one of my sisters but now there is no chance, because he's too busy with his girlfriend. They are planning to be married and he doesn't call us often or spend much time with us because she doesn't want him to."

Nothing forces daughters of divorce to accept the reality that their parent's marriage is truly over as much as the advent of new romantic attachments for either parent. The Stepfamily Foundation states that half of the one hundred twenty million children under thirteen in the United States live with one biological parent and the parent's current partner. Of these sixty million children, half are daughters. According to the United States Census Bureau, the majority of men remarry within three years of divorce. The ambivalence for many of these daughters arises because they want their fathers to be happy, but are afraid that the fathers' new partners will jeopardize whatever relationships they have had with their fathers. When the father's new partner enters the divided, divorced family, the dynamic is altered. Shifts in loyalty evolve, and daughters who have sided with or felt pity for their fathers sometimes change, feeling more for the mother instead.

When Mothers Find New Partners

The majority of mothers and daughters are united by their shared gender and our society's long-standing tradition of girls being nurtured by their mothers both before and after divorce. Previous generations of mothers taught their daughters the importance of domestic life and encouraged them along the way. As Cokie Roberts describes in her book, *We Are Our Mother's Daughters*, historically there was an apprenticeship, where "mothers trained their daughters in domesticity." Many mothers today are role models for their daughters not only in tasks of the home and mothering, but in terms of career and the work world, and ultimately, by example, for relationships with the opposite sex. With four out of ten marriages in the United States being second marriages for one of the parties, many daughters have the opportunity to observe the impact of divorce and remarriage on their mothers, their mothers' friends and on the balance of being mothers, wives and independent women who can support themselves.

"Today there is pressure on our daughters to live in two different worlds," Alice Michaeli, sociologist, explains. "There is the world of the helpful wife and mother. At the same time today's girls must acquire necessary educational credentials and skills." Since the socialization of our daughters incorporates all that is feminine and because mothers and daughters are of the same sex, it stands to reason that daughters relate strongly to their mothers. For many daughters of divorce, as we have seen, adolescence often brings about changes of heart and their sympathy for and identification with one parent may shift. Yet the overriding result, as E. Mavis Hetherington reports in her "Virginia Longitudinal Study" is that most mother/daughter relationships are "close and supportive" in divorced families, while the "mother/son relationships remained more conflictual than those in non-divorced families." Most mothers are challenged by adolescent daughters, without a doubt, as are stepmothers, but despite incidents during this stage, many mothers and daughters share an enduring bond. The equation however, sometimes is shaken not only when the mother has a romantic relationship and/or remarries, but when the father takes the same path thereby introducing a stepmother into his daughters' lives.

Stepmothers who have traveled the same roads as the mothers have often suffered similar consequences of divorce, socially, emotionally and financially. Yet daughters of both mothers and stepmothers often perceive their mothers' remarriages as betrayals because of the new bond established between daughter and mother during the mother's post-divorce, single period. In our society mothers often are perceived as sexless caretakers who have little time or seem undeserving of male attention and romantic love. Some of my interviewees confessed that it was an absolute shock to some daughters that their mothers have both physical and emotional needs and desires. Daughters' misperceptions extend to stepmothers as well. Stepmothers who inherit adolescent stepdaughters often find their relationships confusing and challenging beyond any expectation. Although the triangle of mother/daughter/stepmother is fraught with intense emotions, many mothers and stepmothers who could objectively view the situation recognized and sympathized with each other's plights in dealing with daughters of divorce.

"I have found myself defending Herb's ex-wife, Loretta," begins Denise, a thirty-three-year-old stepmother of eighteen months. "I do see how hard it is for her to plan time with her fiancé and how resistant her daughters are. My own daughters, since they are only six and nine, did not make a fuss over my marriage to Herb. I told them this was how it would be and they knew there was no other choice. The older girls, my stepdaughters, are tough on their mother and tough on me. I see how they talk about Loretta's fiancé, Joel, and how they make fun of him. I guess they make fun of me too, when they are with their mother. And I see how they feel entitled to have their mother all to themselves.

"I have this urge to call up Loretta and tell her it will be okay.

She and I were divorced the same year and met our future mates within a few months of each other. We both have daughters, we both work full-time and we both had to sell our homes during our divorces. She is getting married in June and I want to be supportive. I know how tough it will be for her. The dust hasn't settled here by any means; I can relate to her and I bet deep down she can relate to me. Herb tells me to stop mentioning her and worrying about her, that she is not my concern. But that isn't so. Her life and mine, as divorced and remarried mothers, with two girls to share, sort of brings us together. I would rather work with her as a teammate for the sake of our daughters."

Many stepmothers and mothers revealed they were unprepared by the visceral reactions which their daughters have to their new lives. Stepmothers who have their own daughters to contend with when they find partners sometimes identify with mothers who find partners and have to tolerate their daughters' negative responses. Of the women I interviewed, seventy-five percent of stepmothers with their own daughters and eighty percent of mothers expressed bewilderment at how their daughters behaved in terms of their remarriages. Almost all mothers and stepmothers anticipated some level of negativity from their daughters, but the majority expected that on another level their daughters would be pleased for them and not as antagonistic or distant as they turned out to be.

The ages of the daughters, the conditions of their single mother family units and the length of time that their mothers had been single are all major influences on daughters' feelings when their mothers remarry. Some stepmothers who believe that they have good enough relationships with their stepdaughters to encourage them to be more open and accepting of their mothers' remarriages have rude awakenings. Some daughters' reactions to their mothers' remarriages may not only defy the mother/daughter bond, but can wreak havoc on the stepmother/daughter bond as well. It appears in this situation that the stepmother may be seen as a reminder of the parent's divorce for a stepdaughter who resents this woman even discussing her mother's impending marriage. When this happens, both mothers and stepmothers face a struggle with daughters.

Susanna, one mother with whom I spoke, described her daughters' negative reactions to both her and her ex-husband's new partners. Although Susanna's divorce was final six years ago, and she has been with the same man for five years, her two daughters' attitudes have never been supportive of her relationship or, to a lesser extent, their stepmother's. "I was very careful how I introduced my four children to John. Looking back now, I still believe I made every effort to get it right. My oldest daughter, Jackie, was fourteen when my divorce occurred and she was just beginning to be involved with boys. Sometimes Jackie and I were getting ready for a date at the same time and it seemed like fun. But the minute that John arrived on the scene, the fun ended. Often she would become withdrawn and leave her boyfriend alone in the den with John, refusing to go in and join them. My youngest daughter, Sandie, was delighted that Jackie and I had dates. For a seven-year-old, watching mom and her big sister dress up for dates was fun.

"Four years ago my ex-husband remarried a woman who I think is very good to my girls. Again, I saw that Sandie loved to be with her and bake cookies, put on nail polish and do things young girls enjoy. But just as it happened when John and I became serious, when my ex, Carl, got engaged to Maggie, my older daughter Jackie treated her stepmother just like she treated me, coldly and unfairly. Maggie has a daughter of her own who is grown up and this girl was happy for her mother. So in our extended family, I was able to see examples of how daughters at various ages reacted to their parents' remarriages."

Many daughters who witness their mothers' remarriages are constantly navigating and reevaluating their relationships with their mothers. Sometimes a mother's remarriage causes the daughter to take another look at her stepmother, who may appear more sympathetic and appealing. Discomfort over a mother's remarriage may upset a daughter. I learned in speaking to my interviewees that, whereas fathers are more easily forgiven for their remarriages, mothers are not. In my study, I have heard the voices of many adult daughters of divorce who held this point of view, even if intellectually they knew it was not fair to their mothers.

"I realize," admits Samantha, a thirty-one-year-old daughter of divorce, "that my parents were not going to get back together, whether my mother remarried or not. But I still wanted my mother all to myself and I felt I deserved this because I was the one who took care of her for four years while she was a single mom. I gave up sleepovers at my friends' houses because my mother was so sad when she was alone. I never admitted to her that I enjoyed spending time at my father's and stepmother's house because it would bother her. She was my pal and I was hers. We leaned on each other. I was only nine when the divorce happened, but I understood how much responsibility I had for her happiness.

"Once my mother remarried, everything changed. My mom sent me to my father's and stepmother's more often because she wanted to be alone with her new husband. This not only hurt me, but it started creating problems between my stepmother and me. My step-mother liked having me over but she also wanted time alone with my father. So I felt like an intruder no matter whose house I was in. Now that I am an adult, I can look back and understand my mother's and stepmother's needs. But at the time, I felt used and neglected, particu-larly by my mother."

Many experts believe that when divorced mothers depend upon their daughters for companionship, it creates a hardship for the daughters. Not only does this unnatural relationship get in the way of the child's chance to socialize with her peers, but it also evokes guilt and the daughter feels conflicted. Often this will be the case in the first months or first year after parents' divorce. As time goes on, daughters who once felt put upon become accustomed to being number one in their single mothers' lives. When the mothers meet other men and set-tle into adult relationships and subsequent remarriages, the daughters become confused and feel cast aside. If the stepmother is available to the daughter at this point and they have an independent relationship, the mother is fortunate. For those mothers and stepmothers who have historically not communicated, the mother's remarriage sometimes was a turning point in their relationship. This is not to say, however, that there will not be future issues or competitions.

Though they may do so grudgingly, eventually most daughters accept their mothers' remarriages and new partners. As Judith Wallerstein points out in her study, the mother/daughter relationship is more complex when it entails a divorced family. Yet what Wallerstein describes as the "prolonged push-pull, going from too much closeness to too much distance, which severely affects mothers and daughters in a divorce situation," does, based on my research, level out in time. This I found often occurs as daughters mature and better realize their mothers' desires for second chances at adult relationships. Once these daughters are able to acknowledge their mother's needs, it appears they also bring about greater understanding of and sympathy for their stepmothers.

Double Standard: When the Father Takes a New Partner

When it comes to remarriage and fathers, gender inequality rears its ugly head. Remarriages for fathers has traditionally been largely free of household and child care obligations, though parenting obligations in more modern households have changed and fathers are often more involved. Even so, close to ninety percent of my interviewees witnessed their ex-husbands experiencing difficulties in adjusting to single lives immediately following the divorce especially if the wives precipitated the breakup. Yet most rebounded quickly, moving into new long-term relationships and remarriages. It seems society accepts this path for men while divorced mothers are given the implicit message to proceed with caution in dating for the sake of the children.

Often in divorce, the father moves out, leaving the ex-wife and children in the family home. In fact, a large number of mothers report that their ex-husbands move into hotels after the divorce. The most recent vital statistics show that 23.3 percent of children of divorce live solely with their biological mothers while only 4.4 percent with their biological fathers and only 0.6 percent live with their biological father and stepmother. I found in my interviews that the majority of daughters empathize and identify with their mothers after a divorce has taken place, but a minority do sympathize with their fathers, especially in situations where the father gives up a great deal for his family.

"My ex-husband, Larry," begins Helena, who at fifty has been divorced for fifteen years, "lowered his standard of living quite a bit the day he left our house. I think he did it for several reasons—to get some sympathy from our daughters and to show me he had nowhere to go in the hopes that I would forgive him for his affair and we would reconcile. Well, his living in a hotel didn't sway my opinion about him but I could see it affected the girls; they really felt bad for him. It took him longer to find a house than it did to remarry. It was such a relief when he finally did both, for me and the girls."

Those daughters who feel their fathers have suffered frequently hope that their fathers can find some form of happiness. To this end, these daughters feel that their fathers are more entitled to date than their mothers, reinforcing our culture's double standard. Fathers who are less available to their children because of love interests do not concern daughters to the same extent as when their mothers become involved in relationships and are less available. Of course, there are exceptions to these generalities, as in the case of Jessica, who at twenty-three, suffers the repercussions of her father's decision to live with his girlfriend.

"I feel very loyal to my mother—she is the victim in this divorce," sighs Jessica. "I'm closer with my mother than my father, who doesn't even listen to me. My mother is both a friend and a mother. I would not mind seeing her remarry at all and I wish the best for her. She is dating someone now whom I really like. He has been very good to me about everything, especially since my father is not there for me. I like Eric and hope he and my mother stay together partly because my father pays no attention to me. I feel like a ghost when I am with him. My father would like me to have some kind of relationship with his fiancé, but there is no way that will happen. I have friends who really dislike their mothers' husbands or boyfriends, and yet they like their fathers' girlfriends. I am just the opposite."

Since the majority of daughters under the age of eighteen live with their mothers after their parents' divorces, their relationships with their fathers may be more tenuous and distant. Hetherington, Stanley-Hagan and Anderson report that gender plays a significant role in how children behave after divorce, noting that any disturbances "in social and emotional adjustment in those girls living with their mothers have largely disappeared by two years after divorce in contrast to those daughters in the custody of their fathers who show higher levels of aggression and behavioral problems and fewer incidences of pro-social behavior."

Once fathers had introduced their significant others to their daughters and announced their plans to marry, many daughters wonder if their relationships with their fathers would be jeopardized by this life change. "If these daughters are very close with their father, they are threatened by another woman coming into his life, even if they are happy for their father," explains Dr. Donald Cohen. "Much of this depends on the age of the daughters. But the bottom line is that the daughter may feel she must compete with the new wife for her father."

Some fathers at this stage fail to notice their daughters' apprehension or competitive feelings. Thus, many daughters who often have not seen the most mature behavior exhibited during the divorce period witness their fathers' attachment to other women with misgivings. As the new partners become integral to their fathers' lives, daughters have asked themselves: *Who is this woman? What does she do for my father that my mother could not?* Again, how this plays out often depends on the age of the daughter when the divorce and second marriage take place.

Daughters under ten years of age can, in general, be quite accepting of their fathers' new partners and view them as other mother figures. As Sallie, twenty-seven, whose father remarried when she was eight, explained, "I couldn't get enough mothering. I had a great mother and a great stepmother. I was a little girl and I wanted them both. I wanted it all. But I had friends whose parents divorced when they were in junior high and they didn't see it quite the same way. Those relationships took a beating before everyone settled in."

For Dorothea, thirty, whose stepmother came on the scene when she was seven, there was the promise of a happier father. "I am the oldest of three children. Our mother walked out on us when I was six and we never saw her again. She met a man and they ran off, and they both divorced their spouses to marry each other. Soon after that, our father remarried. Charlotte, my stepmother, was kind and decent. But I still missed my mother and I also lost my status as daddy's little girl. Once my mother left, my father became preoccupied with how he was going to take care of us and with his new marriage. After a while, my father came back to me, so to speak, and I focused more on my relationship with my stepmother since I needed something to fill the void left by my mother."

Although in many cases live-in partners/stepmothers evoke negative reactions from daughters of divorce and unquestionably destroy dreams of their parents' reconciliation, it is clear from Dorothea's story and other daughters with whom I spoke that some are open to the situation.

The correlation between how these daughters react to their new stepmothers often is contingent upon how the stepmothers and fathers interact. If couples are very exclusive and the daughters feel they are unwelcome, this usually takes its toll on the relationship between the fathers and their daughters. If the new couples are welcoming, there is the possibility of forging a bond and having a happy future in those stepfamilies. On the other end of the spectrum lies the over seventy percent of daughters that I interviewed who have admitted having easier times with their fathers' remarriages than their mothers' remarriages. Thus, in many cases, fathers and their new wives have better chances of winning the affections of daughters/stepdaughters than do mothers and their new husbands.

Emmie, a twenty-seven-year-old daughter of divorce, explains why she found her father's remarriage acceptable and her mother's remarriage unacceptable.

"I am bonded with my mother and we are very close," begins Emmie. "I respect her more than anyone in our family even though I was angry when I was in high school that she had to raise us in wretched conditions. At first I liked my stepmother, Lena, because I admired her lifestyle and came to really know and like her. In high school I was not so forgiving or fair to my mother. I think that my sisters and I were much nicer to our father when he married Lena. I regret that we made it so difficult for our mother and her husband. No one ever gave them a chance."

My interviews indicate that like Emmie's stepmother, mothers who become stepmothers are often successful at established relationships with their stepdaughters. However, these mothers sometimes find that their own daughters from previous marriages are not welcoming of their husbands and unreceptive to their mothers' remarriages. These women, who are both remarried mothers and stepmothers, find themselves navigating two rocky paths, one which encourages connection with their stepdaughters and the other which concentrates on the lack of connection between their new husbands and their daughters.

Over sixty percent of remarried mothers in my research reported frustration at how much easier their ex-husbands seemed to adjust to their new wives and daughters. The mother's predicament is worsened by the reality that while stepmothers might not be immediately accepted, many daughters do come to accept them in time. Some mothers are bitter about the break that stepmothers and fathers get and this can be added to the list of negatives that mothers feel about the stepmothers. As the mother struggles to get her own life straightened out in terms of her daughters and her new marriage, the father's ability to easily maneuver through a similar situation is distressing and seems unfair. If the mother has been harsh toward the stepmother, she might lighten her attitude at this point, realizing it does little good for the daughters or either woman. If the daughters have mellowed and were at first vociferous about their new stepmother, the mother can find their change of heart to be promising. She can hope that with time, her remarriage might come to be accepted by the daughters too.

Daughters, as I've said before, are not as likely to blame their fathers for their parents' divorce as they are to blame their mothers. In some cases this is compounded by the fact that the father and step-mother lead a nice, comfortable life while the mother no longer does, which may appear to be further proof to the daughter of the mother's former complicity in the divorce. With this in some cases comes a lack of forgiveness toward the mother and sympathy for the father. It seems ironic that even though girls identify more closely with their mothers, this has little bearing on the daughters' feelings about their fathers when they remarry, compared to their negativity toward the mothers under similar circumstances. Logically, one would expect her gender identification with her mother to bring about the daughter's openness toward the man whom the mother loves. Instead, as Dr. Donald Cohen tells us, "If the daughter is closer to her mother, she will be threatened by someone she is dating. Much of this depends on where the daughter is in her own sexual development. The daughter sees her mother as a victim in the divorce, and may be more sympathetic to her remarriage. If she blames her mother for the divorce, she will be angrier about her remarriage."

Economics of Remarriage
No matter what kind of person a father has chosen as his new spouse, most daughters see these new wives as interlopers who have ended

any chance of the daughters' parents being reunited. To make matters worse, the economic burdens of divorce which usually fall more heavily on mothers, further affect daughters' views of her father and his new partner and the lifestyle the two create together.

"My father was a good provider," begins Felicity, twenty-three, whose parents divorced when she was twelve, "and then he left us for another woman. Even though he never helped my mother care for me and my sisters, I still thought I had a great father. I was hurt by his leaving. To make matters worse, my sisters, my mother and I all suffered financially. My father had a good job but he moved across the country and didn't take responsibility for most of our expenses. I watched our mother work so hard to make ends meet. Finally, years later, I forgave him and accepted my stepmother, because I cannot hold a grudge for the rest of my life. I try not to think of what might have happened, how we could have lived, if he hadn't left."

Some daughters with whom I spoke are acutely aware that their single mothers live deprived existences. Then they see their fathers remarry and their quality of life improves greatly. Suddenly these daughters find their fathers are more well-off than their mothers, especially if their mothers have not remarried. Many daughters witness their stepmothers living the lifestyles the daughters and mothers once had. This baffles many daughters of divorce and may diminish their perception of their mothers. As Judith Wallerstein points out in her book, mothers of young children become absentee parents once divorces occur in order to work and help support the family. The majority of mothers of young children often return to work as a way of feeling less isolated as well. The mother's absence is keenly felt and can be traumatic for young daughters. Older daughters often are not as upset by their mothers' absences, but do become upset when their mothers must return to the workplace out of dire need. When they compare their mothers' situations to their fathers' easier lifestyles, many daughters pity themselves and their mothers for what they have lost.

"The essential issues here are self-esteem and time," explains Dr. Michele Kasson. "The family needs to recognize that the changes in lifestyle do not diminish the mother and the daughter. The mother can teach her daughters about perspectives and values in life that are unrelated to material wealth."

Sexual Rumblings in the New Homes

When parents remarry, there is a honeymoon phase with which daughters must contend. When fathers remarry, for example, their homes may seem filled with sexual and romantic overtones that make daughters feel uncomfortable. Again, much of how the daughter responds to her father, his new wife and their new home is a reflection of how she is treated by both parties and how her mother responds. Thus, once again, the elements of the new triangle are important and influential. Even though most daughters do not live full-time with her fathers and stepmothers, joint-custody arrangements or standard visitations bring these daughters and stepmothers in continual contact.

My interviews with daughters of divorce indicate that most daughters do not view their fathers in the same way as they view their mothers. However, I have observed that divorce sometimes creates the opportunity for fathers to develop closer relationships with their daughters. A father who pays careful attention to his adolescent daughter, in order to preserve what existed between them before the divorce or to improve the relationship, can be for the daughters a kind of mirror reflecting the male population. If this father takes his daughter shopping and makes her feel special, then she is, in some ways, already in competition with other females, much as she would have been with her mother—had the marriage survived—for her father's attention. This situation changes when these fathers bring home new wives.

In many instances, daughters who have discovered their fathers' affections for their new partners at vulnerable times in the daughters' lives, feel they have been deprived. Not only that, but seeing women who have obvious sexual relationships with their fathers can be very painful and daughters' positive affections for their fathers can be shaken. As author Stephanie Stahl points out in her book, *The Love They Lost*, "When a father doesn't give his daughter the attention and love she craves, it can affect the way she relates to men." Thus the father walks a thin line when his sexual/romantic relationship with his new wife causes the daughter to feel threatened.

"I was fourteen years old when my folks divorced," says Lori, who at forty-two still sees the repercussions in her family. "My father remarried three years later. I know that my father met his second wife, my stepmother, on a business trip before my parent's divorce. I didn't fault him, though, because my parent's marriage was not good. It was over long before they made it official. And I knew his new wife made him happy. So I was fine with the marriage. But my younger sister who turned thirteen when my father remarried had a rough time. She viewed our father's remarriage as all about sex because our stepmother was much younger and sexier than our mother. She even blamed our stepmother for breaking up our parents' marriage but I know otherwise. So, while my sister has never accepted our stepmother and hasn't gotten along with our father in many years, I have a great relationship with both of them because I don't accuse or blame or try to get between them. As a result, my sister has sought a father in every man she has dated. Needless to say, she's had a lot of failed relationships and she's not a happy woman."

If the mother is remarried as well, the daughter, particularly in preadolescence or older, may find herself in a sexual, romantic arena in both of her parent's homes. A daughter who is beginning to date and socialize with boys wants her privacy and may feel confused about her feelings when surrounded by all this sexual tension. The idea of her father kissing or making love to his new wife is unnerving and makes the daughter feel awkward as she begins her ventures into dating. However, in the case of the mother showing similar signs of having sexual relationships with men, there may be an even stronger negative reaction from the daughter. According to early studies by E. Mavis Hetherington, girls exhibited poorer adjustments to parents' divorces and remarriages than did boys. For these daughters, the idea of their mother as some other man's wife, can be discouraging and distancing. Hetherington's research and my interviews indicate that for these daughters there is an internalizing and externalizing of behavioral problems and their social skills are below those of girls in intact families.

"I think that I act strangely with my boyfriend because my mother has always had one too," begins Carmen, twenty-one. "Even her getting remarried doesn't help. I still keep imagining what they do together and it freaks me out. I think that she acts very young when she is with him and flirts. So how am I supposed to act with my boyfriend? My little sister doesn't like the idea that our mother and stepfather are upstairs in the bedroom together and so, on weekends she tries to sleep over at friends' homes. She also has changed since our mother remarried, and she makes all these stupid sex jokes.

"We were not like this with our father. We did whisper about him and Jennie, his wife, but we didn't feel as threatened by their relationship. With my mom, it's too 'in my face.' I worry about a lot of things, like what if she gets pregnant? Or what if I bring my boyfriend home and we hear my mother's bed squeaking? Why can't she just be asleep in sweats on the couch in front of the TV—alone? It's too strange for me."

Nevertheless, when fathers remarry and daughters compete with their stepmothers, most daughters find these situations difficult, according to my interviews. Fathers need to be keenly aware of their daughters' needs during this time of transition. Fathers' obligations to their daughters often are compounded by their new wives' hopes that they come first and that the fathers first family comes second. It is not easy for anyone; the daughters with their great needs to be loved and nurtured, the stepmothers who often secretly wish that there were no stepdaughters in the picture and for the spouses, who face the challenges of forging new lives for themselves without sacrificing these daughters and their roles as good parents. Acclimation to their stepfamilies takes daughters from four to seven years, according to divorce expert Patricia Papernow. Until that day arrives, mothers, stepmothers and daughters need to communicate and help each other navigate the uncertain terrain. Although the balance is tentative, it is not impossible, as my research reveals, to reach stable footing and secure effective bonding within the triangle.

CHAPTER 5

How Financial Issues Affect the Triangle

"Money was always an issue in our house after the divorce," Brittany, thirty-one recalls. "I was fourteen when my parents split up and our big house was sold. Before the divorce, our whole family had gone to wonderful, far-off places. Even though the trips were usually my dad's idea, my mom was thrilled to go and happy to expose her children to new places and cultures. After the divorce, vacations with my mother disappeared, while trips for us kids continued with my father and our stepmother, Elena. Somewhere along the way my mother's view of it all changed. She seemed to think we were not entitled to these trips and that we'd somehow become spoiled. She even blamed Elena for the trips and spending too much money but it was always—before and after the divorce—my father who planned our vacations. In this regard, it was our mother who had changed, not us.

"Looking back though, I know my sisters and I did change in some ways too. My father and Elena tried to buy me and my sisters' affection and we gravitated toward them for that reason. We began to see our stepmother as lighter and easier to be with. While our mother talked about not having enough money for health insurance, Elena bought us designer jeans and took us to cool restaurants at the mall for lunch. I guess we were influenced by the power of money."

Some daughters of divorce find themselves in two homes where the climates and lifestyles are diametrically opposed. Although many divorces occur when two people do not share the same idealistic values or view of the world, nothing is as glaring as dissimilar views over money and lifestyle. In regard to members of the triangle, while disparate values between both mothers, fathers and stepmothers extend beyond materialism to those of philosophical natures, over ninety percent of mothers, daughters and stepmothers reported to me that money was one of the most profound points of contention.

Shuttling back and forth between two homes takes its toll on daughters' emotional states. Yet when two homes are in very dissimilar socio-economic brackets, suspicion often emanates from one about the other making the transition even more confusing and unsettling for daughters. Many daughters sense this early on and, by the time they are adolescents, they draw comparisons. In some cases, stepmothers live in big houses and have luxuries their mothers do not have because the fathers are well-off. This is especially traumatic when they see their own mothers scrimp. Many mothers' circumstances are quite dismal, since a woman's standard of living declines by thirty to forty percent on the average, according to Duncan and Hoffman, within the first five years of the divorce and over twenty-five percent of women find themselves impoverished. This deprivation of financial stability becomes a preoccupation for some mothers. Such differences often become accentuated over time and daughters attuned to these schisms may make judgments and take sides.

Some daughters, particularly when they are adolescent or older, choose the more appealing road and the moneyed lives of their fathers and stepmothers. According to the Day/Bahr study, the mean per capita income for men after divorce is twice the mean per capita income for women, even when the father remarries and supports two households. According to one interviewee, money becomes a divisive issue between the mother and stepmother when daughters are swayed by their fathers' and stepmothers' lifestyles. Knowing stepmothers are living more comfortably or even luxuriously while they are suffering financially bothers many mothers. But seeing that this well-to-do life is something their daughters are drawn to, makes some mothers bitter and resentful. For mothers who did not want the divorce, these inequities create even greater animosity toward the stepmothers. If the stepmothers' upgraded situations were clearly precipitated solely by their marriages to the fathers, the mothers feel this is just one more reason to dislike them. In cases where the stepmothers are independently wealthy or successful on their own, many mothers are not as resentful, but surprisingly, quite a few with whom I spoke still are. I found that mothers' reactions to financial disparities do not follow some obvious pattern or trend. Instead they vary depending on the individual and her situation and seem to be more negative if the daughters are drawn into the conflict. Some mothers I interviewed are hostile toward the stepmothers when it comes to inequities in lifestyle in any and every instance no matter the circumstances. Yet other mothers are discriminating about what bothers them and what they find acceptable.

Displeased Mothers

Most daughters realize early on that a lifestyle where one can afford nice things is more pleasant than one filled with apprehension over financial issues. In cases where mothers feel deprived and unhappy about it, especially if they are single, this attitude often spills over into their daughters' lives. Some mothers blame the stepmothers indirectly, because they are the women on the other side, the fathers' sides, and are part of the other family for her daughters. Of course, to a large extent the mothers' opinion about their material and financial statuses are influenced by their own early experiences. For Sally who at twelve became a daughter of divorce and at thirty-three became a single mother to three daughters, ages nine, seven and five, there is a full understanding of why her young daughters like to visit their stepmother's home. Sally also witnessed her own mother's financial trials and remembers well her own reaction to her father's and stepmother's wealthy lifestyle.

"I feel that I have seen it all," Sally reveals, "but I don't behave as if I have. Instead I am angry at Mary, the girls' stepmother, for her constant trips to toy stores, for her endless indulgences. And I know that I was only a bit older when I also was spoiled by a stepmother. It bothered my mother to see me spoiled until she became a stepmother herself and did the same thing with her stepdaughter. But even with that knowledge, I'm still bothered because it's happening to my girls now. I always feel exasperated when the girls go off with Mary and Leon, my ex-husband. I see myself as someone who failed because of my divorce and I am failing further because I can't compete with Mary's ability to give my girls all the things they want. Besides, Mary would never stoop to shop at a discount store. She only patronizes expensive boutiques. So it isn't just the spending on the girls that bothers me, but the message that Mary sends them about the value of a dollar. I doubt that Mary wants to cause trouble and I think she is nice person but her values are not mine, and that is a problem."

Some mothers' behavior becomes extreme and usually they direct this at the fathers. For example, a few mothers with whom I talked have attempted to keep their daughters away from their fathers, claiming that the fathers and stepmothers are "buying" the daughters. In other cases, the mothers choose the stepmothers as the scapegoats and treat them with vicious anger. Most stepmothers who are on the receiving end of this extreme behavior find it alarming. In my research, fifteen percent of the stepmothers interviewed felt that the mothers' attitudes toward them was extreme enough to worry them. In these instances, the stepmothers believed the mothers were withholding information about the daughters and manipulating the daughters' affections so that they would not spend time with the fathers and stepmothers.

"I know that all of Deirdre's anger is directed towards me," says Christy, thirty-five, a stepmother of two girls, aged twelve and ten. "When I go to pick up the kids, she tells me that they are sick and can't get in my car. She calls me at home and tells me that she does not want me buying her kids shoes and that she will take care of it. Every gesture I make, she undermines. She sees me as the one who buys her kids, when really it is Marco, my husband. I am just the one who does the dishes for the kids, makes their beds and tries to be nice. I know how hard it must be and the girls seem so sad to come to our house and to leave their mother. So I try to do things that they'll like and yet I still can't win. Whatever I do sends their mother into a rage.

As was pointed out earlier, when the stepmothers' financial status is improved by their husbands and not by their own earnings, mothers may feel particularly threatened and sense they've been treated unfairly. Some mothers at this stage feel remorse over the divorce, especially if they have not created new lives, post-divorce. To these mothers, the stepmothers' lifestyles further exemplify what they are missing. The other aspect affected concerns values. Mothers who once enjoyed the comfortable lifestyles that the stepmothers now have, no longer see this as appealing. Though the appeal of financial security can not be denied, excessive spending and amassing material goods may be viewed in a new, critical light by mothers. Mothers view the fathers as "spoiling" the daughters and money becomes a weapon between the mother's house and the father's/stepmother's house. This makes the materialism and wealth of her former husband and his new wife all the more distasteful for the mother.

When the daughters are under the age of ten at the time of the divorce, their mothers usually are not battling what the stepmothers offer materially to the same degree as when the daughters are adolescents. That is not to say that young daughters are not influenced by stepmothers who shower them with gifts, but the emotional support of their mothers at this stage of development is much more important to them and compels them to maintain loyalty to their mothers. Later on, as daughters hit adolescence, there is more emphasis placed on looks, labels and material possessions and less emphasis on the need for emotional connections. If the mothers are still struggling financially, some teenage girls will find this a source of embarrassment and turn further from their mothers and more toward their fathers and stepmothers. This gives some stepmothers an unfair power and influence due to their material affluence, in some mothers' eyes.

According to Andrea, a thirty-nine-year-old mother, money has become a weapon used by her daughters' stepmother. "I knew that I would struggle financially when I divorced Chris," begins Andrea. "And I think that my girls were accepting, if not happy, with how things have turned out. This was when they were eight and six. In the past six years though, things have really changed. I imagine that I would have different relationship with Lydia, their stepmother, if it wasn't for the fact that she has become important through money. My girls always liked her, and I was pleased with that, because when they were younger, it put my mind at ease to know their weekends with their father included Lydia. But Lydia has since assumed control of everyone's lives. I suppose I should be grateful that she doesn't use this money against my girls, and keep it all for herself. But instead she is at the opposite end of the spectrum, using her money to buy my girls. I don't agree with this behaviour and, in truth, it is not necessary. The girls liked her before she spent money on them."

Stepmothers and Money

Most stepmothers' histories play into how they treat their stepdaughters in terms of material things. In some cases, the stepmothers are happy to contribute to their stepdaughter's lives, through material goods as well as through time and energy. This is more common when stepmothers begin their relationships with stepdaughters when they girls are young. Young daughters are more open to their stepmothers and the stepmothers are less self-conscious about stepping in. If the relationship between stepmother and stepdaughter is established early, before the age of twelve, it is usually less complicated for all three females. Later on, a stepmother who appears and begins to buy her stepdaughter's affections can be threatening to the mother/daughter bond. I found those mothers who were too secure to let the stepmothers' overtures bother them and were able to view the daughter/stepmother relationship as another female bond for their daughters. Other mothers, however, were watchful of the stepmothers initially, only relenting with the passing of many years.

"One of my fondest memories," recalls Julie, a twenty-year-old stepdaughter, "is when my stepmother bought me my first Barbie doll for my sixth birthday. My mother didn't like it, but I loved it." In my interviews, over sixty percent of stepmothers felt comfortable being a part of the buying process for their stepdaughters, and felt appreciated by their stepdaughters. Of the buying population of stepmothers, close to eighty percent sensed a rise in tension between them and the mothers after purchases were made. Stepmothers also are keenly aware of the mother/daughter bond which allows little penetration from the outside. So, regardless of what stores they shopped in together at a mall on Saturday, by Sunday night the mother and daughter are reunited.

In regard to finances in general, stepmothers' roles in the triangle are complex. Though most are just trying to establish their own identities within the stepfamily, they still have to contend with mothers who are unhappy about money. Of the stepmothers I have interviewed,

ninety percent cited finances and lifestyle as the largest and most prob-
lematic issues between themselves and the mothers. "I feel as if I am
being watched constantly," Rhonda, a thirty-year-old stepmother to a
fourteen-year-old stepdaughter, admitted. "My husband is fifteen years
older than I am and his ex-wife, Laurel, is quite upset about our marriage. She can't really express it except in comments she makes about
how we treat her daughter. This is how it becomes high drama: I buy a
miniskirt for Maddie, my stepdaughter, then Laurel calls my husband
at work and complains about me. All I am doing is trying to please
Maddie and Laurel is making it a problem. If Maddie admires my out-
fit, I know her mother will hear about it and assess how much it costs."

Few stepmothers wish to engage in this kind of triangulation,
especially when they are being evaluated by the mothers. One reason
that lifestyle is so often at the center of the triangle is because it is palpable. A mother cannot see into the private life of the father and the
stepmother, but she can easily come to conclusions based on what car
the stepmother drives, what part of town she lives in and the expensive appearance of her clothing. Stepmothers who have daughters
who have their own stepmothers are, on the whole, better equipped
to deal with the anger and hostility that can arise over this issue.

"There is no easy way to work it out," sighs Veronica, who at
thirty-six has been a stepmother for three years. "I had such good will
when I married Jerry and became a stepmother to his two daughters.
I felt I had an advantage because I had an ex-husband of my own and
one daughter. I thought that the mother and I were on a level playing
field. Heather, their mother, is remarried and seems to be in a similar
income bracket. Yet she so resents my style, my way of taking her two
girls and my daughter to stores and restaurants. Even the children's
movies that I rent are objectionable to Heather. I feel scrutinized and
as if we are in some competition. If Jerry and I get a new car, then
Heather has to. If my daughter, who is the same age as Kerry, my
younger stepdaughter, signs up for an after school gymnastics class,
then Heather signs up Kerry. The watching and comparing is sick. I
don't want any part of it."

If stepmothers and mothers are in the same financial situation,
as described in Veronica's story, and there is still anger generated by
the mothers towards the stepmothers, I found this is often historically

based and may be traced back to the unpleasant divorces between the mothers and fathers. This is especially true in cases where mothers did not want the divorces. In these cases, the stepmother often suffers. This happens even when mothers create new lives, remarry and have more children, because it is the past injury from which the mothers have not recovered. Brenda Szulman, psychotherapist, remarks, "The money becomes a symbol of rage. What money really conveys is the hurt and misunderstanding that occurred in the marriage. This is then transferred through the daughters, in some cases, and from mother to stepmother in some cases."

It seems in many cases that the stepmothers and the mothers are invested in their own causes, and do not always look beyond. They do not consider the 'greater good' for the daughters who navigate tumultuous paths between the two homes of their mothers and stepmothers. When stepmother and mother disagree about money and materialism, daughters may become their pawns. Some stepmothers, as several remarked in my interviews, voiced that from their points of view, they are damned regardless of what they do or don't do for their stepdaughters. One example was a stepmother who bought her stepdaughter her prom dress because the mother could not and found herself precariously positioned. The mother felt relieved and happy for her daughter, but displeased in that she felt diminished by the stepmother's ability to give her daughter what she could not. The stepmother views her act as a simple gesture of kindness towards her stepdaughter, but the mother sees it as a power play. Similar stories were repeated by others. For instance, Matilda, a thirty-year-old single mother, clearly resented her daughter's stepmother, Ellen, for buying Matilda's daughter, Allie, a dress for Allie's sweet sixteen party.

"I believe that Ellen is only generous when it makes her look good," comments Matilda. "I have a joint custody arrangement with my ex-husband and Ellen has my daughter a lot of the time. She is egotistical the same way as my ex-husband Nathan is and all weekend she spoils Allie. Then Allie comes back to me and acts out, demanding everything under the sun because at Nathan and Ellen's she's used to getting whatever she wants.

A group of interviewees indicated that stepmothers can be influenced negatively by the fathers toward the mothers when it comes to material goods. Some stepmothers believe that their husbands' ex-wives have received such excellent settlements that if the daughters want more clothes, more spending money and more after-school activities, these should all be funded by the mothers. Even when mothers are having financial difficulties, some stepmothers may not know because they have been convinced by their husbands that the ex-wives have been well provided for. Of course, in some cases, this is quite true, but not always. Other stepmothers confided to me that they considered the mothers and their daughters overindulged and unmotivated. This point of view was not only expressed by stepmothers who work full-time and have no children, but also by those stepmothers with children of their own who work part-time or are stay-at-home mothers. Sixty-five percent of the stepmothers I interviewed believe their stepdaughters are too materialistic and get their way too often. These stepmothers also view the mothers as self-indulgent to varying degrees, but most stepmothers voiced their primary concerns about the spoiled daughters.

"My stepdaughters, who are thirteen and fifteen, are so spoiled by their mothers that it makes me sick," begins Beth, a stepmother of two years. "I work as a radiologist and I have one daughter from my previous marriage. My message to her is to work hard and be financially independent. I have also told my stepdaughters about this way of thinking and they ignore me. I don't know if it is because I am their stepmother and they don't care what I think or if it is because I do not impress them. My own daughter, who is ten, knows I value independence and hard work and I push her hard in school already. But my stepdaughters' mother doesn't care if they are mediocre students and she doesn't care if they go to college.

"The mother doesn't work and never has. She lives in a huge townhouse and has leisurely days and collects child support. She isn't busy with the girls because they are at school all day and they are not babies. They are at my house every Saturday for the day and I take them with my daughter wherever we go. Sometimes we go to the movies or to the park but they usually ask to go to the mall or to the video store. They do not read books and they love to shop and buy magazines. After a recent visit, I decided that I should meet with their mother and tell her how I feel. We had coffee and I said that I was worried about her girls at school and that they were addicted to shopping. She laughed and said she was never a good student and that she loved clothes. When I went home that night and saw my husband write a child support check, I had to bite my tongue. But I don't intend to give up. I want the girls to hear me and I hope their mother and I can talk about this further."

Stepmothers who are accused by mothers of "buying" the daughters say they have several reasons for extending themselves to their stepdaughters through material goods. Firstly, this will please their husbands, the fathers, and this is of the utmost importance to the stepmothers. Secondly, it hopefully wins the favor of the daughters and this makes for smooth sailing all around, although winning over stepdaughters can be arduous.

As I've indicated before, the daughter's age is a factor in how the stepmother's efforts are received. When stepdaughters are in junior high school through high school, according to my pool of interviewees, they are most open to any opportunity to receive status symbols from their stepmothers and are most easily impressed by them. Stepmothers are not always aware that stepdaughters at this stage would welcome gifts from almost anyone, from their aunts, to their mothers, to their fathers, to their friends, and that they usually are not discriminating, but influenced by our culture to want certain things, be it designer sneakers or designer belts. Stepmothers who wish to ingratiate themselves to their stepdaughters and have ones who are adolescent, often see that it is easier to do so at this juncture and take advantage of the opportunity. But despite what many mothers think, several stepmothers told me they never intended to spoil their stepdaughters. They are just trying to find an opening, a way into the girls' lives so they can feel like a real family.

Mothers and Money

The mothers, daughters and stepdaughters interviewed for this book are from many different socio-economic stratas, yet they share similar views when it comes to the daughters and the materialistic culture in which we live. Their daughters are growing up in an environment which stresses materialism and labels. A *Vanity Fair* article which ran in the September 2001 issue entitled "Ben and Dara Are In Love" exemplifies the adolescent's preoccupation with superficial existence. Dara, who is sixteen and lives with her single mother in New York City, has a "day of beauty" at the Elizabeth Arden Red Door Salon and Spa on Fifth Avenue, which costs four hundred dollars and is a present from her nineteen-year-old boyfriend, Ben. Ben, who wears two thousand dollar suits, describes his father wearing two hundred dollar suits. Clearly the characters in this story do not exemplify typical teenagers. However, whether the youth in question is a sophisticated Manhattanite or their seemingly less cultured rural or suburban counterparts, there are few adolescent daughters today who are not aware of labels spanning from the Gap to Gucci, because the power of the media is so pervasive and influential. Adolescent daughters of divorce cannot help but be swept up in this wave and most believe that status and possessions have tremendous importance. With money viewed as the means to achieve this, the woman with less wealth—whether it is the mother or the stepmother—may feel she is at the mercy of the daughter's whims and is at a distinct disadvantage compared to the other woman in the triangle.

"I feel that I am at such a disadvantage," sighs Marina, who is a thirty-year-old remarried mother. "Whatever I do, I cannot win with Janet, my daughter's stepmother. She has great taste and my daughter is quite taken with this. My ex-husband is now very successful so Janet and he live a luxurious life. My daughter admires this and doesn't understand that even if I had lots of money I would never live like they do or spend the way Janet does. And I wouldn't give to Casey, my daughter, all the things Janet buys her. On top of encouraging Casey to shop and spend every nickel and dime she has, Janet has told Casey she shouldn't baby-sit and that Janet would give her extra spending money instead. I was so bothered by this that I called Janet and told her even if we were the wealthiest people in the world I'd want Casey to learn what it is it to work for one's money. These are my values and I do not want to be undermined by Janet's warped view of the world."

What scares many mothers in Marina's position is not just the corruption of the values they have tried to instill in their daughters, but that the stepmothers will succeed in "buying" these daughters. "The idea that a daughter will be lost to her mother or can be lured away by money," notes Dr. Michele Kassan, "occurs mostly when the daughter is adolescent and she is already pushing her mother away." Nevertheless, it is a frightening possibility most mothers want to avoid. It seems even more likely to happen when the daughter not only enjoys the wealth of her stepmother, but seems captivated by the stepmother's personality and style. Delia, a sixteen-year-old daughter of divorce, finds her stepmother's manner intriguing.

"I have a young, hip stepmother in Joy," says Delia. "She has taken me under her wing. My mother hates when I spend the day with Joy. My mother views her as the enemy because she has bought me so many great things and she really understands my life. In a way I can't imagine Joy with my father and I only think of her as someone there for me. But I don't say this to my mother, because I know that whatever Joy gives me or wherever she takes me, it bothers my mother.

"Two weeks ago Joy and I went to this amazing hair salon and she paid for me to have my hair cut and highlighted. My mother had a fit when I came home and she made me feel terrible, as if I had done something wrong. My mother made me wash my hair and pull it back in a pony tail. Then she muttered about Joy for hours, about how Joy just wastes my father's money. She complained that I might like getting my hair done at fancy places, but will there be enough money left at this rate for me to go to college? Then my mother talked about how Joy lives in our old house and how she goes through money like water. I wish my mother wouldn't do this to me, ruining my times with Joy. I wish that they could be nice to each other and not act like enemies."

What Delia does not understand is that along with a variety of other issues being played out, Delia's mother feels threatened by Delia's solid relationship with Joy. My interviews reveal that this is not uncommon. Often those mothers feel they are the opposite of the stepmothers and thus are appalled to see their daughters drawn to these women. The mothers may become distrustful of the stepmothers, believing that the stepmothers are disingenuous in their behavior towards the daughters. Stepmothers feel in these situations that the mothers are maligning them and trying to poison the daughters' minds against them. Caught in the middle are the daughters who feel they are expected to choose. While their primary loyalty usually falls to their mothers, this causes more guilt when they enjoy time with their stepmothers.

I found that mothers who are jealous over financial issues are invariably bothered by other factors. In my interview pool, forty percent of the stepmother population consisted of women younger than the mothers and almost all of them had established careers for themselves. Only half of the stepmother population had been married before and less than half had children of their own from previous marriages. Thus some mothers who feel they have been replaced with younger women are hit doubly hard because they feel alienated by their inability to identify with the stepmothers. This only serves to escalate difficulties in communication.

Do mothers prefer stepmothers who do not pay attention to their daughters, especially when it comes to material goods and lifestyle? In cases where the stepmother is not financially independent but gains her financial security from her marriage to the father and is not generous toward her stepdaughter with money, friction between mother and stepmother may still arise. In these situations, some mothers are defensive, because their daughters are slighted while the fathers and stepmothers live quite well. I discovered that some stepmothers who did not include their stepdaughters in their lives still get along with the mothers, but when stepmothers are seen as greedy by the mothers, they quickly lose their chances of acceptance. As we know, most mothers are protective of their daughters and while it is one thing for such mothers to feel that the stepmothers are extravagant or flashy, it is quite another to see their daughters denied while the stepmothers are steeped in creature comforts.

"It is absurd for my daughters to go wanting when their father has money and their stepmother is financially independent," comments Jamie, thirty-seven, who is a divorced mother of two daughters. "I am absolutely appalled at how they skimp when it comes to my girls' needs and then they'll take a vacation in the Caribbean. I have been so upset by this, because I expected more from Collette, their stepmother. She is not only successful, but she knows better. She is a smart woman and when my ex-husband tells me that he can't pay for a summer program for the girls and she says nothing, I consider her downright selfish. It isn't that I would ever expect her to foot the bill, but how about some cheerleading for the girls?

"Before my ex-husband married Collette, he never denied the girls anything. When they first got married, I thought it was great that the girls had such a nice stepmother. Next thing I know, my ex-husband is telling me that he is not responsible for this and not able to pay that. And Collette has money, so I can't figure it out why they are so stingy."

In contrast to Jamie's experience, is the story told by Aurora, a forty-three-year-old mother. "At first I didn't like for Polly, my daughter, to spend so much time with Annalee, her stepmother," Aurora tells us. "Polly was only four when Lawrence, her father and I divorced. He married Annalee within a year of our splitting up. Lawrence had made money, but nothing compared to what Annalee had. Annalee was a perfect stepmother from the start, willing to spend time and money on Polly and willing to forge a real connection. I had to admire it, but it made me feel like I had nothing to offer my own daughter. This was ten years ago.

"Over time I have come to understand that Annalee loves my daughter and it gives her pleasure to take care of Polly and spend money on her. So in a way, Annalee is helping me out by helping Polly out. She and I have respect for one another. Nothing bad has happened here. Our relationship has been as good as it can be."

Ideally, if fathers and stepmothers are financially stable, daughters will benefit and mothers will be pleased. Yet clearly, this is not always the case. Despite the population of mothers who did not relish the stepmothers' attempts to buy their daughters and felt threatened, eighty-five percent of the mothers I surveyed still preferred stepmothers to be financially generous with their daughters to those who were not. Apparently, the down side for daughters denied economic stability and opportunities is taken very seriously by mothers. Even competitive mothers will not to bar their daughters from accepting financial support from fathers and stepmothers.

Money Through the Daughter's Eyes

Money can often represent of a confluence of feelings for the daughters. It is what their parents continue to argue about long after the divorce and seems to be at the heart of many issues that pit mother against stepmother. Money, or lack thereof, produces singular results in the mother's living conditions, and since more than half of the sixty million children living with one parent live with their mothers, these effects are a part of their lives as well as their mother's. In cases where the father does well financially after the divorce and the mother does not, the daughters will move between the mother's house and the father's and see great differences in comfort and lifestyle. Money becomes all-important to many of these daughters when they see the imbalance it creates. Another reason money has such power for all three women of divorce is because our society has emphasized it to such a degree. Adolescent girls and young women are the focus of advertisers and merchants. Without question, capitalism has had a direct effect on daughters of divorce, as on all members of society. These daughters observe their mothers and stepmothers and are quick to assess who has an easier time in a material world. "Money is very tangible and one's destiny can be controlled through it," explains sociologist Nechama Tec. "A reduction in the standard of living which affects women in divorce is not lost on the daughters. The daughters sees their mothers suffer and since spending is valued in a capitalist society, the idea of having money is highly exaggerated for them."

"My mother has always thought well of our stepmother, Dorothea," begins Clarissa, who at twenty-three has been a daughter of divorce for eleven years. "Her feeling was that everyone should work together to raise us, my younger brother and me. But when it comes to how Dorothea spends money, my mother gets angry. She becomes critical and makes nasty remarks. Had money been available to us for college, my mother might not have harbored such feelings toward Dorothea. Since Dorothea and my dad were busy on trips and both have high powered jobs, it seemed unfair that they would not help pay for our education. It was my dad who didn't want to pay for college. My mom says that despite that, Dorothea could have contributed some money. If she had convinced my dad to pay, he would have paid. Instead my brother and I took out a lot of student loans and went to state schools.

"I have been a stepdaughter for long enough to know that Dorothea was terrific until there was an issue. The issue was about which college I would attend. Had Dorothea and my dad been willing to help pay, there wouldn't have been problem. But I got pulled in difference directions over this and my relationship with Dorothea suffered."

When daughters feel that their stepmothers exert financial control over them because of their stepmothers' influence with the fathers, it can chip away at otherwise healthy relationships between daughters and stepmothers. Furthermore, when daughters witness stepmothers living luxuriously while their mothers struggle financially, most daughters will defend their mothers. This is a situation where the daughters are "the unwitting 'victims' of the reduced circumstances of their mothers," according to Wendy A. Paterson in her book *Unbroken Homes: Single Parent Mothers Tell Their Stories*. These cases reduce the potential of mothers, daughters and stepmothers to be connected. When this happens, some daughters feel they must choose sides.

"I had to choose my stepmother and father over my mother because of money," Adrienne, a twenty-one-year-old daughter of divorce explains. "I was sixteen when my father remarried and Vera, my stepmother, was not that interested in me. But I tried to have some contact with her because my mother told me to. My mother said that it was the only way that my father would still pay for things. My sister and my brother who were older did not listen to my mom. They disliked Vera and had no relationship with her. I ended up getting what I wanted because I tried to be a part of Vera's and dad's lives. It caused me to be distant from my brother and sister, though. My mother pushed me in this direction even though at the same time she disliked all that Vera stood for. But she never said that, she just told me to be sweet and to spend time with my stepmother.

"I think my sister and brother made a big mistake. If they hadn't been so angry, maybe they'd be in a better position today. It does not pay to be angry, that was what my mother taught me; it pays to be practical. In my case, unlike my siblings, I get along with everyone: my mother and I and my stepmother and I. Even my mother and step-mother talk if they have to. This began about financial support, but it has gone beyond that."

Of the daughters I interviewed, a small percentage reported that both their mothers and stepmothers had money and were able to provide material comforts. This transpired in several ways: either both the mother and stepmother worked, both women were married to men who were successful, both women had impressive divorce set-tlements, or had family money. In such cases, these daughters were exposed to two mother figures who represented financial indepen-dence and means. If both mother and stepmother were materialistic, then the daughters had a double influence of materialism and perhaps both home lives were conducted in a similar fashion.

My talks with mothers, stepdaughters and stepmothers showed that, for daughters of divorce, feeling caught between moth-ers' and stepmothers' lifestyles is quite common. However, in some cases, mothers and stepmothers with similar financial circumstances had more in common and avoided burdening their daughters with lifestyle clashes. For example, when both women work, they often coordinate children's schedules and use cooperation as a means of eas-ing each others' parental burdens. When they reach these optimal conditions, my interviews revealed it is because these women have achieved understandings and mutual respect. Both the mothers and stepmothers juggle their work days and whoever has the more flexi-ble schedule at a given time takes responsibility for the daughters.

Melinda, who at twenty-eight looks back on her childhood skillfully choreographed by her mother and stepmother, believes that she had the best of both worlds. "My mother and stepmother made it clear to me that they both had to work, for money and for self-worth. Not surprisingly, I saw both of them more than I ever saw my father, who also worked hard but was out of the loop when it came to my after-school activities. Neither my mother nor my stepmother wanted me to be a latchkey kid and so they would take turns leaving work to pick me up and take me to ballet or to swimming lessons. This was when I was only seven. As I got older, I stayed at an after-school pro-gram at the school or went to day care. I never knew who would pick me up at the end of the day, my mother or my stepmother, but I knew I could count on one of them to be there."

My interviews indicated that mothers might or might not prejudice their daughters against stepmothers whom they perceive as 'gold digging,' but daughters are keenly sensitive to this syndrome on their own. They observe their stepmothers closely and easily recognize if these women are in their marriages simply to obtain the lifestyles that their fathers can provide. A mother's bias against a stepmother who is living a luxurious life does not always influence the daughters. Despite the common wisdom that surrounds divorced mothers, that they begrudge the stepmother any moneyed life with the father, most daughters revealed that they draw their own conclusions and forge their own relationships.

"My father has been more than fair to my mother, in my opinion," begins Vivian, twenty-seven. "I know how fortunate I have been as a result. My mother might not have liked Kami, my stepmother, years ago, when she first came on the scene, because Kami seemed to be into the lifestyle my dad offered. But after all these years of Kami's kindness and generosity toward me, including paying for my senior year college trip, which I'll never forget, I don't know how anyone can be upset."

Across the board, daughters appreciate mothers and stepmothers who do not conduct financial wars between or through them and do not judge each other's roles in giving these daughters of divorce some of the perks of a world free of financial woes.

Money as Power

Although it was not always the case, an overwhelming majority of the mothers I interviewed reported that divorce represented for them a severe diminishment of funds. The stigma and plight of the single divorced mother in America persists, not only because of social bias, but because of the realities of her economic standing. Of the stepmothers with whom I spoke, those who had children from previous marriages and thus had also been at one time single mothers, almost one hundred percent reported that they were financially more sound because of their remarriages. In a perfect world, the mother and stepmother would be on a par financially but since this is not often the case, daughters of all ages draw comparisons between their mothers' lives and their stepmothers' lives and many see their single mothers suffer.

If a daughter is drawn to the material comforts of life and sees that she can get this from her stepmother, this will not go unnoticed by the mother. In fact, such a situation may make the mother anxious about money, certain that with it comes power and without it comes loss and defeat.

"I sometimes think that I have lost and that my daughters' stepmother has won, because I work two jobs and my husband makes very little money," comments Denise, a thirty-four-year-old mother of two. "My girls are only eleven and eight, and I am appreciative that Amy, their stepmother, has time for them. She has a son from a former marriage who is only ten, so she knows what it is like for me. But she remarried my ex-husband, who has a great job and it makes a difference. I know that my girls find it fun to be with Amy because they enjoy a life with her that is similar to the one they used to have before the divorce. Amy once confided in me that she thought I had a lousy divorce settlement and that I should take my ex back to court. Now, that amazed me. She has never been a show-off about the money. In fact, before she takes the girls anywhere or buys anything, she checks with me.

"So why do I feel that I'm losing my girls and why do I feel like I can't compete? It is definitely about the money, and not so much about Amy as a person. I just feel inferior when I think about their big house in the great neighbourhood, their wonderful vacations and not having to stress when bills arrive or a repair is needed. It is the money that gnaws at me, all the time."

When stepmothers are genuine in their efforts toward daughters, most mothers are appreciative; however, the wounded pride of being poorer may continually haunt some mothers. Some of the mother's anxiety and tension can be lessened if she and the stepmother work together particularly in areas related to money, allowing the mother to retain some power over what happens to her daughters. Brenda Szulman, social worker, remarks, "If the stepmother establishes a relationship with her stepdaughter which includes financial support, it is important that she work it out ahead with the mother and develop a co-parenting situation."

I found in a few cases that mothers, daughters and step-mothers were all diminished financially. Some stepmothers who did not anticipate that their husbands would have financial setbacks find themselves subsidizing their husbands' first families. Some mothers, who have excellent jobs, are suddenly thrown when their ex-husbands cannot pay child support due to unexpected hardships. Then the mothers or stepmothers, have to stretch their incomes for the daughters' sakes. It would be wise for mothers and stepmothers to have considered these scenarios ahead of time, but few have. Both mothers and stepmothers who experienced serious financial setbacks reported to me that they never believed such things could happen.

More seriously, as this book and other research reiterates, the economic consequences of divorce for children can be dire. According to the United States Census Bureau in divorced, single parent families, almost twenty-five percent of children under six and twenty percent under eighteen live in impoverished states. As authors Lamanna and Riedmann remind us in their book, *Marriages and Families*, these poverty rates are not only applicable to minority children. "Over fifteen percent of non-Hispanic white children under eighteen grow up in poverty as well..." write the authors, "the relationship between family type and poverty is consistent across race/ethnic categories: Children in mother-headed single-parent families are significantly more likely to live in poverty than children in married-couple households."

"Unlike my older sisters, I really missed my father after the divorce," Taylor, twenty-three, remembers. "He lived far away and he was pretty poor. He could barely afford the plane ticket, let alone a hotel room, so I hardly ever saw him. I felt horrible for him and for myself. I love my stepfather, but I have never felt torn about my father versus my stepfather. I would just have like to have my father be there for me too.

"I know my father was glad that I grew up in a nice home with my mother and stepfather, but he also felt sorry and inferior, because he does not have as much money. For me, though, it was never about money. I was hoping my father would show up and be part of my life. I just wanted my father back."

Of course, many fathers (the majority, in fact) work hard to support their children. "Despite the conventional wisdom of divorce and fathers," Brondi Borer, divorce attorney, comments, "I have seen fathers living out of cars in order to give their children better lives. I have seen fathers desperate to see their children and in friendly divorce situations, asking the mothers if the children can be with them more than the allotted time."

When Laura, a stepmother of twelve years, discovered that her husband, Jack, had lost his job, she realized that she had to help out for the sake of his children. "I knew there had to be some money coming from me," Laura discloses. "I even helped to pay for my stepdaughter Stacey's wedding, because Jack didn't have enough money to pay. I had never really dealt with Penny, Stacey's mother, before this, but suddenly I was drawn into their lives. And while I had thought that she was nasty all these years, I ended up liking her."

In a similar about-face to Laura's, but from another point of view, Valerie, a single, remarried mother, found herself excusing her former husband from child support when he lost his job. "I told Wyatt to forget about it, until he gets back on his feet," explains Valerie. "I make a living and he has always been responsible. His wife called me up crying to thank me. They had just had a baby and were going through tough times. I didn't see the point in torturing everyone and we had to make an adjustment. It would not have been good for my girls to have more turmoil. I wanted them to see that, even in the face of economic hardship, we can all get along, learn to compromise and work together."

When mothers and stepmothers are able to establish a dialogue based on helping their stepdaughters financially and emotionally, it is the reconstructed family unit which greatly benefits. When grudges and bitterness are set aside, this enlightened attitude takes hold and peace reigns. It is significant that both financial and family values can be threaded throughout any gifts bestowed upon the daughters. For example, if the daughter needs money for college and the stepmother offers to help, the mother can impress upon her daughter the importance of the stepmother's role in the daughter's life and that the gift of education is precious and worthy.

The daughter should not be spoiled by the stepmother but appreciate what she does for her. This applies to small matters as well—value must be placed on the gesture. Lila, a forty-six-year-old single mother, expresses her good feelings about her daughter's stepmother, remarking that their world is richer as a result. "I am happy for my daughter because she and her stepmother spend time together. If they shop, for instance, it becomes a way of reaching out and connecting to each other. I have found we can share my daughter and there will still be enough love left for everyone. If her stepmother buys my daughter a gift, even a somewhat expensive one, I don't make a fuss. I always remind my daughter to thank her stepmother for the thought. I am secure in my relationship with my daughter, and I can't imagine that her stepmother's attention, even if it happens to be less about books and art and more about boutiques, can be bad for her."

When mothers feel as open-minded as Lila about the stepmothers and daughters spending time together in whatever activities they like, then the daughters, I found in my interviews, often feel good about it as well and all three women benefit. Nonetheless, almost half of the daughters interviewed expressed a sense of guilt when they shopped or did other things with their stepmothers. These daughters felt torn and, especially when they approached adolescence and beyond, they noticed distinctions between the two women. Savvy mothers recognize and accept that differences between themselves and stepmothers are more common than not. They do a great service by assuring their daughters that they needn't feel any guilt for enjoying time spent with their stepmothers. Mothers and stepmothers who don't see eye-to-eye but can compromise on how they assert their values offer daughters the best of both worlds.

For daughters of divorce, the material aspects of their dual experiences in the worlds of their mothers and stepmothers can be confusing and frustrating, as evidenced in my interviews. While each woman brings her own life experience to the interpretation of a material world, the concern in spoiling the daughter on the one hand or denying the daughter on the other, is something many mothers and stepmothers wrestle with continually. Of my pool of interviewees of mothers and stepmothers, fifty-five percent felt comfortable communicating the persuasive quality of materialism with each other when it came to the daughters. Interestingly, communication began when both mothers and stepmothers realized the daughters were somewhat out of control in so far as desiring luxuries. As one stepmother described it, "I kept my mouth shut until my fourteen-year-old stepdaughter wanted her belly button pierced and a designer make-up bag. Then I called her mother, who was equally appalled."

In recognizing the power that money has, especially its role in the lives of women of divorce, we have to take into consideration the positions of mother and stepmother. If the mother is overwhelmed and feels impoverished, then money seems an unattainable panacea and the stepmother's lifestyle, if better, can provoke feelings of envy and denial for the mother and her daughter. If the stepmother feels that the mother and daughter receive too much money from the father, then she may feel denied in her position and may not reach out to the daughter or be communicative toward the mother as a result. If mothers and stepmothers can join forces in a united front where finances further the daughters' existences and are not utilized strictly for superficial purposes, then these daughters' values will be more grounded and their lives will be richer for it.

CHAPTER 6

Mothers versus Stepmothers

The historic and mythic antipathy between mother and stepmother still plays out in some triangles, as revealed by Faye, a twenty-five-year-old daughter of divorce. "Our mother influenced us to dislike Terri, our stepmother. I was only eight when my parents divorced and the rest of my childhood was spent watching what my mother went through after the divorce. My sisters and I knew that my father had left us for this woman, and had put his life with us behind him. As I got to know her, I came to my own conclusions where Terri was concerned even before they were married. I saw her as manipulative. She once called the hospital where my father was sick and said she was his wife when she wasn't his wife yet. I resented that.

"The biggest problem for me is the way that the divorce came about. Terri once stormed into our apartment and had a screaming match with my mother. Then she expected us to like her and her daughters. While time has softened the blow and I know that my father needed to be happy, I do not respect Terri the way that I respect my mother. It isn't possible."

One recent school of thought suggests that the impact a parent has upon a child is not necessarily gender-driven, however, my research indicated that the majority of daughters are more influenced by their mothers than their fathers. A natural extension of this mother/daughter bond is that most daughters look to female role models throughout their lives. Not only do mothers have great influence over their daughters, but they are largely responsible for their socialization. For most, the mother/daughter bond is a lifetime connection despite difficult times and what seems the unrelenting challenges of adolescence. The July 2002 issue of *Prevention Magazine* reported that at midlife, eighty-five percent of women acknowledge having a good rapport with their mothers. It is the mother's opinion of the stepmother that so often affects her daughter's attitude toward this woman, the other mother figure.

When fathers/ex-husbands/new husbands and mothers/ex-wives have not put their first marriages to rest, stepmothers/new wives often suffer the consequences. If the family has not regrouped and is not synchronized, then the parents as well as their daughters are not on sure footing. As I discuss in my book, *Second Wives*, if the ex-wife still contacts her ex-husband in a crisis unrelated to the children, big or small, and he quickly responds, he remains a safety net for her. This is not healthy for the husband's new marriage and his new wife often will take exception to the ex-wife's ongoing dependency. Thus, before daughters are even brought into the equation, there may be remnants from the first marriage influencing the second. It is wise if old patterns can be put to rest so that the old triangle of the ex-wife, new wife and the ex-husband can be minimized. This is especially important since the new triangle—comprised of mother, daughter and stepmother—is emerging.

In my research I found that the question of how the divorce occurred has much to do with how the mother views the stepmother. If the father's new marriage is the result of an affair and the mother was jilted, she usually harbors resentment toward the stepmother and makes these feelings known to her daughter. If the mother is remarried and happy, yet dislikes the values and style of the stepmother, she will, in many cases, let her daughter know this as well. If the stepmother has daughters of her own and they live with the father while his own daughters live with their mother and do not see their father regularly, the mother often will show her displeasure and so will her daughters. In any scenario where the mother does not encourage her daughters to be open-minded toward the stepmother, I found the daughters will feel torn if they like their stepmother. "If the mother is against the stepmother," Claire Owen psychologist, remarks, "the daughter will feel guilty every time she enjoys her stepmother's company. Whatever the two do together, the daughter will be uncomfortable."

Mothers Wield Power

Single custodial mothers, according to researchers Twaite, Silitsky and Luchow, turn to some kind of counseling or mental health service more often than any other marital group of women. According to a study conducted by Zaslow, twenty-nine percent of daughters of divorce have issues with their mothers, compared to fourteen percent of daughters in intact families. Mothers often exist as the object of love and hate for their children, as British psychoanalyst Melanie Klein points out in her book, *Love, Hate and Reparation*. In order for the positive to outweigh the negative, according to Klein, the mother cannot be "too closely wrapped up in the child's feelings." It is only when she steps back that she will "get full satisfaction from the possibility of furthering the child's development."

It would be easier if both the mother and stepmother acknowledged that the daughter is the innocent victim of divorce and the one who is truly not in favor of a new life that includes a stepfamily. Most daughters look back and recall their old lives with longing, imagining those times were better than they really were, embellishing the good parts while ignoring the bad. While trying to adapt to life with a stepfamily, many daughters of divorce scrutinize their stepmothers' every action, partly in defense of their mothers and partly in defense of their own loss. Anything from the mundane to the serious may be scrutinized. If a stepdaughter sees that her stepmother is not washing pots the same way as her mother, she will take notice. Some of what goes on between the stepmother and her stepdaughter depends upon the father's sensitivity or insensitivity to the issues. His active involvement and encouragement of a positive relationship between his daughter and his new wife can greatly improve the experience. On the flip side, if he turns a blind eye to the situation, the relationships between stepmother and stepdaughter can suffer.

"I have no real relationship with Gina, my grown stepdaughter," Cathy, forty-three, says with a pained voice, "because my husband keeps me at a distance. It is especially noticeable now, because Gina just had a baby and my husband and his ex-wife are constantly visiting their daughter and granddaughter. They sometimes end up there at the same time, while I'm at home alone, made to feel I don't belong in this family. I feel my husband hasn't done the right thing for me or Gina. At first I tried on my own to be involved in Gina's life but, without the blessing of her father or mother, she would have nothing to do with me. Now there is little I can do to change things. I see clearly now that there is little room for me in this family.

"Still, I can never totally give up hope. All Gina has to do is say the word, and I'll be there for her and her baby. I believe for that to happen, it will take intervention by Gina's mother. So I would love it if she did something to sway Gina to be more open to me. I can only wait and hope."

Ironically, though she feels it was her husband who failed to set up a relationship between her and her stepdaughter, Cathy now believes that it is the responsibility of her stepdaughter's mother to make the first move toward an improved situation. Yet it would be beneficial to everyone if both women as well as the adult daughter would openly discuss the relationship and commit—if that is what they all desire—to improving it together. Author Cherie Burns reminds us in her book, *Stepmotherhood*, that "these relationships are nothing if not optional" and a stepmother must be prepared to face the fact that her stepdaughter may never want a relationship with her. Yet this dire possibility is not the norm in my research. Most daughters I interviewed are looking for something more from both women, and in their quests to have better lives as daughters of divorce, they don't want to hear any negative remarks coming from either woman about the other.

What the stepmother is up against in some cases the strength of the mother/daughter relationship, especially in later years. Even if the mother and daughter have their own issues to sort out, their connection runs much deeper than any current argument and might not allow much room for the stepmother. The stepmother is often times a mother as well, since couples with children constitute a quarter of the remarried population. Yet the stepmother's relationship with her stepdaughter may not manifest as a nurturing experience, despite her maternal instincts. As sociologist Helen Fisher writes in her book, *The First Sex*, "The basic brain chemical oxytocin is also linked to nurturing. Although both sexes produce this pituitary hormone, females produce much more of it—particularly as they give birth." Even when daughters are grown and are far from infancy, mothers' strong maternal ties to their daughters persist and stepmothers are often relegated to more superficial roles. The small daughter, under the age of seven, has a greater chance of developing an attachment to her stepmother because she evokes more of a maternal response in her stepmother and her own quest for mother-love is more inclusive at this stage.

"I think if I had met Renee, my stepmother, when I was still in elementary school, it might have worked out better," Melia, thirty, says. "But I met her when I was already in junior high school. My father met my stepmother while my mother was still single and working hard to make ends meet. I think that colored how I looked at Renee. I saw this woman as the opposite of my mother and she seemed wacky to me. She had no sophistication and was like a country bumpkin. I saw her on my own terms and my father was careful not to scold me or try to change my mind. His willingness to let me form my own opinions helped, but it didn't make me and Renee close."

It seems an odd twist that, within our society, daughters often don't acknowledge the sacrifices and unconditional love of their mothers until a divorce occurs. Of course, this can work in the opposite way too; a woman who has been an exemplary mother during the marriage may appear to her daughter as selfish and self-serving if she is the one to precipitate the break-up. If the mother didn't initiate the divorce, the daughter may be quite sympathetic. Once the mother dates, however, the daughter can feel differently. When a mother who is less available because she is dating, this can effect the relationship her daughter has with her stepmother.

"My stepdaughter appreciates me more since her mother has less time for her," begins Blake, who at forty-nine is the stepmother to a seventeen-year-old daughter. "In the beginning, Kayla did not want to share me with her father. We would go on an annual vacation and my stepdaughter would come and stay in our hotel room. Recently, after eight years of being a patient but second-class citizen as the stepmother, Kayla has become more open toward me. I believe it is because her mother is now living with someone. My concern is that if her mother ends the relationshi,p my stepdaughter will withdraw from me."

Based on my pool of interviewees, mother-hunger as a motivator, even when there is disappointment in the mother, is quite important to the daughters. The mother/daughter bond is so critical to a daughter that if her mother is absent, she will seek out other mother figures. This may not extend to the stepmother, however, because she is too blatant a reminder of the loss the daughter has suffered as a result of the divorce. Therefore, a stepmother who lets her stepdaughter know that she wants a closer relationship takes a big risk. The daughter may be put off, out of loyalty to her mother, even when the daughter's mother is preoccupied with her own love life or her career. A daughter in search of mother love may look to another woman, like her best friend's mother, a teacher or an aunt. The daughter's approach to her stepmother depends upon the history of the relationship. As we know, if the stepmother was the cause of the divorce, there is much less chance that the daughter will reach out to her. If the stepmother arrived on the scene after the divorce and has been consistent and supportive, she could be the recipient of her stepdaughter's affection. Nonetheless, the determining factor in a stepmother's journey toward a meaningful relationship with her stepdaughter is colored to a great degree by the messages about other women which the mother gives to her daughter.

The Prevailing Mother Bond

Feminists such as Betty Friedan noted that the value of motherhood is undermined and confusing to women since it is both appreciated and deprecated simultaneously. Yet, without question, our culture continues to encourage motherhood as the quintessential role for women. To this end, small girls are taught to play with dolls and to practice their mothering techniques. The implicit message for daughters is that girls' childhood experiences and education are preparation for the great event, that of marrying and having children. It is interesting that in my research for my book, *Reclaiming Ourselves*, many young women with whom I spoke are not hell-bent on careers and independence, as were their mothers, but imagine their futures as wives and mothers. In some cases the pervasive attitude is a direct reaction to their baby-boomer mothers who had little success at balancing work and mothering/wifery, ending up divorced and in marginal careers. Some of these daughters have vowed to create more traditional adult lives, where mothering can be important and fulfilling enough on its own. In their view, mothers can have it all. These daughters feel enlightened and plan to approach motherhood without making their mothers' mistakes. According to these idealistic daughters, there will be less divorce and less conflict over career versus at-home-mothering in their lives.

These new attitudes and directions of some younger women cause them to look at their mothers and stepmothers and judge the choices that the older women made and those they overlooked. "My daughters think I blew it by divorcing," explains Nicole. "And they think their father blew it, because he chose such an unfriendly woman to be his second wife, their stepmother. They see me as financially strapped and they wish their stepmother were more generous toward them. She always discourages my ex-husband from spending anything on the girls. That is her way of dealing with them. It is really a shame, because even though I do not want to be with their father. I did want him to be with someone who would make him happy *and* the girls happy.

"What I imagined was that both my ex-husband and I would find happier lives after our divorce. I thought that I would remarry and so would he and that everyone would be civil for the sake of my three daughters. I must have been dreaming. I feel lucky that the girls are all mine because of their stepmother's disinterest, but in a sense they've really lost out."

Most mothers have mixed feelings about the stepmothers, depending on the nature of their divorces, their own personal happiness and their relationships with their daughters following divorce. If the mother has not found her own way in life after the divorce and leans on her daughter, the daughter's growth often is stifled. The mother might not realize that her adolescent daughter tries to please and keep her happy. This is so because the mother is preoccupied with rediscovering her own identity. However, the mother still needs her connection to her daughter. Neither the daughter nor her mother will look gladly to the stepmother if they are immersed in their own struggles. Many daughters will feel too guilty about what is lacking in their mothers' lives and their mothers' loneliness to ever warm up to their father's new wife, particularly if these stepmothers enter the picture at a pivotal time. Mothers, I found, are not as generous of spirit toward stepmothers if the mothers don't feel content with themselves. Even when the mother knows intellectually that her ex-husband is better off married than dating and that her daughter has found her stepmother to be pleasant and forthcoming, the mother can resent that the stepmother has established herself while the mother has not.

On the other hand, the ambivalence that some mothers with whom I spoke voiced toward stepmothers was sometimes mirrored by the stepmothers' own stories. Some stepmothers seem set in their second marriages and fortunate to have found the right mates, yet they may suffer the repercussions of their own divorces. For example, some stepmothers with whom I talked had daughters from previous marriages and were experiencing their own conflicts with their ex-husbands and the husbands' new wives. The high level of stress associated with second marriages that include stepchildren is evidenced in the United States Census report. These marriages fail at a rate of sixty percent and yet half of all Americans are involved with some sort of step-relationship. Ideally, this information should make everyone in the triangle more accepting of each other and more ambitious to bring about a successful stepmother/mother/daughter rapport. Despite what many mothers and daughters believe, remarriage can be an overwhelming experience for the stepmother. The incorporation of the new marriage and the attempt to forge a stepfamily and, if she has her own children, to not lose her daughters in the process, is indeed arduous. Ironically, the mother and stepmother are in similar places and cooperation between the two women would benefit both parties. Yet the two key elements—great maturity and a common goal, that of the daughters' well-being—are required for the mother and stepmother to be unified.

Wendy and Doris provide a good example of how maturity and making the daughter's well-being a top priority can create a positive situation for daughters, even in the face of a strained mother/stepmother relationship. Wendy, thirty-eight, had hoped that her daughters' stepmother, Doris, would be open and loving toward her daughters. "In the beginning, when Doris was dating my ex-husband, she was not only nice to the girls, but nice to me. We watched my oldest daughter perform in the marching band together and once we drove to a school picnic together to be there for my youngest daughter. Then Doris became engaged to Robert and she became a bit cooler. Once they got married, she stopped talking to me. I am disappointed, because I thought we had a good relationship worked out.

"Since Doris is still good to my girls, I don't complain. I know this is very important and I know they are in good hands when she is with them. I feel slighted by her sudden change towards me, but I always put the girls' interests first. I think Doris does the same for them, so it still works out."

Eventually, as daughters grow and mature, they will see past any petty squabbling and view their stepmothers through their own eyes, regardless of their mothers' influences. Even stepmother/stepdaughter relationships that get off to a shaky start have tremendous potential for improvement, and vice versa. If a stepmother implies that she cares for her stepdaughter at first then distances herself, the daughter is aware of the change and judges accordingly. What the daughter needs throughout the adjustment to her parent's divorce and the advent of a stepmother, is for her mother to be steadfast. "The mother should be aware of her daughter's feelings," explains Antoinette Michaels, relationship expert, "and make sure that the daughter does not feel cheated in any way. Adjusting to this new family dynamic takes time, patience and communal effort."

Women who have been in two of the three or in all three roles at various points in their lives are best equipped to deal with other members of the triangle. For they, more than others, know the difficulties, hard decisions and benefits that come with being a daughter/stepdaughter, a mother and a stepmother. There is a natural extension from mothering to stepmothering which can be recognized in positive experiences, such as the one conveyed to me by Zandra. While it may not be a smooth journey, the outcome can be quite rewarding and reflect one's mothering instincts. Zandra, a stepmother for twenty years to Catherine and Becky, has experienced a myriad of feelings over the course of time. The fact that she is a stepdaughter as well as a stepmother and a mother has influenced her openness toward her stepdaughters.

"Catherine was nine, and Becky was only seven when I met them. I did not dislike the girls but I realized that I resented their presence and the fact that they existed. I was much younger than my husband and I had wanted him to come with a clean slate, which was impossible. These girls had a mother and a father and I was his new wife. The custody arrangement gave him every other weekend and I found that I was with the girls much more than their father. As I got to know them, I started to actually enjoy them and to see that they were darling children and special in their own right. I didn't expect it, but they brought out the mother in me.

"Four years later I had my own daughter and that made me appreciate my stepdaughters all the more. Their mother was never very active in their schools or hobbies and because I was, that made me a mother figure to them. I think their mother actually appreciated my involvement, because it was good for her girls, but we never had much of an exchange. I look back now and I realize that the adjustment period took a long while, but my stepdaughters and I began to bond.

"I have encouraged my stepdaughters and my daughter to be close. Their relationship to each other is important to me. I know that my stepmother, who has her own daughters, is someone I can count on and I have great respect for her. I want my stepdaughters to see me that way, too."

Stepmothers Wield Power

As we have seen, the myth of the wicked stepmother dies hard and we need only think of Cinderella or Snow White, eternal fairy tales that make the stepmother larger than life, to know this is true. But more recent portrayals in popular culture, like the film *Stepmom*, show another side of the stepmother/mother power struggle, proving that neither woman is totally flawed or totally perfect. Such films promote the concept of co-parenting and place an emphasis on sharing, rather than winning, to bring about the most benefits for the children of divorce.

Among those stepmothers interviewed, I repeatedly heard that the stepmother has the power. As the new wife and a presence in the father's home, she can not help but influence him and come in contact with her stepdaughter. The mother, in most triangles I studied, retains her power, because as the mother she has the original tie to her daughter. For many daughters of divorce, there have been concerted efforts to be close to their fathers after their parents' divorces. Joint custody is one way to provide this opportunity and is implemented more frequently today than in the past. In joint custody arrangements, daughters are able to see each parent three or four days a week in comparison to seven days a week as they did when their original families lives were intact. With this joint custody schedule, as discussed previously, many daughters still feel uncomfortable when fathers remarry. In traditional psychological terms, this might be attributed to the daughter being usurped and her Oedipal fantasies shaken, perhaps destroyed, by a strange female whose existence removes the daughter from the throne she was placed upon by her father.

Stepmothers come with a variety of stories of their own and some have a keen sense of what they are up against. Therefore it is no wonder that so many of the stepmothers interviewed for this book expressed trepidation when meeting their future stepdaughters for the first time. Some stepmothers are considerably younger than their husbands, have never been married and are hopeful that they and their new husbands will begin families of their own. Other stepmothers are older than their husbands, with their own grown children and ex-husbands. Some may be interested in adult relationships with their husbands, which exclude their stepdaughters, while others may be eager to forge relationships with their stepdaughters. Some stepmothers may have their own daughters of similar ages to their stepdaughters, or there may be great disparities in the daughters' ages. Other stepmothers' custody arrangements might be such that they have primary custody and their new husbands must house their stepchildren while their own children live primarily at their mothers' homes. The list of various scenarios could go on and on. The point is that the advent of stepmothers is a remarkable step into the unknown for daughters and for their mothers. "When the father remarries," Antoinette Michaels, relationship expert comments, "it adds to the complexity of the dynamic between all the individuals: the father, the daughter, the mother and the stepmother."

Many different triangles encompass the members of divorced families. When the stepmother enters the picture, the first triangle is between the stepmother, the father and the daughter. At this juncture, the second triangle begins forming, which is at the heart of this book, that of mother, daughter and stepmother. The underlying triangle— between mother, daughter and father—always exists, and is deeply affected by the stepmother. If the stepmother is aware of the intricacies of the latter triangle, she can make a concerted effort with her step-daughter, regardless of how difficult she is, or how locked into being on her mother's side she is. A wise stepmother will extend herself to her stepdaughters from the start. In the face of the daughter of divorce's suffering, and the end of her former family, which is finalized by her father's new marriage, the fact that the daughter's psyche is fragile is to be expected. At the outset a daughter will usually feel that her mother and stepmother are diametrically opposed or that her stepmother will never be like a mother to her. As she matures and if the relationship is good she will see that her stepmother need not be a mother, but a mother figure, another female role model. In almost every case I stud-ied the mother still very much exists, despite the stepmother's presence.

"In the beginning, I felt I had to give in to my stepdaughter's every request," Rory, thirty-eight, remarks. "But in the past three years, I have backed off. I knew from the day I met Annie, my stepdaughter, that we were very different, but I saw how my husband felt about her and I knew I had to try my best. Once we were married, his ex-wife seemed much more present. On the days Annie was visiting, she made constant references to her mother. Then Annie begged off visiting whenever she could, in order to be with her mother. I think that George would have insisted that Annie come on her appointed days, but I convinced him to have patience and not to force her to come. It just seemed unfair.

"I am definitely conscious of how persuasive I can be with my husband where Annie is concerned. If she wants something and it seems excessive, I will point that out, but if she wants something reasonable like to bring over a friend and he thinks it isn't necessary, then I will plead her case. I see her as changing all the time, and I'm sure that it has to do with being an adolescent. So I try to understand. But when she won't stop talking about her mother or when she eyes me up and down and checks out our home to report to her mother, I distance myself. In the end, I remember that George is in love with me and we have a good life together."

Rory's take on stepmothering incorporates both knowledge of her power and her uncertainty in how to deal with her stepdaughter. Common sense dictates that the kinder the stepmother can be to her stepdaughter, the happier the father/husband will be. My research shows that many new wives fear that their husbands will place their children ahead of them. An even bigger fear for some stepmothers is that these children might opt to live with their fathers as they become older. "Daughters who are in junior high or entering high school often want to live with their fathers," notes Dr. Michele Kasson. "They are separating from their mothers emotionally at this point and think highly of their fathers."

The complication for the daughters is that their stepmothers are living with their fathers and that alters how their fathers will relate to them. Competing with stepmothers for their fathers' attention also can effect how competitive daughters become in other areas of their lives. As author Hope Edelman notes in her book, *Motherless Daughters*, the death of the mother rather than a divorce situation is instructive in seeing how these daughters relate to their stepmothers. "When a daughter grows up perceiving an adult woman as a threat," writes Edelman, "she may unconsciously carry the competitiveness she once felt or still feels towards her stepmother into her adult relationships with other women." It is more fortunate for daughters of divorce, who have not lost their mothers but still have their mothers as well as the opportunity to learn that stepmothers can enhance their lives. If, however, the mother leaves her husband and children behind after the divorce, the loss to the daughters is very similar to having their mother die. In some cases, these daughters are eager to have a stepmother fill the void.

"It took me years," begins Muriel, forty-seven, who has been a stepdaughter since she was in grade school, "to truly appreciate my stepmother. I was so relieved when she came to our home and I was free to be a girl again. I knew that I wanted her to be like a mother to me. My mother simply didn't want to have children and I had to face this and that my mother had left us. In my stepmother I saw a woman who made the commitment to my father to raise his two daughters. I was the older one and I very much wanted this to work. After our mother left, we were so grateful to my stepmother. I was quite sick of acting like a housekeeper and wife. Our stepmother was a good person or she would have been heady with conceit seeing how desperately we wanted her there. We looked to her for her mothering skills, and we counted on her. I suppose she loves my father very much because she took on a huge responsibility."

Almost all daughters of divorce, I found in my interviews, say they do not want to be surrogate wives and while they are willing to do housework and manage homes in order to help fathers after the divorce, few want this situation to continue nor do they see this as their future. A stepmother/second wife obviously takes on that obligation and, in many instances, the daughter's gratitude empowers the stepmother.

Denise, a woman who found herself falling in love with a man who had custody of his children, stated, "I knew that Alfred was exhausted from the demands of taking on the role of a mother, since he lacked the skills." A stepmother of four years, Denise continued, "From the first time I visited him with his children on a weekend, I knew he was over his head. He was trying hard to make arrangements for the twins, who were only eight. He was calling their mother about his older daughter's ballet recital. I was subtle and I moved quietly in the beginning. But I was driving the girls places by the third month. I doubt their mother liked it, but the girls saw my efforts as efficient and they appreciated them.

"This has worked out for everyone, because I made the decision to be civil and respectful to the mother and to reach out to her when it seemed like the right thing to do. My husband needed to have a life free of strife, and he could not handle any bickering between his ex-wife and me. I look at some of my friends and listen to how they complain about their stepchildren and the mother and I think they've made a huge mistake. When children are shared, everyone has to work together."

The concept of mothering as a common goal grants the stepmother more power than any divisive measure she might take. Though in many cases there are high hurdles to get to a place where the stepmother is confident enough in her relationship with the husband and of her mothering skills to reach out to her stepdaughters, it can bring rich rewards. As Sue Patton Thoele writes in her book, *The Courage To Be a Stepmom*, "Stepmothers who feel supported and loved, those who manage to forge strong bonds of communications and have deep, enduring friendships with their husbands, feel that every stepfamily challenge and heartache is worth it."

Daughters Exert Influence

Some of the daughters of divorce to whom I spoke expressed that they feel impotent in the face of their fathers' new marriages, much as they felt impotent in the face of their parents' divorce. Many have conflicting feelings when first seeing their stepmothers. Those who are caretakers for their fathers since the divorce are often relieved that they can behave as daughters again. If they compare their fathers' quality of life to their mothers' and find their mothers' to be lacking, they most often feel, as I've mentioned before, guilty and uneasy. Self-esteem issues for daughters of divorce are often related to the change in socio-economic status for their mothers following the divorce. As Wallerstein's and Corbin's research has revealed, daughters exhibit poor psychological adjustment after the divorce because their mothers lived at a lower income level than the fathers. A daughter will find her father's lifestyle more alluring than her mother's and, before her father remarries, may believe this bounty is hers. For younger daughters, the father seems more powerful because of his ability to spend money and to live well. This diminishes the mother's ability to discipline when the daughters are small, according to authors Twaite, Silitsky and Luchow in *Children of Divorce*. As the daughter grows older, the mother's authority remains weakened, whether she is still single or remarried, and the father's social status remains appealing.

In the majority of cases, we see the stepmother is definitely a factor in how the daughter will be treated financially and emotionally. Many daughters realize how pervasive their stepmothers' influences are and evaluate their own positions with these women.

"I was nine when my father married my stepmother," Penelope, twenty-seven, begins, "and I knew from the start that she was good to me so that my father would love her more. But that was okay, because she really was good to me. I was not happy about their marriage, and my mother got remarried within a few months of my father's wedding, so it was a bit much for me. I am the oldest of three sisters and I definitely felt my father's remarriage more than my little sisters. However, I was more tolerant of my father's remarriage than of my mother's because I mistakenly thought that my mother had wanted the divorce. It wasn't until years later that I learned that my father wanted it too.

"I was raised by my mother and my stepfather while my father and stepmother lived across the country, in California. Though she was good to me when we were together, I missed my father because I was his little tomboy and he had left me and moved far away with his wife. When I was fifteen I moved in with them for two years, to see what it would be like. I was not feeling very confident and this move made me closer to both my father and my stepmother. It has taken me years to get over my parents' divorce and their second marriages. I look at my stepmother today and I see that she always makes an effort and has always tried to be important to me, but she knows she is not my mother."

Teenage daughters are vulnerable whether their parents are divorced or married to each other. While divorce may represent liberation for teenage daughters' mothers and second chances for their fathers, they are profound losses for daughters. My research shows that divorce worsens most daughters' lack of self-esteem and erodes their sense of being grounded. Stepmothers clearly represent new chapters for fathers and at the same time an obliteration of the past for daughters. Whatever went wrong in the marriage, the stepmother/ new wife is proof that the father feels he can do better.

"All I ever wanted was to be a happy family," sighs Antonia, twenty-one, "but when I was thirteen, my mother said she wanted a divorce. I understood her reasons but I believed she should have put us first. Kids at school heard about the divorce and they looked at us differently. We had to sell our house and our father moved to another town. He started to date and he had a girlfriend whom we all thought was smart and nice and whom he eventually married. She brought her son and daughter with her. We were supposed to be the 'Brady Bunch.' Instead it was hellish. Then I found out that my father had had an affair with her while he was still married to my mother. That changed my view of her as a stepmother. I felt that my mother had been very stoic not to ever tell us."

There are several elements of Antonia's interview that illustrate similar strong reactions in other daughters of divorce to whom I spoke. When she describes how she wanted a "happy" family life—an intact family—the same sentiment is echoed in many others' reactions showing how deep-seated the desire for a traditional family is for children. Most daughters dislike unhappiness or discord in their parents' marriages but were willing to tolerate it to maintain the illusion of an intact family.

That it remains the opinion of most daughters that having divorced parents is a fall from grace is striking. Especially since the divorce rate hovers between fifty and sixty percent for first marriages, and sixty-five percent for remarriages involving children from prior marriages. Finally, my research confirms that in cases where the fathers' affairs caused the divorces and the fathers later married their mistresses, the relationships between daughters and their new stepmothers is negatively impacted by the history between them. "Only when I was in a bad marriage myself and had an affair which broke up a family," remarks Nina, a forty-three-year-old daughter of divorce, "was I able to forgive my stepmother for having done the same thing. She had been married to my father for twenty-two years by then. Sometimes you have to live your life, make mistakes and stop judging others."

From a mother's point of view, her ex-husband's affair can cause her to keep her daughters at a distance from their father. Not often does the mother/wife admit that the marriage had deficiencies and that the affair was a symptom of a poor marriage. Instead I found in most of these cases the mothers blamed the stepmother/other woman for instigating the divorce. Often these mothers displace all their anger onto the stepmothers rather than their husbands who were at least equal partners in the affairs. Despite this common attitude, there were those among the mothers I interviewed who understood their husbands had affairs. "The mother can be very astute and recognize that the affair was not due to the other woman but due to the ex-husband's actions," explains Dr. Michele Kasson. "Therefore she might not blame the other woman for the failure of the marriage. She may recognize that the cause of the affair had deeper roots."

Many women think their lives and marriages will never be touched by extramarital affairs and that even if they are, their husbands will never find women as good as them, women worth marrying. Yet statistics indicate otherwise. In 1999, according to *Washington Post* journalist Pamela Gerhardt, approximately one million children witnessed one of their divorced parents remarry. With most men remarrying within three years of divorce, stepmothers enter the picture rather quickly. But it takes two for these affairs to happen and women are engaging in them at a much higher rate than ever before. As Shere Hite's research reveals, the number of women having affairs has risen a staggering seventy percent. The research I conducted for my book *A Passion for More* indicated that over sixty percent of unmarried women were involved with men in extramarital affairs. Thus it can safely be inferred that a substantial number of remarriages after divorces are the results of affairs. It is valuable for the daughters' well-being and adjustment to their new lives after their parents' divorces for mothers to consider how they want to present this information to her daughters. Many daughters can easily be persuaded to think negatively about their fathers' new marriages because of the affairs which preceded them. A stepmother is in a tough spot and can not determine what the daughter has been told by her mother. All she can do is consider the best interests of the daughters, by attempting to establish a healthy rapport with her in the present and the future.

Without their mothers' help in adjusting, it can take years for daughters to separate their mothers' feelings from their own. Sometimes daughters move forward while the mothers are not able to do so. In Talia's case, her bitterness over her husband's affair remains strong today, seventeen years later, while her daughters have moved on. "My daughters were only three and seven when their father asked for a divorce. I think it was traumatic for my older daughter, Zoe, while Elizabeth was too young to know what was happening. I was left alone and sad because I really loved him. It turned out that my ex-husband left me for his best friend's wife. I told my girls all this and so they know who Lorna, their stepmother, is and that she used to be my friend. When the girls were small, I would have to talk to Lorna to make arrangements and it was very painful for me. Once they were in junior high, I let the girls make their own arrangements with Lorna and their father. It has been years since I have had to deal with Lorna directly.

"Since everyone knew everyone, I believe this divorce and my ex-husband's remarriage was more difficult than most other divorce situations. We had an extended group of mutual friends that got divided after the divorce. I've lost friends and so has my ex-husband, yet I see these people around town and we pretend not to know each other. It's very uncomfortable. However, I also see that the divorce has had a positive effect. My girls know how life can turn out and they have made their own decisions concerning their stepmother. I will never get over what happened, but my daughters look at Lorna in another way. They have come to see her as a person who cares about them and has been there for them. I know that they need to have a relationship with her and I'm the one who can't get over it."

If the mother remarries, I found, this often relieves the stepmother and father of a certain scrutiny on both the mother's and daughter's part. Many mothers in such cases become preoccupied with their own lives and then have less time to obsess about their ex-husbands and how the divorce ruined the family. While this makes life easier for the ex-husband and the stepmother, it is often more difficult for the daughters. In my interviews I found that many daughters under twelve felt their mothers were not as available after they remarried. Some of the daughters find themselves spending more time at this point with their fathers and stepmothers while their mothers nurture their new marriages. For the teenage daughter, already embroiled in the push and pull of female adolescence against her mother, the perception of this unavailability many times becomes heightened and results in negative feelings.

"I remember exactly what happened when my mother got engaged," begins Samantha, nineteen. "I was only nine at the time and I began to hate my stepfather. It wasn't against him personally; I was against anyone who would have wanted to marry my mother. My father was already married again and I liked my stepmother. I ended up going to their house more and doing sort of mother-daughter things with Clarissa, my stepmother. This lasted for several years. I still lived with my mother, but I always thought my father's home was a better place.

In junior high I was cool toward my mother because I saw how it got to her. I felt she'd left me for John, my stepfather. I know that I gave them a hard time and my stepmother and father probably thought they'd won me over. In high school I wanted my mother again, and I slowly gravitated back to her. It's really true—the power was all mine because everyone wanted me. What I learned in the end is that your mother will always be your mother through thick and thin, no matter what."

Ongoing mother/daughter friction only heightens complications of parents' remarriages. As E. Mavis Hetherington reports in her Longitudinal Study, "For daughters who were more likely than sons to have had a close, compassionate relationship with their divorced mother, a satisfying marital relationship may be seen as more of a threat." And so the daughters view their stepfather as endangering the very core of closeness they share with their mothers. At this point, the stepmother may seem more appealing than she has in the past. With time, usually the standard four to seven year period, daughters often come to a better understanding of their parents' divorces and subsequent remarriages. After adolescence, a daughter recognizes the complexities of her parents' lives, and of her own. This understanding often results in acceptance, forgiveness and healing.

Invisible Fathers

It helps matters greatly for mothers, daughters and stepmothers if fathers are more visible and take positions that further the relationship between the three females. New wives usually are in desperate need of support in their roles as stepmothers, and mothers want to be reassured that their daughters are still priorities in their ex-husbands' reinvented lives. As evidenced in my interviews, the vast majority of daughters of divorce feel a range of emotions, from loyalty to their mothers, to guilt when they have good relationships with their stepmothers, to the sense that their fathers have forgotten them for their wives. Many fathers fail to notice their daughters' cynicism and belief that they are less important to their fathers. Once these men are invested in their subsequent marriages, parenting roles may seem off-balance or their fathers may seem distant to the daughters.

The manner in which fathers and daughters interact after fathers' remarriages depends to a great extent upon how they and their daughters interacted before the divorces. Another factor is the amount of contention between the adults which the daughters witness. Researchers Twaite, Silitsky and Luchow warn that the level of conflict between parents before, during and after the divorce is directly reflected in the children's poor adjustment in school and with their peers. According to my pool of interviewees, many daughters' perceptions of their parents' divorces and the actual status of the parents' relationships after the divorce is often lost on their fathers and this is reflected in their behaviour when their fathers remarry. It is as if some fathers are oblivious to their daughters' feelings, but the problem is more likely that fathers cannot fathom what the daughters feel. "The daughters are in competition with the stepmother," Antoinette Michaels, relationship expert, explains. "And the father doesn't even notice. That is why fathers sometimes introduce their daughters too soon to this woman. Even if he marries her, there has to be an easy entry."

"My ex-husband, Dan," sighs Lorraine, forty-two, "began to date right away. I doubt he saw how it bothered our girls, Jennifer and Robin. This was six years ago and they were only six and ten at the time. Dan was not really ready to cope with two tender-aged daughters who were upset with him. So he solicited help from his girlfriend. This lasted for a few years and then he and the girlfriend married.

"He had known his new wife back in college and probably thought that this historical connection would mean something to the girls. Of course it meant nothing to them and it simply negated their parent's marriage. The only message to the girls was that their father had made a big mistake marrying their mother and that this new wife was his real destiny. My daughters didn't buy into it and never really forgave him. It's a real shame. He just didn't get it. They spent less and less time with him and now they barely know him."

Far too often, divorced fathers' roles in their daughters' lives diminish, sometimes to the point where they are almost totally uninvolved. This is due in part to the fact that most young daughters live with their mothers who are often named the primary custodial parents after the divorce, while fathers are only given visitation rights. However, divorce attorney Brondi Borer explains that many states allow children over the age of twelve to choose which parent they would prefer to live with. A study in Judith Wallerstein's *The Unexpected Legacy of Divorce* notes that, while there are those divorced fathers who "abandoned their children outright...most fathers in this study fall in between." The reason that contact falls off is because of "second marriages with new children and stepchildren as well as new jobs...," explains the author. We have to bear in mind that these results are from a twenty-five year study and the parenting efforts made by many fathers today are more impressive because of society's encouragement of involved single fathers. Despite low percentages of joint custody, the majority of daughters interviewed for this book have spent some time living with both parents. Thus the fathers' remarriages have tremendous impacts on their daughters and the daughters have an impact on the fathers' new wives.

A sense of devotion plays a large part in how daughters react to their fathers' dating and remarriage and to their long-term approval of stepmothers. "Even though my father introduced my sister and me to all his girlfriends," Joanna, thirty, recalls fifteen years later, "I didn't mind. I was a sophomore in high school when my parents split up. I saw my father as someone who could not be alone and could not face his feelings. My mother was already alone throughout their marriage so we figured she knew how to cope. I sort of took my father's side and I tried to befriend whomever he was dating because I didn't want to worry about him when I wasn't there and he had no one. My mother did not mix her dating life with her children, but my father did. It was almost like he couldn't do it any other way. My sister and I forgave him and we have always been respectful of our stepmother."

The connection between mothers and stepmothers benefits fathers as well and when jealousy subsides, everyone can have a productive life. When the father is more present, the mothers, daughters and stepmothers find their common ground more quickly.

"It can happen that the mother and stepmother form a healthy relationship," Claire Owen, psychotherapist, notes, "but the father is usually involved and both women have to work on it." Fathers are important in laying the ground work for mothers, daughters and stepmothers to interact with civility, a truth which will be explored in greater detail in the next chapter. However, it is the mother's approval of the stepmother which is the key factor in the success of the stepmother/daughter relationship.

CHAPTER 7

Daughters and Fathers in the New Triangle

"My sister, Molly, was a teenager when my father married Arlene ten years ago," recalls Candace, twenty. "Molly had her group of friends and she was able to talk about her feelings with other people. I had no one to talk to and my mother was not willing to talk about the divorce or my father's remarriage. It is really strange, but I ended up talking to my stepmother, Arlene. She actually listened to me. I was young enough that I saw her as another mother figure. Arlene was ready to do things with me so while she was the enemy by definition as a stepmother, she wasn't that in my life.

"Molly didn't have much of a relationship with Arlene and she ignored my bond with her. When we were with my mother, who was the custodial parent, it was this world of just the three of us—my mother, my sister and me. We have always been very close to our mother. But when we were at my father and Arlene's house, Molly was cool and unfriendly to Arlene. And as the day would go on, she would become cool to me, because I was so enthused about being there. It took a long time for Molly to accept Arlene. But Arlene and I have always had a close stepmother/stepdaughter relationship."

In families of two daughters or more, my interviews demonstrate that stepmothers may win one daughter's affection and not the other's. This can be quite disturbing to the fathers and causes schisms between the sisters. Some mothers with whom I spoke were greatly troubled when they saw one daughter suffering in the stepmother/stepdaughter relationship, even if another was flourishing. In many cases this put mothers and stepmothers at odds.

Sisters Divided

Daughters of divorce whose fathers (and mothers) remarry struggle to maintain equilibrium in their weekly schedules which are divided between two households with distinct rules and structures. Aiming to please their parents and wanting to be "good girls" at all costs often become integral parts of their behavior patterns. Daughters will often silence themselves and not express their true feelings for years after their parent's divorce. The research of Hetherington, Cox and Cox finds that many girls from divorced families become depressed and exhibit "over-controlled" behavior.

While the accepted four- to seven-year recovery and bonding period of the stepfamily is supported by my interviewees, my research indicates that, even within this timeframe, daughters do not always rebound completely. Instead, some daughters find some other acceptable reality within the parameters of the subsequent stepfamilies. In other words, the daughters adapt in unhealthy ways to the common tug-of-war of mother versus stepmother.

On the positive side, I found inner reconciliation is a slow but steady process for many of these daughters and, in many cases, sisters soothe and support each other through their parents' divorces and remarriages. However, in other cases, the unexpected occurs: there is a schism between the sisters, caused by differing views of their stepmothers and stepfamilies. Since sisterhood is a powerful bond, when sisters are divided over their parents' divorce and remarriage, the loss felt by each sister is particularly painful.

"As much as I wanted a divorce, I never expected that my daughters would be separated by it," Jacinta, forty-eight, says sadly. "I had raised them to be so close and they are only two years apart in age. I took both of them everywhere, even to work with me on weekends. Their father had no time for them until he remarried and then he wanted them back in his life. He and his wife began showering the girls with gifts. Dawn, my older daughter, bought into it completely while Rosie, my younger daughter, didn't care a bit. She stayed with me when Dawn, who was twelve at the time, moved in with her father and Marnie.

"I'm glad that Rosie stayed with me, but having my girls split up definitely was not my choice or the way I thought it should be. I would have fought it more but Dawn was adamant and I knew she'd only resent me if I tried to stand in her way. My daughters have been raised for the past ten years in two different homes. It's heartbreaking to see these once close sisters act like strangers."

When two daughters are divided, with one sister accessible to her stepmother and the other distant, more complications develop. As in Jacinta's case, the mother suffers upon seeing her daughters so split over their new stepfamily. While it might be satisfying initially for the mother to have one daughter whose allegiance to her is steadfast, it is not healthy for that daughter in the long run, and certainly isn't healthy for the sister relationship. A wise mother knows that, should she remarry, she and her husband might not escape the same alienated reaction her daughter has bestowed upon the father and stepmother. After several years of divided loyalties and miscommunication between sisters, mothers and stepmothers, union is difficult.

Many stepmothers feel that they are outsiders in their stepfamilies and that their husbands and his daughters are firmly bound to each other through their biological links. Stepdaughters who choose to enter the stepmother's home immediately were rare among my interviewees. Such relationships rarely solidify in the early stages of stepfamilies, according to Patricia L. Papernow, author of *Becoming A Stepfamily*. As Papernow writes, "Confusion for all stepparents is heightened by the fact that the biological family members hold firm perceptions of each other's needs, character, strengths and weaknesses. Stepparents, as outsiders, often have a very different point of view, but most find themselves acceding to their mate's interpretation of which kid was at fault and what needed to be done despite their own initial inclinations."

Some stepdaughters with whom I spoke made a separate peace with their stepmothers because it pleased their fathers, despite having sisters who did not approve of nor partake in such gestures. Others were encouraged to make peace by fathers who were forceful in their attempts to remain connected to their daughters and who demonstrated an ability to be inclusive. Most mothers respect this behavior on the fathers' parts. Nonetheless, daughters might not be responsive in the beginning. This can cause friction in both mothers and stepmothers because the daughters can act out in destructive ways.

According to Pam Gerhart's article in the *Washington Post* on February 23, 2000, "When parents remarry, kids may need time to feel at home in the new family." The adjustment for members of the step-family requires enormous effort. And, despite the theory of the seventies and eighties that remarriage was beneficial for children, today we see that remarriage is stressful for the entire stepfamily. Children in stepfamilies are considered more likely to fail academically than children in intact families, at a rate similar to that of children in single parent families. This points to how imperative it is that the father, stepmother and mother prepare themselves for the repercussions of remarriage and anticipate the needs of their daughters by remaining presences in their daughters' lives.

Gender Split

From a gender point of view, divorce usually precipitates certain behaviors in mothers and fathers. Many mothers become immersed in motherly activities and efforts toward their daughters at the outset, as if these are the only resources they have left. This may result in such mothers treating their daughters as confidantes, which is not healthy for either party. Another result is a guilty daughter, who feels she must care for her mother and view her stepmother as the enemy.

Many fathers' act in a way that is all too common for their gender: they downplay their emotions and focus on practical matters. This is an attempt to achieve normalcy in everyone's life, in the face of a new and strange existence of a stepfamily. But I found that being practical and avoiding emotions leads to awkward and difficult moments for fathers. Some wise stepmothers who see that the fathers are having trouble connecting emotionally with their daughters, get involved.

"I made every effort for my husband," Lorna, a fifty-six-year-old stepmother, told me. "It was twenty years ago when I married Bill and decided I would do whatever was necessary for his daughters. Little did I know it would work with my younger stepdaughter, who was nine at the time, and not with her sister, who was thirteen. I sort of hobbled along, trying every way I could to get them to see their father. On the weekends when the girls came, we baked cookies and went shopping, we did projects together and planted a garden. I wanted to be there, to try to make our house a home for them. They were always welcome, but I think my own daughters intimidated them. It certainly was a challenge.

"In the end, my older stepdaughter left home without finishing high school and moved half way across the country. I saw how guilty both Bill and their mother felt. Meanwhile, I had managed to save the younger daughter. She and my oldest, who are eight years apart, became like a big and little sister. So if my other daughter and Bill's older daughter didn't want to fit in, what could I do? I tried everything to keep the family together and, in the end, I accepted my losses and appreciated my gains. Today, we are a family—my one daughter and his one daughter. We have never given up completely on the other two. We are just going to have to wait and see."

The new life for mothers, daughters and stepmothers begins in a healthy way once acceptance has taken place. At this point, the three women let go of the past and move toward the future together. How the fathers work with the stepmothers to hold their stepfamilies together is telltale in this forward movement. Even with the best intentions and efforts on the part of the mother, father and stepmother, however, I witnessed scenarios where stepdaughters were at odds with each other. In such cases, it may be up to the mother and stepmother to put aside their differences and work together to correct the problem. One of the women I interviewed, did exactly this to correct the problems in her relationships. "I finally called their mother," Gabriella explains. "After two years of feuding sisters and my icy relationship with their mother, I could not stand it. I told her we had to do better and it worked." Finding this kind of courage is difficult but twenty-five percent of the population of stepmothers I interviewed had to do just that: bite the bullet and call the mother. Often, I found, mothers are not as reluctant to call stepmothers, as they feel their role as mother entitles them to certain rights and responsibilities. In my study, forty percent of mothers of adolescent and older daughters said they were comfortable calling stepmothers when difficult issues confronted them.

Many mothers, daughters and stepmothers grieve for the loss of their original families even as new stepfamilies emerge. With an awareness of the divorce rate in America, mothers, stepmothers and fathers share personal beliefs that the effects of divorce and remarriage on daughters will diminish with time. However, my studies indicate that the process has many challenges, including the disparate hopes of mothers, and stepmothers as well as deep skepticism of almost all daughters over the age of twelve.

Internal Conflict for Daughters

Though most daughters of divorce want to be close to their fathers, some feel they cannot. Many daughters of divorce are keenly aware of the imbalance in lifestyle, wealth, values and child-rearing methodologies between their mothers and their stepmothers. For daughters who live primarily in one home, there is often both intense curiosity about and disdain for the day-to-day life and goings on in the other home. Younger daughters often long for the noncustodial parent until they arrive at his or her home, and then it is the other, absent parent who they miss. A stepmother's style might not fit with her stepdaughter's ideal and subsequently, the daughter is mystified that her father has adopted the stepmother's way of doing things.

"After my parents' custody case for my sister and me, I never felt easy in either place," sighs Caroline, twenty-three. "I kept missing my mother when I was with my dad. I was glad that my mom had won custody because I thought she needed me more than my father did at the time. My mother and Helena are like night and day. My mother is fashionable and social, Helena is introverted and sensible. Their house is so unlike my mother's. I'm always drawn to my mother's way of doing things."

The power of the mother/daughter bond is only strengthened when the stepmother seems so different and unfamiliar to the step-daughter. Even when a stepmother's differences are looked upon as positive, most daughters persist in longing for their mothers, as Melinda's story reveals.

"My younger sister, June, never seemed to miss our mom when we were at our dad's house," Melinda begins. "June loved our Sylvia's way of running dad's house—she didn't compare it to our mother's at all. Maybe she was so young that she wasn't hooked on how our mother cut the crust off our bologna sandwiches or gave us warm towels right from the dryer. But I saw the differences and I always wished I was at home with my mom when we visited my dad."

Before the divorce occurs, most daughters, depending on their ages, will be conscious of the patterns that exist between their parents. Once the divorce takes place, those patterns are gone, later to be replaced with stepfamilies and their singular rhythms and styles. As Margorie Engel, President and CEO of the Stepfamily Association of America explains, "With remarriage, we're actually creating a new relationship defined by what was, but isn't any longer. With remarriage, we're getting involved with all the people from each other's former marriage."

A daughter who has two stepfamilies might compare one to the other. If she has been closer to her father, she might be more accepting of his remarriage than her mother's. If she has been closer to her mother, she might find her mother's remarriage more acceptable. One sister may identify with her father more strongly than her mother or vice versa and the resulting relationship with the stepparent will reflect those feelings. For many daughters of divorce under the age of eighteen, a substantial amount of time is spent with their father and stepmothers. "If there has been an unhealthy, destructive divorce, a daughter might feel guilty, because her mother doesn't want her to like her stepmother," comments Dr. Donald Cohen. "Or one sister will be very close to the father and the other to the mother and take sides. If the mother feels secure with her daughters, then she won't compete with her father or stepmother."

While the internal conflict in daughters is not precipitated by outside forces, if the parents are still feuding even years after their divorces and new marriages, this hostility worsens the problem for the daughters. These daughters will feel caught in the middle and, as a result, they will struggle emotionally, academically and socially. As cited by Maccoby, Buchanan, Mnookin & Dornbusch in their study, "Postdivorce Roles of Mothers and Fathers in the Lives of Their Children," adolescents who felt they were positioned "between parents" had poorer adjustments. "Adolescents in dual residences appear to benefit more from cooperative co-parenting (or from being shielded from any parental conflict that does exist) and suffer more from being embroiled in parental conflict than do adolescents living primarily with either fathers or mothers," write the authors.

"When I was twenty-one, I married a man with two small daughters and an ex-wife who lived thirty minutes away," recalls Juanita, forty-seven, "I wasn't much older than the oldest daughter, Mira, so I was like a big sister to her. We would go shopping together and I was her cheerleader when she first began to date. The younger daughter, Lara, never wanted that kind of bond with me. She would hang around with her father on visiting weekends, but she never said much to me.

"I just couldn't win Lara over. I couldn't mother her, because she wouldn't allow it. I couldn't be her friend, because she didn't want that either. She would watch Mira with me, but she never crossed over and joined us. Even after the girls were grown up and married, Mira made me feel like family and Lara always kept her distance. I don't know how it changed their relationship or how their mother felt about it, but the two girls were definitely divided over me. The hard part was that I couldn't really treat them equally, because they didn't act the same toward me."

The stepmother's presence represents the official end of the former family. In some cases, this is acceptable and in other cases, daughters feel they have been cheated of a whole family. A step-mother who understands the conflict has her own demons—whether she has children of her own from a previous marriage or not. A mother does not want to see her daughters tortured over their places in the stepfamily, regardless of the mother's own feelings about her ex-husband and his new wife. Daughters of divorce are constant reminders of the past for their mothers, fathers and stepmothers, and, as such, the daughters can take advantage and manipulate the adults or hurt them as they were hurt by the divorce. For those daughters who do take advantage, their actions are reflections of their unre-solved inner conflicts.

Growing Up Too Fast

Preadolescent daughters tend to mature more quickly during and after divorces than do their counterparts in intact families. "Once the daughter matures and her parents are remarried, she is on her own," warns Antoinette Michaels, relationship expert. "The daughter may be exposed to sex, drugs and a fast life." Such a possibility is frightening for parents and stepparents to consider.

"I have watched Ella, my stepdaughter, go from a sweet, inno-cent six-year-old little girl," begins Shelley, forty-one, "to a promiscu-ous twelve-year-old tramp. She now looks and acts like a prostitute. I think so much of this has to do with the divorce. Clark, my husband, keeps battling it out with Barb, the ex-wife, to make some rules and regulations that apply to both homes. Meanwhile, Ella is allowed to do too much because neither parent wants to discipline her properly and be the bad guy. I hear talk on the phone with boys and I know this is just the beginning of our troubles with her. Her sister, Henny, who is in eleventh grade, is a bookworm who doesn't want to face her sexuality. So she is as extreme in her own way as Ella. The girls don't get along like they did when they were younger. The whole thing is very painful for everyone.

"I called their mother, Barb, to talk about how things are getting out of control. We sorted some things out and already I feel much more empowered to help my stepdaughters. It feels safer to parent the girls because Barb and I can talk."

Judith Wallerstein's research concludes that, once daughters of divorce hit adolescence, issues brought about during the divorce appear once again and sometimes manifest in premature sexual acts and unsettled relationships with boys. In my interview pool, some daughters expressed the desire to "get back" at the opposite sex for what transpired between their parents during and after the divorce. These girls feel abandoned by their fathers and act out with male peers.

"I see that my three daughters, who are fourteen, sixteen and eighteen, want to get even with the male population for the way their father treated me," April, forty-six, explains. "My girls, who are all teenagers now, are very precocious and mature. Mostly my girls see boys as a great big joke. When they get boyfriends, they toy with them for a short while then dump them quickly, before they get dropped. It's amazing, because I was always timid when I was dating as teen. I would never have been so bold.

"Until a few years ago, the girls and I were very close. Then they began to date boys and it seemed tied in to seeing their father more. Frank, their father, gave them advice about dating, that I felt showed poor judgment on his part. I expected Frank to give the girls more guidance but I think he wanted to seem cool and knowledgeable. I don't think if we were still married he'd try to be this hip. I think he'd be more cautious about his daughters' plans with boys."

Despite the negative outcome of fatherly advice in April's story, it is evident from my research that daughters who grow up too fast need the love, attention and advice of their fathers just as much as their mothers and even stepmothers. Thus fathers must be more than just presences in their daughters lives; they must be active, involved parents. How they achieve this is not as easy as it appears, for fathers are often unsure of their duties, what is expected of them and their abilities in their roles as parents to daughters.

Confusion for Fathers

In the past fifty years, the role of fathers has changed tremendously. In cases of divorce, this change is dramatic. In a 1991 study by Judith A. Seltzer, "Relationships Between Fathers and Children Who Live Apart," it was reported that only twenty-five percent of divorced fathers see their children once or more per week and twenty-nine percent of divorced fathers call or write once or more each week. Fathers who were responsible for child support regularly kept in touch with their children. Yet, sadly enough thirty-one percent of the fathers, according to Robert Hughes, Jr.'s study, "Demographics of Divorce," had no contact with their children. However, with increased visitation rights, co-parenting and through child support, many fathers remain in touch with their daughters and feel they are a part of their lives. My studies also showed that mothers who encourage fathers to remain involved with daughters are on the right track, no matter what their personal feelings about the fathers may be. If the fathers are still absentee parents, as was the case in twenty-five percent of my interviews, I found that mothers and stepmothers have discussed the problem and tried to work together to fill in the gaps left by fathers. Sometimes mothers and stepmothers together are able to persuade fathers to participate in their daughters lives.

"After the divorce, my father wasn't around and didn't have time for us," says Kaelyn, eighteen. "He was an alcoholic. Then he met Martha and she helped him through it. Martha is not a mother figure to me, but I try to be open to her efforts, because I know she was there when my dad was so broken. She also planned our visits when we were small. She had to do the planning with my mother, which was awkward for them both. But they couldn't rely on my dad to arrange visitations so they didn't have much choice. In the end, I'm happy my dad has Martha instead of being alone. I just wish I had my dad when I was growing up."

In this book that documents the lives of women, specifically mothers, daughters and stepmothers, and their interconnection in the new triangle, we cannot put aside the feelings or the role of fathers as they impact this triangle. In my research not one mother, daughter or stepmother discounted the feelings of the fathers. The father, whether he is a visible or invisible presence, impacts the lives of these three females in addition to having a profound influence upon his daughter and how she views the world of men. The societal structure which limits the responsibilities of parenting for many men also encourages marriage and the safe haven of family. Many men struggle to find a new balance in life once a divorce dissolves the family. Divorced fathers often express their discontentment to both mothers and stepmothers. There is pressure to support two homes and to remain close with their daughters who they no longer see on a daily basis. A narrow construct is set as a model for men's lives—that of family, fatherhood and marriage. It is little wonder that so many men remarry within the first three years of their divorces, as reported by the United States Census Bureau. Whether they benefited or not from their former marriages, these seem to be experiences that they are familiar with and are motivated to repeat.

"I know that Mike, my husband, married me to stop feeling he was alone in the world," admits Renata. "And I don't blame him. The way he was raised was to have a wife and kids and a backyard with Sunday barbecues. He had no intention of getting divorced and Jill, his ex-wife, really knocked the wind out of him when she left him. He was an old-fashioned kind of husband and he didn't know how to recast his life as a single father. He only knew he didn't want to be alone the rest of his life. His girls, Gracie and Amber, were already in high school and busy with their friends.

"I have been good to my stepgirls because of their dad. Gracie has liked my being there but Amber has not. She fails to see that I have helped her father, and that he needed a wife again."

Fathers are usually the first male role models for their daughters. The more involved a father is with his daughter from an early age, the better off she will be in terms of self-esteem, her views of men and her interaction with males in the adult world. Among my interviewees, some daughters' fathers were not as involved with them until the divorces took place. On the flip side, there were those whose fathers somehow lost their footing and grew distant from the daughters due to the logistics and machinations of divorce, remarriage and stepfamilies. Research shows that if one divorced parent undermines the other, the daughters will see through this and come to their own conclusions about each parent and the role she/he has played in raising them. If fathers shirk their responsibilities as parents, both emotionally and financially, daughters of divorce eventually recognize this shortcoming on their own. There is little defense or accusation by mothers or stepmothers that has influence over this.

For fathers who remarry and abandon their daughters, the loss for the daughters is enormous and for the fathers as well. While their new marriages and perhaps new families may take them away from their daughters from previous marriages, it is the neglect which has the greatest repercussions for the daughters. These repercussions often, I found, translate into the basics: food, shelter and clothing—if the father cannot or will not provide these after the remarriages take place, many daughters with whom I spoke felt their fathers no longer valued them. This can impair the daughters emotionally. As Alice Michaeli, sociologist, explains, "The child feels that if she is loved and valued, her parents will provide for her needs. If the child does not have her needs met, she is starting out at a deficit. The daughters have to receive love to give love and in a materialistic society, part of this is through money."

"My ex-husband, Kirk, could not afford to support our children while we were married or once we were divorced and he remarried," Blanche, fifty, tells us. "Kirk's remarriage and new family made him feel inadequate about his first family. So he gave up our two boys and one daughter, who were all under twelve at the time. He seemed to think that if he couldn't pay for them, he didn't deserve them. This wasn't true at all and I ended up with the entire responsibility of raising these three children. The first few years after the divorce, there was no money and I moved us back to the midwest, where I grew up. It was cheaper to live there and I had family to count on. The only problem was that Kirk was far away. I know that the kids missed him and it was a huge adjustment.

"There are those who would say that Kirk was a deadbeat dad. I saw him as a person who felt he had failed at a marriage and at his main responsibility as a father—to pay the children's way. His way out was to start a new family. It took a long time for him to reconnect. My daughter tried the hardest to see him and so she saw him first and later he came around for the boys. In the end, the situation improved. Everyone is grown now and has a relationship with Kirk."

Many daughters' perspectives when their fathers have been absent in all aspects of their lives mirror the feelings that Blanche had as a divorced mother whose children did not see their father. In such cases, many women search for the connection, one as the mother of children of divorce and the other as the daughter of divorce, to the father.

The father's situation warrants attention as well. A man in our society is conditioned to be a provider and to put his career at the center of his life. His wife and children define him further, but when the marriage falls apart, he can embrace his children as a single father and struggle with the many responsibilities now bestowed upon him, try to avoid them or remarry quickly in an attempt to reconstruct his life with new roles.

When a father's role is redefined as a single father, which is followed by another new definition, that of a stepfather, this adjustment can be tricky. The emotional and financial expectations which translate into "caring" for one's daughters can be overwhelming. In Herb Goldberg's essay, "In Harness: The Male Condition," which describes the complexities of living up to and understanding the male's plight, we see that solutions do not always come immediately to the male/father, and his intentions may be thwarted by his own sense of self or lack thereof.

Despite these problems, fathers like Madeleine's stay connected. "My father always made an effort to see me, from the time I was three and he and my mother divorced," recalls Madeleine, twenty-nine. "There was a period when he was out of work and couldn't pay child support. I know he was ashamed of that, but he put on a happy face for my sake and continued spending as much time with me as possible. That is what matters most. My father was a loving parent and I didn't know until I was a teenager that he had business problems. He never let me see that side and he never let it get in the way of being with me. I admire how he balanced the rough times he had at work with being an involved parent. I've heard so many horror stories from other daughters of divorce that I know how lucky I am."

Psychic Stretches

It can be reassuring for both mothers and stepmothers to realize that some of the feelings daughters have about their fathers and stepmothers are not directly their fault. In my study, sixty percent of daughters had good relationships with their mothers but could not tolerate their stepmother. In explaining the reason for their negative attitudes toward their stepmothers, these daughters cited their unhappiness and disappointment with their fathers as the cause. Another factor affecting the attitudes of daughters occurred when sisters were not in harmony in their feelings toward their fathers or mothers. I found this happened in fifty percent of the stories told to me. The poor treatment of stepmothers by daughters is largely related to family pathology and how the relationships played out before the divorce. Mothers and stepmothers who were at odds sometimes discovered that the fathers were actually in the way of the two women joining to form a united front.

"I look back on my marriage to Kevin and I know that I was not prepared for his relationship with Corrine, his daughter, who was thirteen at the time," says Crystal, forty-five, a stepmother for ten years. "Corrine was the youngest of three girls, and the older two had married quite young and were not living nearby. I believe that they had married in their early twenties as a way to escape the pain of their parents' divorce and dealing with the stepfamilies. Their decision made Corrine an only child of sorts. Joanne, her mother, was also a daughter of divorce so she knew that she and I should talk, for Corrine's sake. Both of us were worried about her school work and she seemed very down. Of course I thought that Kevin was a terrific father, because I wanted to believe only the best about him. It took me a long time to see that he spoiled Corrine and didn't listen to her and what her needs were. Joanne and I are both practical women and we spoke with Kevin about how Corrine felt. I think his pride was hurt, but he learned to deal with Corrine in a different way. He was less superficial and more involved with her feelings. In the end, everyone has profited and my stepdaughter is much better off. I wish that I had had more information on how divorce affects children when I first married."

The research conducted by Paul Amato and Bruce Keith concurs with other studies which reveal that children of divorce often plummet academically, socially and psychologically. Their research includes adult children of divorce who have exhibited similar results. Any interpersonal conflict—whether between mothers and fathers, mothers and stepmothers, fathers and stepmothers—affects the well-being of daughters of any age. The most important ingredient in functioning post-divorce families and stepfamilies is the sense that everyone is working together. In order to make this happen, the adults, in particular, benefit from understanding each other's experiences, expectations and goals. Mothers and stepmothers in my study were more willing to have conversations when the topic was a serious one such as the relationships between daughters and their fathers. On the other hand, fathers seemed more inclined to distance themselves from conflicts in their daughters' lives than share their concerns with their wives or ex-wives. So, though it is important for fathers to be more actively involved parents, practically speaking, mothers and stepmothers will likely shoulder the burden of working to resolve daughters' problems. Hopefully this will change; however, on the positive side, many of the mothers and stepmothers I interviewed are aware of the fathers' shortcomings in this area. Sixty-five percent of stepmothers and close to seventy-five percent of mothers felt it important to share their concerns with each other. These concerns included not only the fathers' roles as parents, but as influences on the effectiveness of the triangle of mother, daughter and stepmother.

CHAPTER 8

Trying Circumstances/
New Connections

"I think that my father married Annette, my stepmother, because she was like my mother," begins Penny, thirty. "Annette has been my stepmother for nearly twenty years. She has always been good to me and a good mother to her own children. Though we are not very close, we are friendly.

"Both my mother and stepmother have similar stories and backgrounds. Both of them have good credentials and great jobs. Although I was surrounded by these two strong women, it took me awhile to develop my self-esteem. Even with role models like Annette and my mother, the divorce was so traumatic. Still, I have learned to see what my mother and stepmother have to offer."

Though initially reluctant, eventually some daughters of divorce discover that their stepmothers can be instrumental in their lives. If not precisely mother figures, some stepmothers become confidantes and staunch supporters particularly for adolescent and adult daughters. When the stepmother is a divorcee with her own children, as Annette was in the previous example, I have found that many daughters draw comparisons between their stepmothers' mothering and their own mothers' ability to parent. I learned that daughters, in some cases, were more sympathetic to their stepmothers' plight than to their own mothers'.

Similarly, stepmothers who care about their stepdaughters and are respectful of the stepdaughters' mothers certainly improve the quality of life for daughters of divorce. My research offers a valuable lesson for mothers, daughters and stepmothers: peaceful co-existence between the three can come about but often only after a long period of time. This passage requires patience, tolerance and communication. As with all players in divorce, whether children, parents or stepparents, communication is key. Dr. Ronnie Burak advocates family meetings where all members vent. These are not to be blaming sessions, but vehicles for everyone in the stepfamily to hear each other's feelings, even if there are no instant solutions. "The daughters who are able to express themselves do much better than the daughters who hold it in," comments Dr. Burak. "A family meeting gives the daughters a chance to do this. Everyone gets to say what is on his or her minds."

The Complexity of Mothers and Daughters

The bond between most mothers and daughters survives adolescence and the damage of divorce. Whatever negativity has transpired during these tumultuous years, most mother/daughter relationships improve over time. Adult mother/daughter bonds are usually so strong that they have profound effects on the daughters.

Since most mothers have also been the ones to nurture their children when small, their attachment is even stronger. A primary explanation is because women are societally groomed for such a job and the majority of men are not, that their attachment usually is less strong in the formative years. Carol Gilligan's book *In a Different Voice* points to the fact that daughters are often viewed as extensions of their mothers: "Girls, in identifying themselves as female, experience themselves as like their mothers, thus fusing the experience of attachment with the process of identity formation." I believe that if we take this to the next degree, some of the mothering aspects of stepmother relationships appeal to daughters of divorce, much in the same way that aunts or close female friends of the mothers can be role models and mother figures.

Mother/daughter relationships alter with age, for both parties, and this, I found in talking to all the members of the new triangle, can have significant effects upon daughter/stepmother relationships as well. Some adolescent daughters of divorce who mature in their mid-twenties begin to be more open to both their mothers and their stepmothers at this stage. As Karen Fingerman, Ph.D, author of *Aging Mothers and Their Daughters: A Study of Mixed Emotions*, observes, most mothers and daughters are deeply invested in each other and this sometimes creates conflict, but also can be positive. During the struggle to become an adult woman, some daughters do not embrace the same values as their mothers. Some can be self-absorbed. Later, when the two women are older, according to Fingerman, the feelings on both sides become more mutual. The underlying theme is that most mothers and daughters love one another so much that they overlook each other's flaws. Many stepmothers who witness the conflict between mothers and daughters and their unbreakable bond may presume they will never have the impact a mother has. However, as the next story reveals, stepmothers can have great influence over their stepdaughters.

"My mother and grandmother were the only two people who made me feel safe once my parents were divorced and remarried," begins Marlene, thirty-one. "My parents divorced when I was four. I was the only child. I remember waking up in the middle of the night and running into my mom's bedroom because my father had always consoled me when I had nightmares. After the divorce, he wasn't there but my mother was. It made me think my mother would always be there for me but my father wouldn't. Then everything changed because both my parents remarried the same year. I was only six and I lived with my mother. Suddenly, she had two older stepdaughters. They never felt like family to me, although my mother pushed really hard for it.

"My father's new wife had no children and together they wen on to have two girls and two boys. I thought of these younger siblings as family and I played with them when they were little. This brought me back into my father's life. But it wasn't him that I was drawn to, it was my stepmother. I began to respect her and see her as a role model. She is a successful attorney and I have always been amazed how she balances a career and children. She has really made an impression on me."

Daughters typically react in various ways to their mothers' choices vis-à-vis careers and parenting. This is especially true of career-oriented mothers and their daughters. These daughters may follow their mothers' footsteps, pursue serious careers, marry, have children and some eventually divorce. Or daughters may seek other routes by not emphasizing their careers and instead become stay-at-home mothers. Still others may seek a balance between the two, choosing motherhood, work and marriage, with a determination not be divorced, not to follow their mothers or stepmothers in this regard.

Some of these daughters, though they may be close to their mothers, question their mothers' and stepmothers' patterns. The majority of adult daughters of divorce in my study, have a strong capacity for looking back on their upbringings to try to avoid the mistakes that their mothers, and in some of the cases, their stepmothers, have made. Whether daughters choose different paths or follow their mother's paths, it is clear is that attachment to their mothers is not reflected in the decisions these daughters make for themselves.

The Arm's-length Stepmother

None of the daughters of divorce to whom I spoke felt an instant closeness to their stepmothers. It has been acknowledged already that stepmothers do not find their roles easy and their ability to be recognized and accepted often is hard earned and prolonged. In her essay, "Women in Stepfamilies: The Fairy Godmother, the Wicked Witch and Cinderella Reconstructed," Anne Bernstein states, "Females may be more sensitive to the quality of relationship within each family dyad: their emotional seismographs identify problems earlier, when the difficulties are more subtle, and their dissatisfaction with family relationships matter more in reckoning their general life satisfaction."

Many of the issues in the mother/daughter/stepmother triangle which have been discussed thus far play out individually. A key ingredient to the triangle's success is that all of the players are open to the idea of the threesome connecting. Daughters' responses to their stepmothers depend largely on their age, the intricacies of their parents' divorces and how many years have elapsed since these divorces. In some instances, stepmothers and their stepdaughters have windows of opportunity. If the relationship between the daughters and their stepmothers become successful, some daughters get from their stepmothers what they might not get from their mothers. I also found that the stepmothers' efforts to communicate with their husbands, their stepdaughters, their own daughters (if they have any), and ex-wives can prosper in time, if not initially.

Jill, one of the daughters of divorce who contributed her story, is twenty-nine. She was ten years old when her parents divorced. Six months afterward, her father remarried and moved several towns away. "After a joint-custody arrangement was agreed upon, my father remarried and moved, which took a toll on me. It took me several years to get close to Betty, my stepmother, because at first I didn't want her around. I wanted my father to myself. I couldn't understand why he had to remarry. In all fairness to my stepmother, she tried very hard to be there for me. And ultimately I benefited from her care.

"Once my stepmother and I became close, our stepfamily began to make sense and I found it a source of strength. I knew that I had two homes. It wasn't my first choice, for my parents to be divorced, but I adjusted because it was my reality. The thing about Betty that has always impressed me is that she hung in despite my initial rejection. Now I really appreciate that."

One extreme feminist view of the role of mother is that it is oppressive and demanding for women and that society further demoralizes women by minimizing their strengths and successes in other areas of life. Many stepmothers do not interpret stepmotherhood as a form of mothering and this is both an advantage and a disadvantage. When daughters of divorce are age ten and up, the stepmother and her stepdaughters need to forge their own relationship. This is less about mothering a young girl and more about forming a support system for the daughter as she enters adolescence and adulthood. In these instances, there can be plenty of false starts and disappointments. Stepmothers' contributions vary—they can be stepmothers nominally or can become active participants in their stepdaughters' lives.

Sonya, who has been a stepmother to her fifteen-year-old stepdaughter since the girl was seven, feels that she made every effort to be a participant. "Chantelle was a darling child and I tried to be there for her in every way," Sonya tells us. "Her father and I took her on vacations and we attended every school play. On school nights, I helped Chantelle with her homework and made sure she was organized for the next morning. But I never deluded myself that I was her mother—she had a mother who was ten minutes away. We both knew that I was just her...stepmother, I suppose. Had we begun when Chantelle was in sixth grade or junior high, I would not have stood a chance. I saw one of my closest friends as she suffered daily with her stepdaughters. I knew I was blessed by circumstances—that I'd married Byron so early on in Chantelle's life.

"I think that what we share is a mutual respect and a knowledge that comes from living under the same roof for enough years. I find this an agreeable situation since I know how unfriendly some stepdaughters and stepmothers can be. I figure that the groundwork has been established and that we both made the gestures to bring about the right result."

As has been pointed out earlier, since there are no precedents for how stepmothers are to behave with their stepdaughters and what is expected of them, I have discovered that stepmothers often position themselves in a variety of ways. Some stepmothers find their ability to communicate with their husbands is sometimes stymied during their stepdaughters' visits. They have the sense that they are invisible during those hours or days, which only heightens the discomfort of such situations. Some stepmothers feel that their stepdaughters compared them to their mothers and found the women wanting. The uneasiness some stepmothers feel can harm their marriages, because it can come between the couples. Stepmothers who adhere to the idea that their relationships with their stepdaughters will succeed simply because they are of the same sex, may be disappointed. The same gender theory that applies to daughters and their mothers, who share a socialization and physiology, does not apply to stepmothers. They and their stepdaughters are, many times, in opposite corners, despite their gender connection.

"My stepdaughter and I do not see eye to eye," sighs Carmen, forty, "so I've distanced myself, as a way of keeping things peaceful. She is twelve years old and whenever she comes to stay, she finds ways to criticize me and our new house. She says to Leo, my husband, that she can't believe how flowery the wallpaper is and how bright the couch is. She constantly compares our house to her mother's house and she says her room here isn't big enough. Leo has asked me to be more patient with her and with her older sister, but I'm fed up and tired of being told how great her mom is. I've told Leo that maybe he should take the girls out for dinner without me when they come over.

"I want to please Leo and I don't want him to suffer because of me, but I've had it with my stepdaughters' rude behavior and negative remarks. I have never interacted with their mother and sometimes I think I'd feel less isolated as a stepmother if I did know the mother. If the girls could see that we get along, then maybe they would know that I am not the enemy, and we could all be happier."

Although many fathers/husbands adore both their daughters and their wives, it is not always easy for them to juggle the needs of the two camps when there is an emotional distance or conflict between them. As the late divorce expert Emily Vischer commented in a speech she delivered at the *Stepfamily Association of America* conference in February of 2000, the stepmother does not see her stepchildren quite as her husband does. Under any circumstance with stepchildren, the step-mother needs to feel appreciated and when she feels rejected, her task becomes more difficult. On the other hand, if the stepmother is able to build a relationship with her stepdaughter, then this sets the stage for later positive experiences for the daughter with other women. "An adolescent daughter might be pushing away from her mother but does not need to push away from her stepmother," explains Dr. Michele Kasson. "The care the daughter gets from her mother might not be accepted during early adolescence, but the stepmother's gestures might be accepted, because the stepmother and stepdaughter are not entwined."

Past Affairs and Future Mothering

In many cases I found a bias against stepmothers who were both causes behind divorces and the object of affection of the fathers. This is understandable. These cases may trigger what Judith Wallerstein terms the 'sleeper effect' which is observed in some daughters of divorce. In such cases daughters will seem fine for years after their parents' divorces transpire, then one day the impact of the divorce will suddenly hit them, turning their lives upside-down.

Some stepmothers to whom I spoke were former lovers of the daughters' fathers and some were substantially younger than their husbands, perhaps closer in age to the daughters. Some single mothers found this threatening and competition ensued. This escalated discord. Those mothers who were accepting recognized that, even if their divorces were precipitated by affairs, the fact is these women are now the stepmothers. I continually found that the less animosity and hostility, the better the situation is for the daughters. "Once this woman becomes the stepmother, a mother who refrains from calling her the wicked witch of the west is doing her daughter a great favor," comments Dr. Ronnie Burak. "A mother who influences her daughter against her stepmother is undermining the chance for her daughter to feel any security and happiness in the stepfamily."

"I have noticed that stepmothers who had prevously had affairs with the men they later married really hate the ex-wives," Brittany, a thirty-seven-year-old stepmother and daughter of divorce, begins. "I wonder if it is guilt that motivates them? I know that my own stepmother had had an affair with my father and I doubt that my mother even cared. But my stepmother had all these issues. And the example set before me was confusing. A home wrecker has her own issues. My experience as a stepdaughter made me very aware of the consequences. One of my best friends broke up a marriage, but I knew that wasn't for me. Instead I chose to be with a man who had a daughter and was already divorced for some time, because I needed clean start.

"I am so careful with my stepdaughter because of my experience as a stepdaughter. I do not try to be only her friend and I do not try to be only a mother figure. My stepmother is half way between my age and my mother's. That made me very uncomfortable when I was a teenager. And it also made me defensive for my mother. I didn't want her to feel old and ugly because Lynette, my stepmother, was so much younger. I eventually opened myself to Lynette but even after she and I formed some kind of bond, the divorce haunted me."

Unlike Brittany, thirty-three-year-old Alexandra did not experience a slew of negative feelings as result of her father's affair and subsequent marriage. Of course, as she explains, it wasn't always easy either. "I know that my father and mother were not well suited for each other," Alexandra recalls. "And it was an unhappy family, although everyone did a good job of pretending. Then my parents got divorced when I was eight and my dad married Lucia. Four years later my brother and I found out they got divorced because our father had had an affair with Lucia. I had really liked my stepmother, but when I found this out, it made me uncomfortable and I had to revisit the divorce years later.

"Ultimately though, I got past the pain, mostly because my mom and Lucia were always very nice to each other. They truly got

along and they set a good example for me. It made me feel secure
regardless of what had caused the divorce and remarriage."

When one considers the fact that forty-three percent of all marriages are remarriages for at least one of the adults, as reported by the
1995 Monthly Vital Statistics Report, it stands to reason that mothers
and stepmothers have knowledge of each other's situation. The rate at
which this population of divorced women will remarry varies according to ethnic group, a fact borne out by the 1998 United States Census
Report. After five years, remarriage occurred for fifty-three percent of
white women, thirty percent of Latina women and twenty-five percent
of African-American women. Whether or not these remarried women
as mothers and stepmothers can develop a rapport with one another
depends largely upon the nature of the divorce and, more importantly, upon the outlook of both women. This means that some ex-
wives and new wives, especially when they have daughters/step-
daughters in common, are able to find middle ground at least and
solid rapport at best. The end product, that of a close relationship
between the daughter of divorce and her stepmother and a successful
liaison between the mother and stepmother, can preempt the history
of the divorce. Among my interviewees, when this transpires, it is a
positive event, which bodes well for the present and the future happiness of all three women of the new triangle.

Disparate Values

"I was only nineteen when I married and had a baby," recalls Cheryl,
who is thirty-eight. "I was clueless when it came to marriage and children. I think my marriage was doomed to fail but I stuck it out for
years because of my girls. I did not remarry but my ex-husband did
quickly. He married a woman named Libbie and while I hope he's
happy, I wish he had married someone with values more like mine. I
don't mean she should be a clone, but I wish she could have had similar opinions about money and things like homework. Because Libbie
cared so little about my girls being in a home with good values and
she just didn't want to deal with kids, I felt my girls suffered. Also,
the girls sort of split over Libbie and Henry's way of doing things. Erin
sides with her dad while my younger daughter, Mindy, sides with me.

"Erin and Mindy do not approach their new world in the same
way. Erin embraces my ex-husband's wealth, material possessions and

fancy friends. Mindy ignores that scene, preferring to stay by my side leading a much quieter life. Whatever closeness the girls had before the divorce is gone now."

My research indicated that disparate values between two households can be quite disturbing for many daughters of divorce. Although these daughters are caught in the middle, my pool of interviewees indicates that their divorced mothers suffer for these differences more than the stepmothers or the daughters. As documented, many struggling single mothers who remarry are able to re-establish themselves financially. As Mary Ann Mason observes in *"The Modern American Stepfamily: Problems and Possibilities,"* a woman's income is increased by three times once she remarries. Thus a single mother who remarries is, in theory, able to buy her daughter more than when she was a single mother. However, one cannot automatically assume that the mother's values, simply because she has the means, are in synch with her ex-husband's. As evidenced in the interviews, money becomes a weapon in many divorces. Some mothers who have remarried feel strongly that their daughters should not be showered with possessions while their ex-husbands feel differently. Often this is because many noncustodial fathers feel guilt over seeing their daughters infrequently and take their duties as providers to the extreme with expensive gifts.

As daughters shuttle back and forth, the distinctions in their mothers' and fathers' values is seen by the girls and often reported to both parents. This increases tension between the two households which takes its toll on the daughters' emotional states. Often when the two homes are so dissimilar, suspicion emanates from one about the other and the daughters sense this. As the late divorce expert Emily Vischer described it in her speech entitled "Love Under Siege," if there is no trust between the two families, "the two households see each other as enemies." As the next story illustrates, it is often up to the mother to work through these differences for the sake of the daughters.

"Problems concerning my three daughters have hovered over me since the divorce began," Helen, forty-eight, begins. "The girls are adopted from China and my ex-husband's live-in partner is also from Asia. The girls are very concerned that when they are out with Tassy, their stepmother, people will assume she is their mother. Their loyalty is to me, without question, and this extra twist, that their stepmother is also Asian, adds to their discomfort in a strange way. I see that going back and forth between their father and stepmother's place and mine is difficult for them.

"I have made it clear to the girls that I do not want to get in the way of their having a comfort level with Tassy, and I want them to feel welcome in both homes. I think that Tassy has made an effort for the girls and I encourage them to have a connection to her. Mostly I do this because if Lee, my ex-husband, had to choose, I fear he would put the girls second to this relationship and I do not want that to happen. If I cannot find a way to make our values, his and mine, more alike, at least I can try to work with Tassy. I need to believe that my three daughters are well cared for in both homes, no matter how differently these homes are run. That is my goal."

For all three females involved, the mother, daughter and stepmother, the invisible presence of the earlier family has a lasting effect on the new family units. It doesn't matter where a daughter lives—her mother's and stepfather's home or her father's and stepmother's—because the influence of the other family is constantly felt. Mothers and stepmothers are not immune to this same feeling. For example, a stepmother may hesitate to make decisions concerning her stepdaughter, because thoughts of the mother—and her approval or disapproval—are looming in the back of her mind. Similarly, a mother may worry when her stepdaughter is visiting her father that the stepmother will make the wrong decision for the stepdaughter or make decisions without consulting the mother. Throughout all of this, the real question becomes, who is the ultimate family to these daughters, the one to take responsibility and make decisions? A study conducted by F.F. Furstenberg, found that thirty-one percent of children would not consider a stepmother or stepfather as a part of their families, even if they lived together. Forty-one percent did not include stepsisters or stepbrothers as part of the family. Fifteen percent of stepparents who had been stepparenting for years also did not include their live-in stepchildren as part of their families. Apparently, the perplexity in defining roles exists for the adult members of these triangles as well as for the children.

"I never know if I should count my stepsiblings on my father's side when I explain my family to new friends," comments Dale, thirty-five. "Here I am, married with a child and I'm still uncertain who my family is. My parents divorced when I was in first grade and my father remarried a woman with three older children. I did not see these stepsiblings much because of their custody schedule. It seemed that whenever I was visiting my father, they were visiting their father. And when I was living with my mother, during the week, they were living with their mother and my father. I tried not to think about this too much, because then I felt left out. Meanwhile, my mother and stepfather had two boys together and my stepfather had one older daughter from his first marriage. When I described my family to outsiders, I didn't feel the need to include my father's stepchildren but I thought I should include my stepsister and my half brothers. I guess that's because I was at my mother's house most of the time and because my stepsister and I became closer after my half brothers were born—we both adored the boys.

"Still, I felt torn between the two families. They were so different. For example, in both families there were forms of discipline but not the same kind of discipline. My mother and stepfather were more strict while my father and stepmother were a bit laid back. In some ways it was confusing as a child yet in other ways, strangely, it was comforting to know I had two places to live and that each was safe."

Once parents are divorced and remarry, the hope for each parent is that he or she finds a partner who is simpatico with his or her view of the world. Daughters of divorce like Dale will feel more secure if their two homes have less contention than their former nuclear families had. Some teenage daughters with whom I spoke feel more secure when their fathers and stepmothers put forth a united front. While the fathers' closeness to their new wives may also be threatening to these daughters, peaceful home lives can be reassuring and offer stability. The more secure stepmothers are in their marriages, the more they are willing to reach out to their stepdaughters. Of my interviewees, one of the most common complaints of new wives were that their husbands had not closed the door on their first marriages, mostly because of the shared parenting of their daughters. This residual attachment to first wives causes many stepmothers to feel uncertain in their places as stepmothers and isolated by the relationship of father, ex-wife and daughter. The mother and the father must work together as parents yet create separate homes with respectful and appropriate distance between the two households. Only then will daughters have the security they need and stepmothers have the certainty they need while a better working relationship between the parents is created.

Whatever respect stepmothers receive from their stepdaughters, fathers should be instrumental in demanding more. As my studies show, daughters (adolescents in particular) may not recognize their stepmothers as mother figures and another kind of relationship develops over time. The stepmother and stepdaughter do not have to adore one another and indeed such situations might take years of mutual history to resolve, but respect and a sense of belonging need to exist. Some fathers abdicate their roles and place their new wives in the role of primary parent, especially to daughters under the age of twelve. Often these men left their wives alone to parent the children during their first marriages, and knowing this may make many stepmothers uneasy. While dealing with the burden of parenthood, stepmothers in this position may also have to face angry mothers. When they learn of the fathers' dissolution of his responsibilities, some mothers become furious and might feel their parental powers have been usurped; thus they come to resent custodial time allotted to the father and stepmother. "Obviously the mother is suspicious of the stepmother in the beginning," remarks Dr. Ronnie Burak. "If she learns that the stepmother is doing the parenting for the father, she feels deceived and worries her daughters are being cheated. Therefore, the father must be an active parent, whether he is remarried or not."

Repeatedly stepmothers reminded me that they didn't choose to be stepmothers. I found few stepmothers who actively sought the position. The now obsolete school of thought, prevalent during the 1950s, was that stepparenting would 'fix' a broken family. In a divorce or widowed situation, remarriage was considered the panacea, as if finding another partner would automatically provide a daughter with a stable home. However, the Stepfamily Foundation reports that fifty percent of children will experience second divorces before they are eighteen years old. As divorce continues to impact the population, it has become clear that the "Band Aid" philosophy of the mid-twentieth century holds little weight. In-depth studies on divorce have revealed its impact on all family members, and, as is evidenced by this book, the seriousness of the consequences on the roles of the new members of the triangle.

These consequences are apparent in Bari's story. "I would not have married Rodney had I known that his daughters and ex-wife would be so impossible," sighs Bari, thirty-four. "This has been going on for three years and it has gotten worse. Leigh and Alexis are now thirteen and seventeen and it's impossible to have them in our house. I really love my husband but I don't think he's on my side when it comes to his daughters. Part of it is that they are very spoiled; they always get their way and there is no discipline. Rodney says he left because he couldn't handle Janice, his ex-wife's take on how to raise the girls and her demands. But another reason they behave so badly, I think, is that they are still angry about the divorce. They were mad at their father and once we married, they were mad at me.

"The problem is Rodney won't talk to me about Leigh and Alexis and their behavior. It's like he can't face the fact that his divorce has anything to do with it. If he ignores the problem, he doesn't have to shoulder any of the blame. And his ex-wife is worse; she lets the kids run wild and won't listen to anything I have to say about taking control. So I'm left alone to discipline these girls when they visit us. I have rules and I'd like Rodney to stand by me on this. I need him to snap out of it and be on my side because it's getting worse."

When two homes are opposite in their approaches to raising the daughters, the unification of stepfamily couples is imperative. This requires open communication and an ongoing dialogue about the daughters and the condition of the stepfamilies between spouses and ex-spouses. This way of coparenting is important even before behavioral problems occur. It should be considered a pre-emptive measure and a healthy approach to raising well-adjusted daughters. Together each couple should establish the rules and boundaries of their stepfamilies.

Most daughters of divorce do not initially appreciate these limitations and many constantly compare one household to the other. I found, however, if each stepfamily has rules of some kind, even if they are relaxed, as long as they are implemented by the parent and agreed to by the stepparent, this helps the daughter to feel grounded. Also, an awareness that both mother and stepmother are in touch about the rules for the daughter, as well as her schedule or plans, has great value in providing stability. "Children do get away with a lot during the divorce and once the parents settle down and remarry, limits need to be set," notes Antoinette Michaels, relationship expert. "In a remarriage, the daughters recognize the commitment that their parents have made and eventually adjust and adapt to their new homes and new rules."

The story of Julianne, who is in her late twenties, illustrates this. "Until I was fourteen, I saw my father every other weekend. My parents divorced when I was three so I was accustomed to this routine. I think I was so young that the divorce and remarriages of both my parents were normal to me. I noticed early on how different my mother and stepfather were from my father and stepmother. My mother pressured me to believe that my stepfather was like a father to me. He is a father figure but she had so many expectations. I was almost forced to see him as my father.

"My father never did that with Tessa, his wife and he seemed much more involved with me without making us into a big happy family. Tessa never told me what to do while Hal, my stepfather, was a more authoritative person. Tessa and I get along on a surface level because that is all that has been offered to me and it works. When I was a little girl she did not extend herself either, but she was always decent to me. My stepfather was much more of a factor in my life. My mother's home and my father's home are like two different worlds."

Like Julianne, Jennifer, another daughter of divorce, has adjusted to the differences in her parent's homes and new marriages. "My parents divorced seven years ago and my mother remarried three years ago," Jennifer, twenty-one, tells us. "My stepfather and I get along well enough, but it us my stepmother that I'm really drawn to. My father remarried two years ago. I love Ruby, my stepmother. She is quite unlike my mother, and gives me another way of looking at things. Ruby is a younger woman than my mother and she knows about clothes and guys. She has been a great example of how a woman should pursue her career. Ruby is an attorney and works very hard. I think she and my dad have a good marriage."

Most daughters of divorce I found are aware of the patterns that exist between their parents and in their stepfamilies, even if they feel powerless to do anything to change them. In many instances, the parents' way of dealing with each other outlives the marriage. One way of settling old scores is to triumphantly move on, as seen in the many tales of remarriage and stepfamilies shared by my interviewees. During this time, new loyalties form and old patterns are challenged, creating some

uneasy situations. However, in time, the mother, daughter and stepmother eventually find their places in the new families and figure out
the shared responsibilities and adjustments to stepfamily life.

Stepfamilies: Mothers and Stepmothers

"I have witnessed my mother and my stepmother struggle as second
wives in stepfamilies," Patricia, twenty-six, begins. "I am even a part
of both of their struggles. There were days when I tortured both of
them. When it all began I was thirteen and my feeling was that, since
I had suffered, they had to suffer also. My mother did not worry about
my sister Elana and I liking Colleen, our stepmother. She was too worried about getting us to like Trip, her new husband. I think she figured our father could worry about us liking Colleen it wasn't her job.

"Neither my mom nor Colleen ever said anything negative
about each other. Elana and I laughed a lot about how Colleen cooked
or baked a cake. We were being cruel and unfair. Our father didn't like
it, but he was too busy trying to win us back and fighting custody battles. None of my parents' fighting over us seemed to affect our stepmother. Colleen never said a bad word and when it all was finally
worked out, my sister and I felt relief. I took me years to believe in
this new life and my parents' new marriages and new homes. In a
way, the two houses were about the same thing—both of my parents
trying again to be married and to succeed at it and still care for their
daughters. Today I appreciate my two stepfamilies."

The divided loyalties of the stepfamily members undermine the
family's success and causes the foundation to be more precarious than
it already is. The very allotment of time, the designated day of the week
for the daughters to visit one parent or the other, is a constant reminder
that the daughter is a product of divorce and a fractured family. At the
same time, the responsibilities required of the adult members of the
stepfamily can be arduous and unrelenting. A stepmother who tried to
keep her distance still senses the devices of the players and the constant
flux of rescheduling and coordinating with the other parent. Research
conducted by Furstenberg and Associates indicates that the influence of
mothers is more palpable in the stepmother's home than is the influence
of fathers in the stepfather's home. According to the study, mothers call
stepmothers' homes to speak with their children and to discuss scheduling. Problems and conflicts are abundant. It is little wonder that some

stepmothers are delighted when their stepdaughters begin college and are out on their own. The day-to-day planning abates, granting the stepmother a reprieve. Yet the stepfamily unit remains and joint ventures continue over time, including holidays and milestones such as graduations, weddings and births.

My research indicates that it often takes years before the mother and stepmother achieve their separate peace, either as a team, linked together by their common concern—the welfare of the daughters—or as individuals who respect each other. The disparate values that seemed an overwhelming delineation between the daughter's two families lessen over time as the daughter adjusts to dissimilar but equal styles of her mother's and her father's homes. Mothers and stepmothers who have achieved mutual trust and have worked together for their daughters' sakes have performed the best jobs possible. As Brenda Szulman, psychotherapist, views it, a healthy development occurs at this point. "In time, the narcissism of the mother eases and the rivalry between the mother and stepmother is less," says Szulman. "Then the daughters enter into the next stage, where she is more open to her stepmother and, in turn, the stepmother feels she can reach out to her stepdaughter."

Agatha, who had no children of her own, was divorced for four years before remarrying and becoming a stepmother. "My husband's ex-wife, Tina, was too much in the picture for me," begins Agatha, forty-six. "She was larger than life and I simply couldn't get inside the family in any direction. Theresa, my stepdaughter was the biggest problem. She was ten when I first met her. My stepsons were never an issue, but Theresa really intimidated me. She was thirteen when I officially became her stepmom instead of her father's live-in girlfriend. When she was little, she seemed to be curious about me but her mother discouraged our relationship. That set the tone for what followed.

"Ironically, Tina now has mellowed in her attitude, because she has her own stepdaughter to deal with and she sees it isn't so easy. Her stepdaughter's mother is not so keen on her and now she knows how it feels. I believe that she is sorry for the damage she caused. Today we are forging a new relationship. Tina and I actually have many of the same problems in our careers and with our husbands and stepchildren, so we talk and make arrangements when necessary. As a result, Tina has come to realize that there is value in having me in her life."

When daughters are part of successfully blended families they can move into adulthood taking their own positive experiences to marriages, and can be open to becoming stepmothers themselves. When stepdaughters have negative experiences, they often have some trepidation in marrying or becoming stepmothers. The fantasy of having fairy-tale marriages can still exist for some daughters of divorce, even when they recognize issues inherent in real life situations. Having solid role models who set examples for them helps. "I know I will succeed as a young stepmother, and it doesn't scare me," Brianna, thirty, tells us. "My stepmother set the example for me."

Changing Realities

It is unfortunate when stepfamilies are created and recreated by loss, but this is sometimes the case as it is with other relationships in our lives. In the wake of the attack on America on September 11, 2001, people of all ages have come to question their lives, to reassess their choices and perhaps change patterns. For a mother and stepmother, this might translate into being more accepting of one another. For a daughter of divorce, the double support she has in two stepfamilies suddenly may become more precious and reassuring. Connections once questioned now may become more valuable than ever before and those that are deficient but meaningful are repaired or enriched. Such changes will most certainly improve the connections formed by mothers, daughters and stepmothers in the new triangle.

"I have noticed that my hostile stepdaughter has definitely become more receptive in the past few months," begins Pauline, forty-nine, a stepmother of five years. "My other two stepdaughters were never difficult but my oldest stepdaughter, who can be difficult and never quite included me, now seems to be warmer and easier to be with. I also see that having two families, ours and their mother's, seems to be reassuring for her. My husband, Arnie, and I have sat down with his four children, who range in age from fourteen to twenty-one, and my two girls, who are nineteen and twenty-four, and talked about how each of us feels about the changes in America and the terrible loss from the World Trade Center.

"I told them that this is no time to be feuding or having petty thoughts. Innocent people died and we have to band together, as a country, as a community and as a stepfamily. Whatever differences we had in the past, it is time to let them go. I think the children heard me, and I know that their mother has the same sentiments. It is time to begin anew."

In this difficult time, perhaps not only will former relationships be less contentious and easier to cultivate, but the extended stepfamily may come to be seen as a safer haven. For those recently widowed women, a future in which there may be a new group of stepfamilies is manifest. However, these new families will not be a result of divorce, but born of tragedy. Leanne, forty, is a daughter of divorce who was raised by her mother and stepfather. The World Trade Center tragedy affected those close to her. "My two best friends lost their husbands who were firefighters and both of them have small children. I have watched these women as they try to create new lives for themselves and their children. It is only a matter of time before they may remarry. And this is natural—no one wants to be alone forever. And I know how much stability my mother got from my stepfather."

For those women and men who were widowed as a result of this tragedy, future stepfamilies will be born of sadness and loss. The depth of this loss is extreme and yet these future stepfamilies hold promise and hope of rebuilding lives now torn apart. And like other stepfamilies, the new triangles which will be formed will need to be nurtured—this time with special sensitivity so that the many grieving children grow up with love surrounding them.

CHAPTER 9

Regrouping in Stepfamilies: Stepdaughters, Stepsisters and Half Sisters

"My stepsister, Toni and I are the same age," Lydia, twenty-two, begins, "but we are not too close. When my father married her mother, he moved away and took his new wife and Toni with him, leaving me and my sisters behind. My sisters and I held it against Toni that her mother had broken up our family and that sort of killed any chance of our having a relationship.

"My sisters and I lived with our mother and we visited our father, but not too often because it's a long plane ride. Maybe if he hadn't moved so far, it would have been different and we would be more of a stepfamily. Instead we would visit in the summers and for some holidays. It's funny that I forgive my father after all this time. I can't hold a grudge forever so I decided to make it work. I have a relationship with my stepmother, although I don't consider her a mother. But I can talk to her and she tries to be supportive. So the only person who I can't be close with is my stepsister. I really think it is because she got my father when I was only ten and I missed him so terribly. She had the benefit of growing up with him around and I didn't."

The Michigan Family Forum reports that over fifty percent of families in America today are stepfamilies. Over fifty percent of daughters live in stepfamilies and many believe they make the concessions necessary to be parts of these units. Among those members of the triangle with whom I spoke, I learned that if the stepmother has daughters of her own, the competition with her husband's daughters can be quite fierce. Stepmothers have double responsibility, for their stepdaughters and their own daughters, who, if adolescent, are often as negative toward their mothers and vociferous as their stepsisters. Most of the stepmothers voiced the intention to accept this responsibility by including in the family units their stepdaughters and to soothe their own daughters, which proved easier said than done. Along with the physical complications engendered by stepsiblings, such as sharing bedrooms and competing for space in new stepfamilies, there is a large emotional component to stepsibling relationships.

The formation of stepfamilies is not easy for any of the members. As Dr. Ronnie Burak views it, "The stepmother is overwhelmed by her responsibilities," says Dr. Burak. "She has a new marriage, which is the reason that this family came together, and she is spending so much time on her stepdaughters and daughters that the marriage gets put on the back burner." From the stepdaughters'/daughters' perspective, I found there is a sense of uncertainty in having not only a stepmother but stepsisters. For the daughter whose father is remarried to a woman who has her own daughter close to her age, the new marriage may be doubly disconcerting. These daughters deal not only with stepmothers but stepsisters who live in their fathers' homes. In many cases, the stepsisters have better lifestyles than the daughters, because they benefit from their stepfathers success.

Competition

Competition between stepmothers and their stepdaughters for the attention of the fathers also may exist between mothers and daughters. Author Nancy Friday points out in her book, *My Mother/My Self*, that daughters remind mothers of their age and fading youth, which stirs competition in some women. These mothers compete with their daughters for the attention of men. In an intact family, according to Friday, this manifests in a jealousy over the father and it can unnerve the mother. In some stepfamilies, stepdaughters compete with their stepmothers thus causing further problems. Some stepmothers may actively compete by wearing flamboyant clothes and acting in provocative ways. Other stepmothers feel unattractive and ancient when compared to their young, beautiful stepdaughters—the stepmothers' self-esteem and sense of place sometimes is eroded in their new marriages.

Cheri, one stepmother with whom I spoke, voiced this lament. "I know that my stepdaughters, who are grown, see me as direct competition for their father," said Cheri, who is in her mid-forties and has been a stepmother for five years. "These women now are in their early thirties, and both of them still solicit their father every chance they get. They look to him to take them out to fancy restaurants for dinner, to pay for clothes and toys for their children and to pay for their vacations. My husband doesn't understand that I find this frustrating. Every time he buys me something or takes me somewhere, they want it too. If they were teenagers or young girls, I would be more open to their neediness, to the way they are always clamoring for 'daddy.'

"I am a younger than Robert's first wife but, compared to my stepdaughters, I feel old and worn. They are very attractive young women and they compete with me for their father's attention. The bottom line is that I don't spend time with them. In marrying this man I have ended up in a constant battle with my stepdaughters to spend time with my husband. I believe that his daughters are more important to him, if he had to choose. We are definitely not the stepfamily I imagined we would be."

The myth that stepfamilies are like conventional families is one that dies hard. It is only by living one's life "in step" that one actually realizes how deep-seated some of the problems are. When competition between the stepmother and her stepdaughters arises, it intensifies the tension, as shown in Cheri's story. My interview with Cheri closed with her voicing disappointment that the stepfamily in which she is now a part is quite different from what she expected and hoped for. Her realizations were voiced by others to whom I spoke. Though many stepmothers who married when their husband's daughters were adults expected things to go smoothly, that was not always true despite the fact there is no visitation or scrambling for weekend plans. Still, the competition persists with many older stepdaughters. The constant struggle for the husbands' attention in stepfamilies affects stepmothers/new wives of all ages and stages, whether there are adult, adolescent or young stepdaughters.

Not only is there a competition and a vying for attention, but a stepmother often is rejected by her stepchildren, according to Genevieve Clapp's book, *Divorce and New Beginnings*, because she is an outsider and the stepchildren resent her presence. Daughters are more stressed than are sons by the arrival of a new stepparent. As Clapp observes, "Girls are also more likely to feel threatened and displaced by stepmothers, since daughters are often elevated to the prestigious status of 'woman of the house' in their single dad's homes."

One stepmother—but certainly not the only one—who felt the sting of this rejection was Brett. "I know that my stepdaughter does not want me in her life," discloses Brett, forty-nine, a stepmother of a twenty-three-year-old stepdaughter. "I want to be accepted, but the problem is that Eliza is so close to her mother and very defensive about her. Hamilton, my husband, and I have a daughter, Robin, who is fourteen, and she is the apple of my eye, naturally. When we planned a confirmation for Robin, Eliza wanted a very expensive dress to wear and I thought my husband should have said no, since my stepdaughter didn't even care about the event, she just wanted to compete with us. Instead he agreed because he said that I was getting something special and Robin was getting the same.

"Eliza lived with her mother until two years ago, but came to our house frequently. She always checked out what we had that was new and watched Robin very closely to see what she had. The way that Eliza watches my daughter and me erodes the relationship between us. And there is little possibility of being close when she is always measuring and positioning herself to get more."

The problems of stepmothering versus mothering is evidenced in an article by Karen Compton which appeared in the December 2000 issue of *Self* magazine. In "I Never Thought I'd Be a Stepmom," Compton describes some of the problems that cropped up when she became a stepmother of two boys. Though she didn't have stepdaughters, the issues raised through her experiences with stepsons are ones which cross gender lines. "At first I just stared at them, my nose pressed to the glass of Stuart's former life," Compton writes. "It was like looking into a crystal ball—not at his future but at his past." The past can be threatening to stepmothers and the stepchildren are a constant reminder of that past.

Some daughters of divorce with whom I spoke feel that, although their father has remarried, his first allegiance should be to them. In this situation, the stepmother must be either very accepting or the new marriage will have serious problems because of the demands of the stepdaughters. The Stepfamily Foundation reports that forty-six percent of second marriages fail with the primary reason being the stepchildren. For the stepdaughter who feels she is the winner in 'the competition,' seeing problems occur between her father and stepmother may prove to be a heady experience.

"My parents' divorce and my father's remarriage happened back to back and my sisters and I never had a chance to catch our breath," says Natasha, twenty-three, whose father has been remarried for five years. "Luckily, my dad does the same thing he did in his first marriage, which is to totally obsess over my sisters and me. My mother felt neglected or got tired of it or something. I know my dad chose Gayle as his second wife because she's different from my mother. She's sort of low-key about my father's devotion to us and she doesn't complain. If anything, my father is more attentive to me than before the divorce. I definitely feel like I am the winner. That's not to say I don't like my stepmother, because I do. We all do. It's just that we spend more time with my dad than she does. That's how my father likes it. I think he see his children as some kind of reflection of him. He takes us seriously, more seriously than my mother ever does. And Gayle follows his lead or else there would be competition."

Though Natasha sees her relationship with her stepmother as a competition she has won, many daughters, particularly adolescent daughters, search for ways to understand relationships and thus find their places, according to author Dianne Hales in her book *Just Like a Woman*. "Statistically, parents of teen girls are much more likely to divorce than those of teen boys," explains Hales. The daughters "may feel resentful or rejected if their parents' marriages fail." I found in my interviews that the emotional loss caused by divorce often becomes co-mingled with the physical loss and financial loss—changing every aspect of life as the daughter has known it. Then her father remarries and she suffers another loss, the loss of her hope for a second chance for her parents. The stepmother's presence is quite traumatic for some daughters. It is obvious that a stepmother cannot replace the mother and most stepmothers do not attempt to do so. Meanwhile, some daughters feel they are being replaced by their stepmothers and their stepsisters who have taken over the daughters' territory in their fathers' homes. Regardless of how the stepmother extends herself to her stepdaughter, the stepdaughter is not her daughter and all parties are painfully aware of this. This profound forfeiture colors all aspects of some daughters' lives. Almost every daughter of divorce is firmly entrenched for years in longing for the intact family that has been dismantled by the divorce.

Judith, who has been a stepmother for thirty-four years, became close to one of her stepdaughters immediately immediately after she married the girls' father. "My stepdaughters were nine and twelve when I married their father," Judith recalls. "Lila, my younger stepdaughter, accepted our marriage right from the start. But her sister, Angela, did not. She was very resentful that her parents had divorced and that her life had changed drastically. I tried to win her over but Angela had difficulty accepting her new stepfamily and after a while I just let it go.

"On the other hand, Lila was so happy to be a part of our family. There was an immediate connection. I had a three-year-old daughter from my first marriage and Lila adored her. This endeared her to me even more. As the years went by and Lila had her share of difficulties, I always defended her. I did this because I remember how readily she accepted and joined our stepfamily. Angela never cared to be a part of our group and the minute she graduated from high school, Angela moved across the country."

Parents expect daughters to adjust to new families and new homes. In truth most daughters are both parts of the new families and yet outsiders, all at the same time. For many to whom I spoke, upon their father's (or mother's) remarriages, the impact of divorce hits them again, this time with more finality. While an eight-year-old daughter perceives her parents' divorce differently than a sixteen-year-old daughter, for both the impact of it will be with them throughout their lives. Though the women of the new triangle are each affected in their own ways by divorce, loss of self-esteem seems a pervasive result for all three females. Authors Gerald L. Kleiman and Myrna M. Weissman point out in their essay *Depressions Among Women* that "direct loss and separation" can lead to depression.

Women cite basic unhappiness as their main reason for wanting to divorce, according to the *Journal of Marriage & Family*, with incompatibility and emotional abuse as the second and third most common reasons. Surprisingly enough, according to Crawford and Unger in their book *Women and Gender*, despite some feelings of "anger, helplessness and ambivalence," women are less troubled than men by the outcome of divorce. This may be why men remarry more quickly—they need to fill the void and have companionship. While this may suit the father's needs, their daughters unwittingly become stepdaughters in the process. Of course mothers' altered lives also have effects upon the daughters. Whether or not the mothers choose remarriages, their daughters' self-esteem and security are put in jeopardy. Remarriage represents hope for the adults, yet is complicated by the shadows of the past. For daughters, remarriages represent the death of a particular hope—the hope that their parents will reunite. And, in some cases, remarriages, like Kate's, result in the death of daughters' ties to one of her parents.

"My parents divorced when I was a baby and my mother remarried quickly," says Kate, who is forty-four. "My father remarried and his wife did not want to see us at all. The fact that he listened to her was so painful for us. I never knew if my mother fought for us or if his wife talked him into giving us up. It was easier in those days to have the same name as your stepfather and to seem a part of a family, so my stepfather adopted us. All these years later, I still wonder how my father could let us go and what kind of woman would force her husband to make such a choice."

Today, divorce is not the anomaly it was in the 1950's and 1960's when the picture-perfect lives of the characters on the *Donna Reed Show* and *Ozzie and Harriet* were held up to television viewers as ideals we all should embrace. In the United States today, seventy-five percent of divorced mothers and eighty percent of divorced fathers remarry, as reported by the *American Psychologist*. The daughters of these remarriages witness rearranged families in the lives of both their mothers and their fathers. While children and parents adjust to single parenting within two to three years, according to Hetherington and Chingempeel, it is when the custodial parent remarries within a three to five year period that most children have a longer period of adjustment.

"It was too much for me," explains Gloria, twenty-two, whose parents divorced when she was fifteen and remarried within three years. "I couldn't find my place. I went away to school but when I came home, I didn't know what 'home' meant. It took me a long time to figure it out. There was no home as I knew it, there was just my mother's place or my father's. I ended up staying at my mother's more, because her husband was not around much. My father's wife, my stepmother, has really tried. Our poor relationship isn't her fault, but it isn't mine either. I keep hoping that time will pass and I'll get older and meet someone and make my own way. Then I'll feel less sad."

Stepmother as Intruder

According to *Psychology Today*, when the father shows affection toward his new wife or there are sexual overtures, it is more uncomfortable for daughters than for sons. Among my interviewees I found that their stepmothers are seen as unwelcome rivals by many stepdaughters and can strain post-divorce relationships between daughters and their fathers. Many stepmothers appear unconscious of these tenuous situations when they first marry, and few are prepared ahead of time for the repercussions of their husbands' divorces and remarriages on their stepdaughters. The daughters often direct their anger and frustration at their stepmothers. It would be advantageous for the stepmother to take stock of the family she is about to enter. For instance, if her husband is too invested in his daughters, the future new wife/stepmother will suffer for this interaction. Her husband might not have room in his life for the new marriage and his daughters will not want the stepmother to have any impact upon them or their relations with their father.

What becomes so arduous for many daughters to whom I spoke is the idea that their fathers have chosen women, virtual strangers, as companions for the second half of their lives. These daughters not only see themselves as being replaced by their stepmothers, but they also see that these stepmothers are replacing their mothers. "The daughter wants to be that special person in her father's life," relationship expert Antoinette Michaels comments. "She finds it difficult enough to share her father with her mother, but now she must share her father with a stepmother. She is competitive with the stepmother and competitive with her mother as well." Many stepdaughters harbor these sentiments, making unpleasant situations for their fathers and their new wives and placing added pressure on their marriages. It is little wonder that the divorce rate for second marriages with children is at sixty-six percent in the United States today, according to the United States Census Bureau.

"My stepmother, Karen, was my father's girlfriend for three years before he married her," Pamela, twenty-nine, begins. "And I suppose that helped us, because we had time to get used to her. She was so nice in the beginning, although she definitely changed once she became his wife. Early on she took my two younger sisters and me everywhere and bought us things. Karen listened to us when we were worried about school or boys, so she seemed really interested in our lives. This was ten years ago and our mother was already living with someone. We saw Karen as someone who could make us a family again.

"But once Karen and my father married, their relationship became very different and she wasn't as warm any more. Suddenly she made demands on him. He seemed torn, because he was trying to please us and please her. In the early stages, he pleased us first but later, he felt he had to put her first. If we had not been older, it would have been worse. I got married young to get away from the family and I moved to another part of the country. My little sister suffered the most, because I left her behind with two sets of parents who were incredibly preoccupied with their own lives."

When the father's girlfriend becomes the stepmother, she often changes in the way she treats her stepdaughters. According to my respondents, this change is a common occurrence, yet it still comes as a surprise to most daughters. Early on some daughters and stepmothers form a bond of sorts, even if it is a superficial one based on shopping or going to the movies. Therefore, this same stepmother's lack of patience and good will after the wedding is unanticipated. From the point of view of the stepmothers to whom I spoke about this problem, most felt when they became brides they deserved to be treated better than they had been when they were just girlfriends. Many felt that, once married, they and their husbands' lives were a priority. It is a delicate balancing act, and often a no-win situation. As Perdita Kirkness Norwood writes in *The Enlightened Stepmother*, this new bride/stepmother wants her husband to give her "emotional security and romantic attention." So while her stepdaughters consider her an interloper, she considers them an obstacle to her needs. Often times the daughter and stepmother are in opposing positions yet the desire the same thing: to be first in the eyes of the father/husband.

A wise stepmother attempts to win her stepdaughters over early. The stepmother takes her cues from her husband and, if he is close with his daughters, then she will both try to be close and give her husband and his daughters room to maintain their closeness. "How the stepmother reacts to her stepdaughter depends on the configuration of the father's relationship with his daughter," explains Nechama Tec, sociologist. "A stepmother will worry that she will lose her husband if she is not nice to his daughters. If the father is on good terms with his daughters, the stepmother wants to cement the relationship." But this is not always easy.

One of the stepmothers to whom I spoke expressed the difficulties of this situation. "Initially I took cues from my husband Rick, when we were first married," Adele, thirty-nine, told me, "and he wanted my relationship with his daughters to be warm and fuzzy. It never happened and after four years of marriage, I don't feel I need to try anymore. I am more open to saying what I want and to persuading my husband about certain things. We moved to California for business last year and Rick's custody arrangement changed as a result. I think he misses not only his daughters, but the Midwest. At first I felt slightly guilty about that, since I had convinced him this was a good move. And then I realized that I was entitled to the life I wanted with him. I became tired of having to put his daughters first. I showed him how we could have a life that was about us and that his girls would survive."

I found among some of my respondents evidence of the cold war that can ensue as a result of some stepmothers' assertions and claims for attention from their husbands. Many stepmothers do not choose this path, but for those who do, the good will and respect for their husbands' relationships with their daughters ends. Many daughters caught in this situation sense their stepmothers' feelings and how complicated this makes family life for their fathers. The daughters' relentless fantasies that the original family may reunite often comes to the forefront once again. Any steps forward are negated by this further rejection of the stepfamily and, especially, the stepmother.

Being an effective stepmother is not for everyone, as evidenced by my pool of interviewees. There were an abundance of stepmothers who did not anticipate how complicated their roles could be and secretly wanted only their husbands, free of their daughters. Other stepmothers tacitly accept that their husbands come with daughters and ex-wives in tow, but do not reach out to the daughters. This is unfortunate and can be detrimental to the daughters. "The exclusionary behavior of the father and stepmother can become a problem when there are children present because they are neglected," remarks sociologist, Alice Michaeli. "Stepparents should understand that children need stability and to be included." Nonetheless, it is a daunting task for the stepmother, especially if she sees her stepdaughters are very jealous of her marriage to their father. As I note in my book, *Second Wives*, some stepmothers feel forced into fighting fiercely for their share of time with their husbands. Boundaries need to be established by husbands/fathers early on to protect the remarriages. The support of the husband/father is imperative for the new wife/stepmother, otherwise the ex-wife and her children can severely damage the new marriages.

On the other hand, some stepmothers have genuine feelings of affection for their husbands' daughters. Nevertheless, there often is a component of pleasing their husbands in the mix. Among the stepmothers to whom I spoke, there were several who continue their efforts at building relationships with their stepdaughters, despite the girls' resistance. These women deserve much credit. "We have to remember that divorce and remarriage are very disruptive for children under any conditions," remarks Nechama Tec, sociologist. "The stepmother can be very giving, especially before she marries the father. If this does not diminish once the stepmother is more certain of her husband, then her feelings for her stepdaughter are genuine."

Suzanne, one woman I interviewed, has tried hard to be a giving stepmother. "My stepdaughters were always welcome in my home," says Suzanne, sixty-three, a stepmother to two stepdaughters. "Gabriella was only ten and Olivia was twelve when I married their father. I have extended myself to them for many years. I also befriended their mother, because I thought it was important. When I first married Roy, their father, I didn't like that he was on the phone so much with Allison, his ex-wife. After a while I saw that there were so many issues with the girls. I decided it would be better if we could all get along. I also saw that he needed help with his daughters and I knew that I was capable. I helped them get into a religious day school and afterward into college. I value education and I thought it was the one thing I could give the girls.

"I don't know how Allison really felt but I'm sure she had mixed feelings about my involvement with her girls. But the results speak for themselves. As far as being a family, Roy, Allison, the girls and myself, it wasn't what I expected in life but it became my reality so I embraced it. I have friends who have walked away from their stepchildren. I knew I would never do that. I am very proud of my efforts and I think we have enriched each other's lives."

Some stepmothers are seen as interlopers and their true intentions are questioned by mothers and their daughters. But if a stepmother welcomes her stepdaughters into her life with love and without expectations or demands, in time her efforts are often rewarded. When mothers do not feel threatened and daughters are open to other female role models, stepmothers, stepdaughters and fathers can thrive. The homes created by these stepfamilies can be mutually satisfying. Author Shere Hite points out in *Women and Love: A Cultural Revolution In Progress*, "As women think through their personal lives, try to understand them and the men they love, they are critiquing the world and envisioning a new one."

Stepmothers' Daughters

My interviews showed that comparisons drawn between stepmothers' daughters and their husbands' daughters occur frequently. If the daughters are close in age, the comparisons are more direct. These comparisons exist on many levels and may include comments and feelings about disparities in social strata, finances, religions and family values. The demands of incorporating stepdaughters into families are magnified tenfold when the stepmothers have their own daughters. To complicate the situation further, a stepmother's daughters may end up living with their mother and stepfather. To the daughter of divorce, seeing these girls living with her father is a blow, especially since, as discussed, her own living conditions with her mother may have suffered after her parent's divorce.

Another issue that may cause problems for stepmothers and their daughters is how little they may truly know about their husbands and stepchildren until they are immersed in their new stepfamilies. Only then does the dysfunction of the original family spill forth. Stepmothers may not have the time they want to spend with their own daughters if they constantly encounter difficult behavior in their stepdaughters. this behavior may be due to deep-seated problems in the original families or the dysfunction which often ensues after parents divorce. Researcher E. Mavis Hetherington points out that single mothers have much less autonomy and disciplining skills with adolescent children than they did when the family was cohesive unit. In the midst of the feelings of betrayal and confusion after the original families dissolve, disruptive behaviour may develop in daughters and stepmothers, especially, are caught off-guard.

In looking at the roles of stepmothers who have daughters of their own, we cannot deny the demands of juggling the needs of their own daughters with the needs of their stepdaughters. When daughters in these cases spend time with their fathers and stepmothers and the stepmothers' children, there often occur disparities in feelings for natural children versus stepchildren. Stepmothers do not love their stepdaughters the way that they love their own daughters. When there are two sets of daughters from former marriages, it can become competitive. This only adds to the difficulties of building new marriages.

"I have my own daughter and a stepdaughter," begins Marilyn, thirty-seven, a stepmother of six years. "I naively thought that my daughter, Carmela, and my stepdaughter, Anne Marie, would be close when I married Felix. And now I see it isn't possible. There is too much competition. I know I don't help matters, but my daughter comes first with me. I have watched these girls grow up together and it hasn't been easy. I know that if I hadn't married Felix, I'd be in the same financial position as my stepdaughter and her mother. It's sad to think that their loss is my gain, but my daughter, Carmela, and I have a great life, because I married this man. My stepdaughter, Anne Marie, and her mother are always scraping by. I know that seeing how comfortable we are upsets Anne Marie when she visits and that creates more tension. I wish I knew how to fix things, but I don't."

When Jacqueline Kennedy Onassis married Aristotle Onassis, his daughter Christina was not pleased. Although photographs of

Aristotle Onassis with Jackie's children, Caroline and John, were published in the press, a photograph of the blended family, which included children from both sets of previous marriages, was not. As a single parent, Jacqueline Onassis's priority was to raise her own children. I found among my respondents that while an age difference such as that between Christina Onassis and Caroline Kennedy often works in favor of a close relationship between two stepsisters, one clearly did not develop between the two famous daughters and is not always the case.

My interviews with daughters who become stepsisters showed the girls often experienced two different scenarios. Either the girls were dissimilar in age and they bonded because there was no competition or they were similar in age and equality was more elusive as a result. In such cases, fathers favored their own daughters but in some cases spent more time with their stepdaughters. Likewise, stepmothers favored their own daughters but most did not allow their stepdaughters' needs to preempt their daughters'.

"I know exactly how my stepsister, Serena, must feel," Angelina, eighteen, explains, "because I cannot escape my stepfamily anywhere I go and I bet she can't either. My mother remarried Serena's father Al about two years ago. I live with them and Serena is the visitor on weekends. It must be so hard for her, because her father got the house in the divorce and I am in her older sister's bedroom. Her older sister just eloped. I'm sure all this stepfamily stuff had something to do with her running off to be married. Al is nice enough to me, but he's not my father. I would spend more time with my father, but he married a woman named Cindy and moved two hours away. And his wife has a daughter exactly my age. So it goes on and on, all of us in the same boat and not liking it."

What is evident through my research is the fact that daughters of any age do better with stepmothers and stepsisters when their mothers are open to the relationship possibilities for their daughters and when there is little conflict between divorced parents. Similarly, stepmothers do best when they and their stepdaughters have no preconceived notions and the husbands/fathers have worked out their relationships with their adolescent or adult daughters prior to their remarriages.

Arrival of the Half Sister

Matters are often complicated further when fathers and stepmothers have children of their own. Some stepdaughters feel that they are outcasts because the babies, their half sisters, are the products of a new, happy marriage, one which represents the present and the future. These stepdaughters see themselves, on the other hand, as products of a past marriage which had failed. Despite the strength of some stepmother/stepdaughter bonds, the arrival of children into new stepfamilies alters everyone's relationships. Sometimes differences in how stepdaughters have been raised and how half sisters are raised create competition. If both the husband and wife have their own daughters, these stepsisters suddenly find they are in the same boat. "Once there is a new baby," remarks Dr. Ronnie Burak, "the stepsisters often bond together. The lives of these girls keep changing and they find solace in one another. What we have to remember is that most of these daughters did not want the divorce, the new marriage, nor the stepsiblings or half siblings. All of this is happening to them and none of it is their choice."

Among stepmothers who had no children of their own before their new marriages, having baby daughters sometimes causes negative comparisons between their own new daughters and their stepdaughters. Even in those stories I heard where stepmothers adore their stepchildren, feelings toward stepchildren often change with the birth of a child. "I loved my stepkids and would have done anything for them," Marilee tells us. "I met them when they were only seven and nine. My husband had joint custody and I feel I helped raise them. When they were twelve and fourteen, I had a baby girl. I fell in love with my baby and my stepdaughters suddenly seemed like outsiders. I realized they were not my children. I guess I never thought about it that way until I gave birth. Over the years I have found myself comparing my daughter to my stepdaughters and for me my daughter is much more special. It's not even close, really."

Most remarriages that fail do so within the first seven years. The *Journal of Marriage and Family* reports that, in fifty percent of second marriages where the wife is under forty-six, a child will be born within two years. Whether the remarriage succeeds or not, a half sibling born into a stepfamily has a profound effect on the precarious structure of the unit. In many cases I found these newborn daughters evoke deep feelings from older half sisters, and in some cases, strengthen the stepfamily.

Sherilyn was never fond of her stepmother, Tracey, but found herself bonding with the older woman after her half sister Becca was born. "I remember reading *Pat the Bunny* to my baby half sister, Becca. Although Tracey hovered over me, I pretended that I was Becca's mother/sister/protector. I was only fourteen and she was six months old. I found myself spending time with Tracey in order to be with Becca. The initial desire I had when I learned that Tracey was pregnant was to make the baby disappear, but that went away quickly and completely. Instead I became devoted to her and I became closer to my stepmother.

"Ten years later, I know that the best thing that happened to me was Becca's birth. I remember her toothless grin and her small hands. For all my half sister's life, I have been her protector and I have watched over her. Our entire stepfamily changed the day that she arrived, and even my stepsister, who was always creating a stir, softened. Even though I never wanted my parents to divorce and I never wanted Tracey as a stepmother, in the end, it worked out anyway and what good came out of the divorce is in Becca, who is loved by all of us."

Just as the birth of a new child brought Sherilyn closer to her stepmother, a strengthening of family bonds can be felt at this time by a stepmother for her stepdaughters. "I wanted to be a perfect stepmother and I thought I was doing a pretty good job," Brenda, fifty-five, remarks, "until I had my own daughter. Then I knew that I didn't love my stepdaughters as I loved my daughter. But we all loved Camilla, the baby. We simply adored her and that brought us together. My stepdaughters, who were in their late teens when Camilla was born, became more dear to me, because of how they mothered the baby. We would jokingly call her 'our baby.'

"I had no qualms about sharing Camilla with the girls, and I welcomed their love for her. It's so ironic that it took a new child to make me see the wonderful stepdaughters I already had."

Although in many cases the new baby bonds the family, in some it does not. When a half sibling is born into the stepfamily, the daughter of divorce faces another enormous adjustment, on the heels of her initial adjustment to her parent's divorce and the second adjustment to her father's remarriage and the formation of a stepfamily. Many daughters' perspectives change when children are born to fathers and stepmothers. Some daughters feel they are nothing more than remnants of past failed marriages and they fear their parents and stepparents will also view them as such. "It is a super-human job for the stepmother to make everyone happy," observes Dr. Ronnie Burak. "While the stepmother may be wonderful toward her stepdaughters, she does not treat them as she treats her own daughter from a previous or present marriage." When a man remarries a woman who has a daughter and then the wife gives birth to a daughter, the man's daughter from his first marriage may feel quite isolated in this new strange stepfamily. "For me," says Leigh, nineteen, "it was too much when my little sister was born. First, my father married Nancy and her daughter Tiffany lived with them. Nancy was nice to me but was always much more loving toward Tiffany. Then Melissa was born and I'd go over there and they'd be falling all over her. I thought I had no place in this family for awhile. Then Tiffany got jealous of Melissa too and that gave us something to bond over."

Interestingly, I found the birth of a new baby sister sometimes bonds stepsisters who had formerly been unfriendly. In some cases the arrival of the new baby displeases the stepsisters and can be threatening for both. Occasionally, this brings the stepsisters together, as exemplified by the story of Leigh and Tiffany. On the other hand, in some cases, both stepsisters grow together, because they share a love for their half sister. This often is true when the stepsisters are as enchanted as their parents are with their new sibling. Of course, if one stepsister does not like the idea of a baby sister and the other stepsister does, this may drive even friendly stepsisters apart. How a stepmother handles the birth of her new daughter is pivotal to help in preventing stepdaughters from feeling displaced or unhappy.

"I made the decision that our stepfamily would work," begins Roberta, sixty. "At forty-two I became pregnant and so my stepdaughter, Lacey, and my own daughter, Kimberly, gained a baby sister. I had more parenting instincts than either Denny, my husband, or his ex-wife. I had made it my business to watch over both my daughter and stepdaughter. I was the disciplinarian, because no one else was. And this role caused me to be involved with my stepdaughter's life. I really believe that both girls were drawn to the baby from day one. I emphasized a sense of family and that helped. We already existed as a family unit so Tina's birth just completed the picture."

The five years that had elapsed between Roberta's remarriage and the birth of her daughter gave the stepfamily a period of time to settle in. The acting out of adolescent daughters when their parents remarry can eventually dissipate, although Hetherington and Associates found that girls take more than two years to stop acting out after their parents remarry. Therefore, giving daughters and stepdaughters some time to adjust to the stepfamily before bringing a new baby into the picture is a wise move on the part of the stepmother. When their daughters and stepdaughters are happier, the half-sister will not only be well received, but cherished.

After new children are born into stepfamilies, I found that the sensitivity of stepmothers to their older daughters' and stepdaughters' issues in having half sisters was valuable. These stepmothers did not saddle the older girls with baby-sitting duties and anticipated the changes in their marriages and the alterations in their stepfamilies due to the babies. "If there is a large age difference between the stepdaughter and her half sister, it becomes possible for the older stepsisters to derive increased self-esteem from caring for her younger half sister," Dr. Michele Kasson notes. When the baby becomes the object of affection, and stepmothers and stepdaughters are united in their mutual affection, the positive outcome can last a lifetime.

"I learned when my daughter was born that there is nothing like having a baby," explains Paige, fifty-five, a stepmother of sixteen years. "I had spent so much time with Leslie, my stepdaughter, before I married Bert that she and I had become close. Leslie was like a surrogate daughter to me. Lauren, my daughter, was born the first year I was married. Leslie loved her baby sister almost as much as I did. Needless to say, I felt blessed.

"Today the girls are fifteen and twenty-five and act like full sisters. They are connected way beyond anything I could have anticipated or hoped for. Their sister bond is about them and how they have each other in this world. If I couldn't have two daughters, this is the closest thing there is."

Not every half sister story I heard was as rosy as the one Paige told me. Some daughters of divorce felt they had been disregarded by their parents for new marriages. In these cases, the births of baby sisters made things often complicated daughters' issues further, yet still brought happiness and joy to otherwise negative situations. "I love my half sister, Emilie, even though my father did everything wrong and so did my stepmother," sighs Wendy, twenty-nine. "My stepmother has been an excellent example of what not to do and so has my stepfather. I often think of how extremely different life would have been had my parents stayed together. Instead there are all these new problems in the stepfamilies, on both sides.

"I tried to be close with my stepmother to please my father, but mostly because of Emilie. She is sixteen and so is my other half sister, Pamela, my mother's daughter. The year I turned twelve, I ended up getting two new half sisters—that is pretty amazing. And no matter what has gone on with either stepfamilies, I see these sisters as full sisters and I love them very much."

For many sisters there is a fierce solidarity that gets them through a myriad of circumstances. This testimony to sisterhood is often able to transcend the trauma of parental divorce and remarriage as well as the machinations of dysfunctional stepfamily members.

The Mother's Approval

When fathers and mothers remarry, daughters of divorce confided these new unions are not always easy on them. Their mothers' approval or disapproval of the stepmothers greatly influenced the relationships that formed between daughters and stepmothers. Once they remarry, mothers usually are more approving of new stepmothers than when the mothers are single. Those mothers who perceive the stepmothers as attempting to take their daughters away from them will not accept the stepmothers. When mothers grant their daughters permission to pursue their own relationships with their stepmothers and stepfamilies, though it is leads them down a long and bumpy road, the new relationships that result can enrich the daughters' lives.

In some scenarios I heard, mothers who created new families of their own were still resentful of stepmothers. Natalie, one of these resentful mothers, lives with Todd who has recently begun a new career. She is adamant that her daughter's stepmother is not a true mother figure. "Diana, my daughter's stepmother and I speak once a month," Natalie, forty-one, told me. "We keep our conversations limited to the children's schedules. I know how tempted she is to befriend my daughter, Kelly, who is twelve, but I've made it clear that Kelly does not need another mother. I believe that my feelings on this subject have won out, because Kelly has also conveyed this to Diana. At the same time, I trust Diana with Kelly, who was only eight when the divorce came through and a joint custody arrangement was set up. I know she is a good mother to her own boys and extends her good judgment to Kelly."

Clara echoes Natalie's sentiments. As a divorced mother to twin ten-year-old daughters, she is cautious in not allowing their stepmother total access.

"Steve, my ex-husband, remarried Elyse when the girls were only seven. This remarriage is a happy one, as I see it. I think that one reason it works for Elyse is that the girls were so young when she married Steve, and they simply let her in. I would never be negative about her and I do give tacit approval. But I do not push the girls in Elyse's direction and on a night when I have a date, I prefer to hire a sitter than take the girls there, even though they always offer to watch them. I want to keep some boundaries and I want the girls to know that I am their real mother and Elyse is only their stepmother. Still, something positive exists between Elyse and my daughters."

One important factor in daughters' acceptance of stepmothers is the original cause of the divorce. If the father precipitated the divorce and he is thriving in his new marriage while the mother is in a less than optimal situation, many daughters may feel they must stand by their mothers and thus reject their stepmothers. Other important factors are the daughters' ages and the custody arrangements. Those daughters who are emotionally bound to their mothers and spend most of their time with their mothers, find it more difficult to accept stepmothers. If the custodial mother remarries however, the daughters reaction often changes. In her 1993 Virginia Longitudinal Study of Divorce and Remarriage, E. Mavis Hetherington reported that "with preadolescent children, especially with daughters, a close marital relationship [in remarriage] was associated with high levels of negative

behavior from children toward both the mother and the stepfather."
However, Hetherington's outcome conflicts with research conducted by
Zill, Morrison and Coiro in their 1993 study *Long-term Effects of Parental
Divorce on Parent-Child Relationships*. Zill and his colleagues found that
children who are under the age of eleven at the time of divorce for the
most part get past their pain quickly and display positive behavior. It
isn't until young adulthood, Zill's research indicates, that a negative
behavior as a result of parental divorce is apparent in many stepdaughters.

These two studies with opposing points of view remind us
that individual circumstances change outcomes. When we look at the
triangle created by mother, daughter and stepmother, repeatedly we
see that if divorces are the result of affairs and stepmothers are the former lovers, there is much less chance of daughters developing close
relationships with their stepmothers since these women are seen as
guilty participants in the break-up of the original marriage and family.
However, some daughters yearn for connections to their fathers,
despite their fathers' affairs and subsequent marriages. Some of these
daughters make efforts to bond with their stepmothers, because the
daughters value relationships with their fathers. "If the father cheated,
the daughter may still want to be with the family," relationship expert,
Antoinette Michaels, concludes. "She cannot tolerate feeling abandoned by him and the rejection of the family only makes her more
desirous of approval by a male."

"I have gotten over my father's affair and remarriage after all
these years," Lorraine, forty-one, tells us. "I was nineteen when my
father and mother divorced. My father went on to marry his lover. I
don't think it was right what he did but I know my parents' marriage
was very troubled. It was going to end sooner or later, whether he had
an affair or not. I didn't see him much as a child because my mother
wouldn't allow it. Now that I'm an adult, I want to have contact with
my dad. So, even though it was difficult, I forgave my father and made
the decision to seek a relationship with him and my stepmother."

After having a troubled marriage which ends in divorce, a
daughter tends to side with one parent over the other. This is not
always gender based, although daughters are quite often aligned with
their mothers. This is, in part, because most of them live with their

mothers after the divorce and because of female bonding and identification. "In a divorce situation," comments Dr. Donald Cohen, "the bottom line is who is seen as the victim. If the mother left the father or the father left the mother, the daughter defends whichever parent seems more vulnerable and she is more open to that parent moving on, remarrying and building a new life."

In reviewing the substance of the triangle created by mother, stepmother and daughter, we have to bear in mind the underlying history of the divorce and the prior marriage. Whatever contentious feelings remain, it is necessary for the adults to make a concerted effort to behave civilly toward one another. If the mother harbors negative feelings toward the father and they spill over into her attitude toward the stepmother, this gets in the way of a healthy relationship between the mother and stepmother. Such enmity complicates matters for the daughter, who feels she has to choose a side. For many with whom I've spoken, the mother's acceptance of the stepmother is key to the daughter's success in having positive relationships with both women. When good will is generated by these two women, it only enhances and strengthens the emotional well-being of the daughters whom they influence so greatly. With cooperation from fathers and open communication between mothers, daughters and stepmothers, the opportunity for mutually satisfying family lives for all the members of these stepfamilies is made possible.

CHAPTER 10

Co-mothering: Failures and Successes

"My mother walked out on us when I was in grade school," recalls Phoebe forty-eight, her downcast face mirroring the sadness in her voice. "I didn't see her again for several years. She ran off with another man and left my father, my two little sisters and me. Suddenly I was in charge and it was overwhelming. So when my father brought home his new wife, a few months later, I was relieved. My father insinuated that we children had destroyed his first marriage and he was determined we would not destroy his second. We were definitely told too often by our father how important his new wife was and how we better not screw things up. I didn't want to lose another mother figure, so I tried very hard to bond with Sophie, my step-mother, not just for my father but for myself.

"My stepmother became my friend and we learned to be mother and daughter together. I never was able to figure out why my mother did not want us in the way that my stepmother did. And my father didn't want to talk about the reasons for my mother leaving. Denial was a big part of his coping or lack of it. Soon after, my mother came back into my life. I visited with her often, but I still lived with my father and stepmother. My stepmother and my mother worked things out between them and this helped me feel more secure. But whenever I longed for my mother, it affected my relationship with my stepmother and I had unbelievable guilt. Still, I couldn't help but gravitate toward my mother at times."

In many of the stepfamilies with young daughters that I studied, much day-to-day parenting is shouldered by mothers and stepmothers. Although a great many fathers today are more involved with their children than fathers in the past, stepmothers, more than ever before, have hands-on relationships with their stepdaughters as well. In the cases of stepmothers who have entered the picture early on, when their stepdaughters are under the age of nine, connections between daughters and stepmothers are more easily established. For these young daughters, co-parenting really becomes co-mothering as the mothers and stepmothers take over these duties.

As daughters grow up, the way in which stepmothers and their stepdaughters interact changes, but for a great number the early attachment remains. Of the sixty-five percent of remarriages that become stepfamilies, according to the Stepfamily Association of America, the majority of stepmothers are seriously invested in their roles. There is also a group of stepmothers who confided to me that they feel that, despite their attempts to form positive relationships with their stepdaughters and the girls' mothers, there are many difficulties and little appreciation.

False Expectations

In listening to many experiences of stepmothers, mothers and daughters, it became apparent that an unrealistic optimism pervades many brand-new stepfamilies but then fades quickly as the reality of co-mothering surfaces. For many mothers and stepmothers, the problems involved with co-mothering and stepparenting are difficult and confusing. As I have noted before, problems with these roles contribute significantly to the sixty percent rate of divorce for remarriages. Stepchildren cause tremendous stress in many of these second or third marriages.

One of the primary reasons for early conflicts, as I have pointed out earlier, is that stepmothers are not always prepared for their roles. Doug and Naomi Mosely, authors of *Making Your Second Marriage a First Class Success* note that most men feel obligated to be good fathers to their first family and their second wives may resent this. Meanwhile stepmothers are making efforts to be "motherly" toward their stepdaughters although their efforts may be ill-served.

All that the daughter wants, as Dr. Ronnie Burak points out, is to be loved by her father as he has always loved her. "'Don't be my mother' is the first cry of the stepdaughter, especially an adolescent one," begins Dr. Burak. "Her second plea to her stepmother is to allow her to still have time with her father alone. The stepdaughter also needs time to get accustomed to her stepmother. The daughter wants friendship from her stepmother more than mothering. Most of all, she wants her stepmother to recognize her feelings." Unaware stepmothers, in some cases, remain outsiders despite attempts at bonding with stepdaughters.

All members of the triangle and the father need sensitivity in order for co-mothering to succeed. If each adult is able to recognize the daughter as the innocent victim in the divorce and to respect her need for stability, there is a much better chance that the daughter's life will be rich in love and security. Yet in forty percent of my interviews, I found that each woman in the triangle has her own agenda, and the daughter's needs are often sacrificed.

The difficulties faced are made apparent by one of my interviews. Analise, eighteen, observed how her father's subsequent marriage evoked an unexpectedly strong response from her mother. "My stepmother, Margie, is really nice, but that doesn't matter to me," Analise begins. "I was thirteen when my parents divorced. For a while everything was fine. Then my father started dating Margie and my mother got angry. Before that, I had two divorced, single parents and it was sort of balanced. I would have liked it better if my parents had stayed married, but I understood that it hadn't worked out. For four years, until my father and Margie got married, I would go back and forth between both my mother's and my father's houses. My mom and dad were both worried about me. Then Margie came along and she tried very hard to get me to like her. Seeing that was hard for my mother. It got harder for my parents to get along like they used to, before Margie. My mom was always polite to Margie if they spoke, but I knew she didn't like her."

When there is contention between stepmothers and mothers as there was in Analise's case, successful co-mothering is not possible. Nothing makes daughters feel as secure as the sense that their mothers and stepmothers are equipped and want to co-mother. Regardless of what circumstances precipitated the divorce, the goal of both women should be a successful co-mothering campaign. This cannot be emphasized enough. When divorced fathers remarry, the majority of these remarriages take place within the first three years after their divorces. In these cases, mothers and stepmothers have to work together to help daughters adjust to these new realities even though many of these daughters may resist in the beginning.

Time can be beneficial in the co-mothering efforts of mothers and stepmothers and is essential for daughters of divorce, according to my research. When stepmothers are cautious about how they enter their stepfamilies, and tread lightly at first, they will be better able to provide a solid foundation for the daughters. This is especially true when there is shared custody or liberal visitation arrangements. This also applies to daughters who no longer are in a custody situation, which legally occurs at age eighteen in some states, twenty-one in others. Many of these daughters, I found, still see both parents on a steady basis and their stepmothers and mothers are still integral parts of their lives.

"I doubt my stepdaughters appreciated my efforts until they were mothers themselves," begins Christine, sixty-two, a stepmother for twenty-five years. "But I never gave up, because I wanted to be a part of their lives. I realized that their approval of me had to come from their mother. Fortunately, I was able to build a relationship with Sheila, the girls' mother. The fact that my stepdaughters, Cora and Delia, were only six and eight when I married Dean was a positive thing. I made myself available to them and I was definitely a positive influence in their lives. Dean wasn't any good at talking to Sheila, and after a while I decided it would be better if she and I spoke directly. Since the girls were small we couldn't afford any misunderstandings about their weekend plans—so it was best if the two mothers spoke. Later, when they got older, there were other problems. Adolescent daughters, in any kind of family, especially those with single or divorced mothers, have issues. I defended the girls when it was necessary. And when Cora eloped, I thought we should all go visit her and her new husband. So we did, Sheila, her husband, Dean and myself. That was how I thought it had to be and I was the one to make it happen. The four of us raised these girls together and that made them stronger."

Some mothers and stepmothers with whom I spoke resist the concept of co-mothering at first, while others fantasize that it can be the solution to all their problems. The middle ground consists of mothers and stepmothers who realize the potential of co-mothering and are open to it, but it will not fix every problem that transpires with daughters. Furthermore, mothers and stepmothers must be realistic and recognize that, due to the other woman's disinterest, anger or other issues, the possibility of co-mothering may not exist. In my research, I found that many stepmothers are more aware of the value of their joint efforts with their stepdaughters' mothers than are the mothers. Most mothers felt that the less contention for the daughters as they moved from their mothers' homes to their fathers' and stepmothers' homes, the better, but they resisted co-mothering (at least initially). My research also indicates that daughters who have both sets of parents/stepparents involved in their lives fare much better in adulthood. Most daughters become aware as they mature of the tremendous strides it takes to form a team of mother and stepmother.

I found that co-mothering, when it works, becomes a significant part of the exchange between mother and stepmother. The daughters have a safety net, because their mothers and stepmothers are working together to give them the best environment in both homes. This is taken to a higher degree when the gender specificity of mothers and stepmothers as a cohesive unit in the raising of the daughters becomes apparent to the daughters. They then have this feminine model in their future lives. In the short and long run, co-mothering between mother and stepmother brings many benefits to the daughters of divorce.

Holidays

Even in the best of circumstances, holidays are loaded down with expectations and, very often, disappointments. Holiday celebrations peel way the layers of a dysfunctional family. When mothers and stepmothers are involved there is often a repressed power play between them which manifests in divided holidays. Tugs-of-war between members of the triangle only escalate the underlying issues and the manipulations. Many daughters of divorce feel torn between their two families who want them to be present at the same events. Some parents will win out and have their daughters in their homes for more hours of these meaningful days.

To make matters worse, for some daughters the holidays are cruel reminders of their losses. They observe friends with intact families who do not have to divide their time on these special occasions between two or more homes. These events, from the daughters' points of view, rarely seem to be shared equally.

"I have dreaded holidays and birthdays for so long," Lydia, twenty-three, confesses. "My parents divorced when I was ten and there was a custody battle. After they settled in court and I ended up living with my mother, there were fights over holidays. As I remember it, holidays were not such a big deal when my parents were married. But once my mother and father divorced, holidays became very important. My mother told me she was afraid to divorce my father for years, because she didn't know what she would do on Christmas without her children. Then it happened, and she had to face her fear. There have been Christmases that we have not spent with my mother. My stepmother, Olga, did the best she could to make those times festive but without my mom, they didn't even seem Christmases to me.

"When I was young, no matter which parent I ended up with, I always missed the absent one. Now that I am an adult, I make up my own mind about where to be on a given holiday or I avoid both sets of parents and just go out with friends. That sick feeling in the pit of my stomach over holidays is finally gone, because I can escape."

Despite the mother and stepmother making positive strides in co-mothering, their efforts can be seriously undermined by unpleasantness during holidays. The disparate manner of dealing with holiday events and family vacations and the scheduling conflicts that follow can cause a rift in the delicate co-mothering action. If the stepmother and mother have a pleasant working rapport, it can be undermined by the pressure of holidays and school vacations. Some mothers who find themselves concerned about their own territory reconsider their decision to get along with the stepmothers. Some stepmothers question why they have gone out of their way for the mothers and daughters in the midst of the arguments over holiday time and vacations. As Amy Reisen, divorce attorney, sees it, when

mothers and stepmothers are drawn into holiday battles, they sometimes lose sight of their commitments to their children. "The first goal
is to work in concert over the issues so they are resolved during the
divorce and not after," Reisen points out. "Any lingering issue can
impact the quality of co-parenting and co-mothering and puts the
daughters in the middle." For the daughters, holidays and vacations
collectively represent how different life is in their mothers' and stepmothers' homes.

Our society has no prescriptive roles for the members of the
new triangle: stepmothers, mothers and stepdaughters. When it
comes to holidays and vacations, this lack of a prescribed role creates
confusion and tension among daughters, mothers and stepmothers.
The best-laid plans for happy holiday dinners unravel quickly in difficult stepfamily situations. The loss for the daughters is more acute
during holidays when the perfect image of family is both implicit and
explicit. "No one knows exactly what the role of the stepmother
should be," explains sociologist Alice Michaeli. "We need the mecha-
nisms to create a role for the stepparent. These children look at their
stepparents, especially at family occasions and can only think, 'You
are not my mother' or 'You are not my father.'"

Ideally, stepmothers and mothers would identify with each
other's pain and hope, thus they could work together to ease their
daughters'/stepdaughters' situations. For instance, if the mother has
her own unhappy stepdaughter to contend with on Thanksgiving, she
should communicate to her daughter, who is due at her father's house
for a turkey dinner that the stepmother will be trying her best. In this
case, the mother will advise her daughter to be tolerant and open.
That is the best kind of scenario but reality doesn't always turn out
that way, according to my interviewees.

At the age of thirty-five, Alexis found herself in a relationship
with two blatantly hostile stepdaughters whose feelings were fueled
by their mother. Holidays brought the negativity to the forefront. Ten
years later, the progress is slow but steady.

"When I married Craig, these girls were not babies, but
teenagers," Alexis begins. "My older stepdaughter went away to school
and now lives across the country and it has not been a problem. My

younger stepdaughter, Natasha, has been trouble for years. It's been rocky to say the least, partially because there is so much contention between my husband and Yvette, the mother.

"During holidays it was the worst. Yvette confused the plans on purpose. So if she arranged for us to have Natasha on Christmas day, she sent her over on Christmas Eve. Or if we were to have Natasha for dinner on her birthday, she would call and say it was too late, that Natasha was too tired. This was mean spirited and malicious. I remember the time we had the balloons and cake and Yvette canceled on Natasha's behalf. I felt terrible for my husband since this was his child. This past year I called Yvette before the holidays and told her we had to work things out together. Yvette agreed to be more of a team player and the holidays actually went smoothly. It is better this way for us as parents, and for Natasha."

If the stepmother takes her cues from the mother and both women are part of the process on holidays and birthdays, it will work better for everyone. Mothers and stepmothers should be sensitive to the daughters' needs and, instead of making daughters feel torn apart on holidays, the two can make plans together so the children can enjoy themselves. When this happens, I found, daughters of divorce who were anxious about pleasing two families came to feel supported and more secure. "If the mother and stepmother are able to cooperate," advises Dr. Ronnie Burak, "the daughters end up with a much easier task on the holidays. The adults have to exhibit a maturity in order for the daughters to benefit."

Past Histories/Present Conflicts

There are instances among the members of the triangles where embattled divorces caused long-standing anger, which in turn later is reflected in the inability of mothers and stepmothers to communicate and co-mother. If mothers and fathers do not communicate, even for the sake of the children, stepmothers enter a combative arena. In some of these cases, the nature of the divorce and the stepmothers' arrival are played out repeatedly, unless the mothers are able to get beyond what occurred in the past. Similarly, when stepmothers have been influenced by their husbands to dislike the mothers, it is more difficult for the stepmothers to build connections to the mothers.

The daughter's need to be loved by her father remains an important factor in overcoming tensions between the adults. Many stepmothers' early intentions in their marriages are to accommodate their husbands insofar as his daughters are concerned, but this plan may, I found, be stymied by a bitter mother. A typical scenario I came across occurred when a daughter has been living with her mother and the stepmother attempts to become a second mother figure. When a mother senses this, she holds on more tightly to her daughter. At this point, if the damage of the past relationships between the mother and father is not reconciled, the mother may prevent the daughter and step-mother from creating a bond. A wise stepmother can play a part in resolving this by encouraging her husband to be less angry with his ex-wife and work to put past problems behind them. Once such a recon-ciliation is put into effect, a more stable, healthy environment is estab-lished for the daughter as the stepmother and mother are able to begin dialogues and plant the seeds of co-mothering. The daughter, feeling more secure, is then free to reaffirm her relationship with her mother and begin a positive, rewarding relationship with her stepmother.

"My parents got divorced when I was eleven and I spent the better part of my childhood thinking I was hurting either my mother's feelings or my stepmother's feelings," begins Stella, twenty-seven. "When my father married Eugenia, my stepmother, I wanted all mem-ories of my parents' divorce to disappear so I could get to know Eugenia. And the only way that we could move forward was if she and my mom could both be there for me. At first, though, they had trou-ble talking to one another. So I didn't feel comfortable talking about my home life with my mother when visiting my dad and stepmother, and vice versa. Finally, my mother and Eugenia began to talk because they both cared about me. That was when the divorce bothered me less. But it took a long time; it didn't happen overnight, just because I wanted it to."

For many daughters of divorce, the discord between their divorced parents is an ongoing saga. When mothers and stepmothers begin to forge relationships, most daughters are skeptical at first. This I found to be especially applicable to those daughters whose parents have had difficulty co-parenting. If their parents have been unsteady in their behavior as divorced parents, the daughters question how the mother and stepmother can be trusted as a unit. When mothers and stepmothers recognize the lack of wisdom in these actions and make a concerted effort to let go of the past, this not only enables the daughters to feel more secure, but allows the triangle formed by these three women to position a new positive relationship for the future.

Dispelling Old Patterns

"My parents fought about the same things when they were married as when they had remarried other people," recalls Lucinda, thirty-one. "I was only fifteen at the time and at first I supported my mother's decision. Then our lives changed and my sisters and I ended up being in a joint-custody situation where the same scenes with my parents were acted out repeatedly. I am the oldest sister and I think I was the most upset by this and we gave our stepmother a hard time at first. My middle sister, Elaine, who was twelve, was thrilled when our father married Maureen. She even imagined having stepsiblings and stepparents as good things. I thought she was nuts.

"My little sister, who was nine, was oblivious and overwhelmed at the same time. She was the reason that my mother and stepmother began to talk and became allies. Maureen saw how my mother and father played each other and she said she would have no part of it. She was a no-nonsense person who wanted to get things right. She sort of won my mother over with her positive attitude. She was kind of a referee at first, then a buffer and then finally, a true friend to me and to my sisters. That was when I began to think that with my mother and Maureen on our side, things would work out."

When fathers remarry, the question becomes, how will daughters of divorce bond with their stepmothers and to what effect? A most willing and forthcoming stepmother will find little room for her efforts if the father, the mother and the daughters are locked into the negative patterns of former families. Some daughters find themselves surrounded by their parents' old behaviors, even though they now have stepmothers. When the stepmother is bold and intercedes, I learned in my interviews, her presence can break old patterns and her communication with the mother can be instrumental in healing old wounds and forging a co-mothering alliance.

Aurora, a stepmother of seventeen years, knew that her step-daughter acted as a sponge cleaning up the negative emotional messes created by her parents. After observing Dory, her stepdaughter, who was twelve at the time, Aurora stepped in. "I saw that my step-daughter was the loser as long as her mother and father were unable to stop being immature," Aurora, forty-seven, explains. "I was young and had no experience in mothering, but I cared about Dory from the start and I thought Steve and Belle were crazy to upset her further. She is an only child and she needed to feel safe.

"I ended up being the one to comfort Dory and to take her places. I felt very much like she became my priority. She was the walking wounded. In the end, I became a mediator of sorts; I was Belle's advocate and the voice of reason to Steve. Belle and I began to share our concerns about Dory. It took five years for us to trust each other but it made a difference in the quality of everyone's life."

Ninety percent of the stepmothers I interviewed told me that they did not, as I've indicated previously, anticipate all the aspects of stepmothering which they encountered. As Kathryn Harrison argued in her *New York Times* piece, "Pity the Poor Stepmom," stepmothers get a raw deal and mothers, in their criticism of stepmothers, are 'relentless.' Harrison writes: "And stepmothers, no matter how devoted are hampered by a combination of factors unique to their particular situations: a lack of basic factual knowledge about the child, the complicating presence of the biological mother, the hostility of stepchildren traumatized by divorce, the father's unwillingness to interfere, and their own senses of alienation from the original family."

Conversely, I found some stepmothers undergo positive transformations in their attitudes towards the daughters. One commonly cited example was the tentative stepmother who, after some time begins to pay more attention to her stepdaughter and the two eventually bond. The mother usually is more hesitant about the sincerity of the stepmother's behavior than her daughter, but if she sees her daughter is happy with her stepmother, the mother might soften toward her too. Both women, in a co-mothering manner, often feel less accommodating toward daughters when they are difficult adolescents. Yet the different thresholds of tolerance of mother and stepmother are reflected in their roles and personalities. Another scenario I found is that, despite a productive co-mothering contract, a trying daughter will push both women's buttons to the extent that both mothers and step-mothers revert to earlier suspicious views of each other.

"I know that Hank misread Corinne when it came to the girls," sighs Antonia, a forty-three-year-old single mother. "I knew that her initial interest in my daughters was disingenuous and that it wouldn't last. In the beginning when Hank and Corinne were dating, Corinne took the girls here and there, mostly to toy stores and movies. She bought them whatever they asked for. But when it came to the hard part of parenting—the day-to-day stuff—Corinne didn't try very hard. Several times when the girls were visiting their father's for the week-end and one of them got sick, Corinne or Hank would call me to have me pick up the sick child and take her to the doctor, as if they were incapable of driving to the pediatrician's office.

"Once Corinne and Hank were engaged, Corinne stopped going out of her way to be nice to my girls. When they got married, she actually convinced Hank to see the girls less; I suppose she did this so that they could spend more time together as a couple I can understand that, but my girls are still young and have had so much loss in their lives. The idea the Corinne and their father are not as available upsets them. I find myself covering for Corinne when she disappoints my kids the same way I used to cover for their father. I want Corinne to be involved with my girls, because it is good for them."

In contrast to Antonia's view of her daughters' stepmother as disingenuous and quickly receding from the daughter's picture once the stepmothers' marriage was sealed, Hannah, a stepmother for twenty-five years, has sustained a meaningful relationship with her two stepdaughters. Even after her divorce from their father, this pat-tern never faltered. "I have known Sydney and Katrina since they were five and eight years old. Kyle, their father, had the standard custody arrangement of Wednesday night dinners and every other weekend. It was a prerequisite of the marriage that these girls would be welcome in our home. I was so young and eager to please I was willing to do anything, and I loved the idea of caring for two little girls.

"From the start, their mother and I got along. She was ten years older than I and she had already remarried a man who seemed very pleasant. When my own daughter, Arielle, was born, I made sure that Sydney and Katrina felt like they were part of this new family. Although Kyle and I split up five years ago, I still see Sydney and Katrina. We have relationships that go beyond blood ties or marriages. I genuinely love my stepdaughters."

Some stepmothers whom I interviewed were not only prepared for their responsibilities, but felt open right from the start toward their stepdaughters' mothers despite being intolerant of their husband's old patterns with their former families. When old patterns reemerge, however, I found that some mothers and stepmothers are able to work out differences for the daughters' sakes and for their own sakes, while others are not. "If one of the partners or both of the partners have unresolved issues," explains Antoinette Michaels, relationship expert, "the health of the mother and stepmother is reflected in their co-mothering. When the divorced family is dysfunctional, the kids become pawns and the mother and stepmother are in a contest." The co-mothering propels the mothers, daughters and stepmothers forward to make the most of their future, always with the well-being of the daughters in mind.

According to those daughters of divorce who feel dissatisfied, life became confusing when their stepmothers became less accommodating to them. Such daughters began to think this was how the stepmother must be in 'real life,' when she wasn't trying to win her husband and his daughters over. The mother also begins to wonder if the stepmother is not quite as sweet and willing as she first seemed. When the stepmother changes her welcoming behavior, it can be traumatic for the daughter. At this juncture, a strong co-mothering foundation can make all the difference as seen in the experience of Brianna, one the daughters of divorce to whom I spoke.

"I cannot describe the difference in how Josephine acted after she married my dad a year ago," sighs Brianna, eighteen. "When they were dating, she and I would do so many things together. She drove me to my friends' houses and picked me up. She'd take us all to a movie on weekends. This was five years ago, when my dad had lots of girlfriends and Josephine wanted to be the one. In a way, I chose her, because my dad asked me if I liked her best and I said yes. I was just hoping he'd finally stop dating. Besides, my mom liked Josephine too, so that sealed the deal.

"Lately I've been thinking that Josephine has changed and has much less interest in spending time with me. She's even excluded me from time she spends with my dad. Mom cared about that too when she was married to my dad, but Josephine is really into spending time alone with him. And I feel like my dad doesn't pay as much attention to me anymore. So I told my mom and she said she would talk to Josephine and explain things. I'm hoping this will help. I want it to be like it was before; that was fine for me."

Mothers and stepmothers whom I interviewed are bound by their affection for the daughters and their mutual desire to make life as pleasant as possible for them. To this end, they become co-mothers, which is a relatively new phenomenon and one which can prove quite successful.

What affects some daughters of divorce is when their stepmothers alter their behavior in specific incidents, because of their fathers. The stepmother's position is precarious at times, and her reaction may be based on her husband's attachment and way of dealing with his daughters. Yet when the mother and stepmother have a good co-mothering history either the mother (in many cases) or the stepmother can intercede and adjust the relationship for the good of the daughters.

Supporting the Daughters

There are no guidelines for divorced mothers and stepmothers in their assigned roles. Yet there are millions of women filing these positions. A surprising part of divorce and stepmothering for adult women is the unrelenting need for support. "I didn't think it would require such constant attention," Michelle, a stepmother of four years, confides. "I keep waiting for everything to be alright but it doesn't happen like that. When my stepdaughter's mother remarried, my stepdaughter, Marcie, had a meltdown. Until then, Marcie had two separate worlds, then she was put in another place and it was too much for her, too many changes. It impaired the progress in our relationship."

The daughter of divorce lives in a precarious world where what seems stable may not be stable at all. Changes make the daughter shaky and unsure. Even the back-and-forth from one stepfamily to the other, is not easy after years of practice. When the stepmother and daughter have begun to build a kind of rapport, it helps. The healthiest of relationships for the daughter and her stepmother are those that grow over a period of testing. Eventually, daughters learn to develop separate relationships with their mothers, stepmothers and fathers and are able to balance a blending of mother and father, on special occasions, and mother and stepmother on an ongoing basis.

Although everyone seems to be floundering at the start of a divorce and stepfamily situation, it seems that the stepmother might be in the most difficult of positions. As Anne C. Bernstein writes in her essay, *Women in Stepfamilies: The Fairy Godmother, the Wicked Witch, and Cinderella Reconstructed*, it is the "Ozzie and Harriet" theory of the American family that causes stepmothers to feel inadequate. Bernstein describes "deficiency comparison," in which the stepfamily is viewed as inferior to the nuclear family. However, she also writes, "significant differences between groups can overshadow the most important findings of all: that majorities of parents and stepparents from both sexes are both involved in and satisfied with stepfamily life."

A positive view of stepfamilies is encouraging and uplifting for the mother, daughter, stepmother relationships, as evidenced in my interview with Marguerite, a stepmother for eleven years.

"Rebecca, my stepdaughter, and I have built a close relationship," Marguerite, thirty-eight, tells us. "I think this is because Clarise, her mother, allowed it. I was able to be a part of her life and it seemed that Clarise wanted that. Clarise married a nice man who also extended himself to Rebecca and this has been wonderful. I have two sons from my first marriage who are older and Rebecca's stepfather has two sons. So she has a special place because she remains the only girl and the baby in two stepfamilies.

"I think the key to the success of our stepfamily is that there is not any fighting between her parents. Both parents seem to have moved on in their lives. Their healthy attitude can be seen in how Rebecca has thrived socially and academically."

The support of parents and stepparents and their amicable relationships with each other makes a huge difference in creating a happy, stable life for a daughter of divorce, as seen in Margeurite's story. Sadly, not all daughters are so blessed. When a daughter loses her mother, there is a new set of problems facing the stepmother. As documented in Hope Edelman's Book, *Motherless Daughters*, she found that her pool of interviewees expressed both negative and positive feelings toward their stepmothers, but many daughters missed their mothers too much be able to forge a relationship with their stepmothers. For daughters of divorce, there is the chance for a successful triangle of mother, daughter and stepmother—after overcoming the hurdles and obstacles, whereas daughters of widowers can never even hope for such an outcome. As Dr. Ronnie Burak points out, "If the stepmother does not have children of her own or only has boys, she will likely see a relationship with her stepdaughter as an opportunity. But if the stepdaughter can't get past the grief and pain of her mother's death, that opportunity may never present itself. It only is the stepdaughter has come to terms with the loss of her mother, and if the stepmother is patient, compassionate and encourages the sharing of fond memories of the mother, that the two have a chance to establish a mother-daughter relationship."

For mothers, daughters and stepmothers, the delicate fabric of their relationships may be unravelled or strengthened and solidified by a loved one's death or one member of the triangle's life-threatening illness. Harriet, a stepmother, discovered how meaningful her link to her stepdaughter's mother was when the girl became gravely ill. "When my stepdaughter, Delaney, was diagnosed with cancer," begins Harriet, fifty-six, "I saw how much more important her health was than the silly feuds that Delaney's mother, Eva, and my husband engaged in—feuds in which I always ended up in the middle. Once this happened to Delaney and her life was on the line, everyone pulled together. Eva and I suddenly saw the value we each had in Delaney's life, as the two women who had raised her. I went with Eva to interview specialists, and we kept each other company in the hospital. Initially, we were doing it all for Delaney, but at some point we realized we were also there to support each other.

"Delaney's recovery has been a miracle to us all. I think seeing her parents, stepparents and stepsiblings put their petty bickering behind them and come together helped Delaney feel safer and more secure in her time of great fear and uncertainty; I think knowing she had a real, loving family that truly cared for her helped pull Delaney through it."

Though Harriet's story is an inspiring one, it needn't take the blow of a child's life-threatening illness to bring stepfamilies together. It does, however, take patience, an open mind, a willingness to compromise and, of course, love.

The concept of co-mothering is complex, as I have seen through first-hand interviews. My research shows that seventy percent of stepmothers often feel left out and inadequate, envious that their stepdaughters' loyalties to their mothers seem to overshadow any chance of connecting with their stepdaughters. Daughters, on the other hand, often feel displaced, uprooted, put upon, cheated of a whole family as they are pulled between two parents. Even in the best of conditions, in happy stepfamilies, these emotions still exist for many daughters of divorce. As Dr. Margorie Engel, President and CEO of the Stepfamily Association of America, reminds us, children are defensive and their behavior toward a stepparent "may have little to do with the stepparent and much to do with prior experience." However, Dr. Engel also points out that stepmothers have an opportunity to help reestablish empathy and attachment in the extended family. She urges all to consider the possibility of the original parents as forming "parenting coalitions, increasing their ability to manage change (completing the separation from and dissolution of the first marriage) and developing constructive ways of dealing with stepparents."

It is only with time, determination, broadened views and deep commitment that each triangle member—the mother, daughter and stepmother—can begin to work as a team, building a positive present and promising future for themselves and the generations to come.

CHAPTER 11

When Daughters Grow Up: Long-term Implications of the Triangle

The failure or success of triangle cooperation and communication can best be seen when the daughters of divorce become adults.

"I don't believe in marriage the way some of my friends do," begins Francesca, twenty-nine. "I don't dream of the perfect day or the perfect man. Because my parents were divorced when I was in grade school, I am very cynical about love and marriage. Our lives changed so much when they divorced that I barely remember the big house we all lived in. My older sisters remember and they talk about it to this day, as if they were robbed of something special. My mother never remarried but my father remarried a woman named Henrietta, who has been a wonderful role model. She has a daughter from her first marriage who is a few years younger than I am and we always got along.

"On the surface, my life seems happy and stable, but what my parent's divorce and subsequent stepfamily life has done is discourage me from becoming serious with any man. It's almost as if I would rather blow off a man than be intimate, because I've been so disappointed in my parents. I can't imagine being able to have a successful family life, a husband and children—I don't feel equipped for that sort of life. My dating pattern is to see one person exclusively for a while and then do something to make the relationship impossible to continue. I put up obstacles at every turn and sabotage the relationship. I think that if I do that, I won't be hurt."

As I've noted, sixty percent of all second marriages fail and children of divorce are twice as likely to have their own failed marriages as those children from intact families, according to the National Opinion Research Council. While by sheer numbers, divorce has become a more accepted institution, the impact it has on children cannot be ignored or underestimated. There are contrasting studies for adult children of divorce. Judith Wallerstein and Sandra Blakeslee's research, explored in their book *Second Chances*, indicates that thirty percent of children of divorce have long-term issues in forming relationships as adults. In comparison, E. Mavis Hetherington's research states that approximately twenty-five percent of children of divorce suffer from long-term difficulties in relationships compared to only ten percent of children from intact families. In my interviews with daughters of divorce, only fifty percent of daughters over twelve stated that they desired relationships with their stepmothers initially. However, by the time these daughters reached their twenties, many felt they had established successful connections to their stepmothers, while remaining close to their mothers.

Circumstances of Divorce

Circumstances, both positive and negative, of parents' divorces and their fathers' remarriages continue to reverberate throughout daughters' lives. Many daughters whose fathers have abandoned their families are, understandably, hesitant to marry and have families of their own. According to those with whom I spoke, when these daughters begin to date and form intimate connections with the opposite sex, the betrayals of their mothers by their fathers haunt them. In a great many of these cases, trust becomes an issue, since these daughters know that their mothers could not trust their fathers and those daughters who are privy to their stepmothers' stories can be intimidated further.

"It hardly matters that my father left my mother for someone else," begins Ginger, twenty-five, "because his leaving was more than we could handle. I couldn't understand the details of what my mother said, because I was only six, but I heard her complain on the phone to our grandmother that our father had a girlfriend. That stuck in my mind, and I've always known it wasn't the right thing to do. My father left my mother alone to raise my sisters and me and to support us our mother had to clean houses. This was what I grew up with: knowing my father found another woman and my mother was left counting food stamps and scrubbing strangers' floors.

"In junior high, boys started really paying attention to me. I either liked them too much or didn't care at all. I acted the same toward them whether I cared or I didn't care. I suppose it was a defense. I was promiscuous and I smoked cigarettes—sometimes I drank. Deep down I was very sad because of what my father had done. This went on for a few years and then I got tired of feeling so badly. When I was twenty-one I became engaged to a nice guy. I loved him and thought it would be safe to trust him. He broke the engagement and since then I haven't been able to trust again. It seems so unfair—I thought I had found someone unlike my father, but my fiancé also broke my heart. That was when I called my stepmother and asked to see her. I had to know her side of the story to understand my dad, to understand myself and my future."

In some cases stepmothers intercede and stabilize relationships for the daughters and their fathers, encouraging the fathers to remain parts of their daughters' lives. Some of the stepmothers to whom I spoke were compassionate and understanding, because these step-mothers have children of their own or simply recognized the value of the father/daughter bond. When this occurred these daughters had fewer abandonment issues, because their fathers were present and not tugged by both their new wives and their daughters. This is true regardless of the nature of the divorce. An involved father contributes to his daughter's positive attitudes toward dating and marriage. When their stepmothers set examples by being inclusive, many of the daughters were grateful. "I have seen instances where the stepmother is truly there for her stepdaughters, in every way," comments Brenda Szulman, psychotherapist. "But the daughters need their father to be a good parent too and these daughters ask, 'Why wasn't our mother able to protect us from the divorce and hold the family together?' Even when the stepmother is great and the father is involved, this question gnaws at daughters."

One stepmother who persuaded her husband to recognize the importance of his being a presence in his daughter's life was Joyce. "I have encouraged my husband Rocco to spend time with his daughter since we began dating," Joyce, fifty-one, tells us. "I know that her mother wanted very much to keep the kids away from Rocco, but he fought for his time with them. He has never missed a day to see them, particularly my stepdaughter, Serena, who is fifteen. I have wanted to become close to her and it hasn't been easy. I think that she sees me as a home-wrecker and her mother has fed her this myth. The truth is, I did not start to date Rocco until his divorce was underway. I want Serena to know that, because I do not want to be misjudged. On the other hand, I have also learned in the past four years that what matters here is not what goes on between Serena and myself, but what goes on with Rocco and Serena.

"It is amazing how things change, because Serena, despite what she's been told, has come to me, realizing that I totally support her relationship with her father. She knows that her mother does not and Serena sees that my influence has helped her. I notice how happy Rocco is when he comes back from a day with his daughter. I doubt he ever thought he would spend a whole day with just Serena. And had he stayed married, he wouldn't have. It was the divorce that forced him to be a better father. And while I am still waiting for my day with Serena, as long as Rocco is happy, I'm happy."

The key for daughters and stepmothers in building relationships that work is acceptance on both parts of each other's roles. As Margorie Engel, President and CEO of Stepfamily Association of America, explains, "The relationship between stepparents and stepchildren is not and never will be the same as the relationship between biological parents and their children." That is not to say that these relationships do not have merit of their own. And in some cases I found these relations grow as daughters mature.

"I see that my daughter, Winifred, who is thirteen, longs for our intact family that dissolved six years ago," Tilda, forty-two, relates. "And that has made it harder for her with her stepmother, Henrietta. In a strange way, it has nothing to do with Henrietta, and she really does like her, separate from the divorce and all that happened afterward. Maybe if Jose, my ex-husband, and I had been more careful during the divorce and when we each remarried, it would have made it easier on Winnie. When I cheerlead for Henrietta, as a stepmother and for my present husband, Gabe, I am giving a message to Winnie that this is her reality. She has two stepfamilies instead of the conventional nuclear family.

"When Henrietta and I make plans for Winnie or when I talk to Jose about something to do with Winnie and she is aware of our conversations, I think she feels safer. I try to show her I am putting the ugliness of the divorce to rest. I hold my marriage and Jose's and Henrietta's marriage up to Winnie as the future. It might not be what she imagined it would be, but it works."

Influences at Work

In the usual four- to seven-year-period required to regroup after a divorce, accepting a stepmother or stepfather as surrogate parent figure often becomes possible. This is an enriching experience for daughters of divorce. At this point, the relationship between the stepmother and her stepdaughter begins to stand on its own as the past begins to recede and a tangible present, which includes the stepmother, takes shape.

"My intention, from the start," begins Dara, forty-seven, a stepmother of six years, "was to be a good mother to my daughters and a good stepmother to my stepdaughters. Who knew it would be so complicated? I found myself feeling isolated yet I was surrounded by people. I had Cal's kids, a daughter and a son, my girls and our invisible ex-spouses, all in our house on weekends. At first no one listened to me or Cal. In my mind, Audrey, the first wife, had too much influence over her girls for me to ever have any input. I wanted the transition to go smoothly and be comfortable. I didn't think that was too much to ask for.

"One day, about a year ago, Lisa, my younger stepdaughter, called me from her college dorm room and told me she was studying film, which is my speciality. She began to ask me questions about courses and about certain directors and I felt as if I'd had some influence upon her after all. It was quite gratifying. Her mother was aware of her choice of study and she had consulted me. Then, my older stepdaughter called asking for my advice about someone she was dating. She had met his father and stepmother and somehow that gave me more credibility in her eyes. It suddenly seemed that this world of divorce and remarriage had some good possibilities for the future after all."

When stepmothers have no children of their own and try to establish relationships with their stepdaughters, the paths can be more arduous and the rewards seem more elusive. However, in comparison to the mother/stepfather family, the father/stepmother family often has more potential in terms of the daughter of divorce and her stepparent forming a bond. In part it is our societal construct that keeps the stepfather at a distance in the stepfamily and causes him to remain an outsider. Although Ahrons & Wallisch's study found that stepmothers felt even more detached than stepfathers, my interviews contradicted this in that seventy percent of stepmothers with whom I spoke are invested in building some kind of rapport with their stepdaughters and this continues as the stepdaughters mature and establish lives of their own.

As I have noted, my research shows that a daughter's approach to men often is colored by her parents' divorce, her mother's status after the divorce, her father's remarriage and her stepmother's ideals. In time, many stepdaughters accept that there is room in their lives for both their mothers and stepmothers. As the years pass, mothers and stepmothers often come to the same conclusion and this is liberating for all three women. For the daughter there is the sense that she is unburdened as she has reconciled her feelings of antagonism.

Seven Stages of Stepfamily

The heightened awareness of most seasoned mothers, fathers, stepmothers and ultimately the daughters of divorce, only revolutionizes the chances of success. As Patricia L. Papernow explains in outlining the seven stages of becoming a stepfamily, as the daughters mature and begin lives of their own, the stages are recognizable in the experiences of mothers, daughters and stepdaughters.

In her book, *Becoming a Stepfamily: Patterns of Development In Remarried Families*, psychologist Patricia L. Papernow outlines "the stepfamily cycle" and the "normal stages of stepfamily development." Naming seven stages for adults and children of divorce, Dr. Papernow points out that adults and children do not move at the same speed through these seven stages. The stages consist of: fantasy, immersion, awareness, mobilization, action, contact, resolution. While these stages are applicable to every person in a stepfamily, they seem particularly relevant to mothers, stepmothers and the daughters as they blossom into young women who experience love relationships of their own. The final stage, resolution, is testimony to a stepfamily that succeeds. The stepfamily in this stage, can "cherish what is resolved and reliable about stepfamily living," writes Papernow. The stepfamily also recognizes the grief that is inherent in the stepfamily and focus on "unresolved issues." In the ongoing machinations of the stepfamily, the daughter of divorce belongs to both a unit comprised of her father and stepmother, a unit comprised of her mother with or without a stepfather, and she is an entity unto herself: a sum of her experiences as a daughter of divorce. All three women who have achieved the resolution stage are able to deal with the positives and negatives of the triangle.

Peer Marriages

Most daughters of divorce with whom I spoke have witnessed a less than equal relationship between their two parents. As many of these daughters reach adulthood, they are able to evaluate what transpired in their parents' failed marriages and compare them to their fathers' and stepmothers' relationships. If the stepmother and father and/or the mother and stepfather have marriages that exist between two equals, it is a paradigm for the daughters. Seeing these new, successful peer marriages, daughters begin to understand not only what was lacking in their mother's and father's failed marriage but what is possible in marriage.

"I think I would have viewed my mother in a different light if she had not seemed to act the same way toward my stepfather as she had toward my father," remarks Florence, thirty-two. "I kept thinking that she never evolved, never realized how traditional and 'wifey' she was in all her habits and beliefs. I suppose that my stepmother, Sondra, was more of the type of role model I valued. Once Sondra and my dad married, they put together a marriage of equals. Sondra is an author and my father is a scientist. They both worked long hours and loved their work. There was no role playing and no conventional housekeeping in their home. In a way, this was quite healthy for me.

"Because my mother was locked into this more conventional way of looking at marriage, she wanted me to behave more like the perfect daughter. My stepmother did not expect that. I don't know if she didn't have the time or just didn't believe in it, but I liked the way that she and my father worked together. Their marriage gave me a sense that I too could have that kind of respect from a husband and not just hang around the house deferring to him, which was what my mother did."

Once an unequal nuclear family has dissolved, it is the step-family which offers the daughters a chance to see an egalitarian marriage. A father who has responsibility for his daughters might be much more likely to share in the workings of day-to-day family life than a father in a traditional, nuclear family. This expansive view often extends to his new wife's work and personal needs. A step-mother who sees her husband's efforts made on behalf of the step-family will feel respected and be appreciative. If she has been married before and this element was lacking from her first marriage, she is all the more grateful. In a best case scenario, the father and his ex-wife can co-parent better at this stage and this too can become a more equal equation.

"In my first marriage, my husband did not think that my goals or dreams mattered as much as his," Charlene, forty-four, begins. "We were always pleasing him, the girls and I. It seemed there was no other way. When we divorced, I worried that my daughters would not have much self-esteem because I definitely lacked it in the marriage. Both Roberto and I remarried, and somehow we both got it right the second time. My husband is so kind and decent and we are a team. This is not only healthy for each of us, but for the girls, who are now eighteen and fifteen. It amazes me that after all that I went through to be heard in my first marriage, Roberto chose a tough-minded career woman who simply won't cower before him. Carlotta, who is considerably younger than I am, is the opposite of me. I never found this threatening, because I found someone special right after the divorce. I like to believe that my divorce and remarriage have taught my daughters what they can have in life, and that if they are not happy, they can change things. I also think that Carlotta gives them another picture—of someone who demands equality. I never knew how to do that in my first marriage and the second time, I met someone who treated me as an equal and this gave me courage. The message conveyed to the girls is that women are to be treated fairly and that marriage is a shared proposition and even if it doesn't work out that way in the first marriage, at least they see it can happen on the second try."

The concept of peer marriage, one that is egalitarian in every aspect, where the two couples share responsibilities, exemplifies a true partnership. While this did not exist for much of the generation that raised their children in the fifties and sixties, the divorce rate was also lower. Peer marriages are unlike conventional marriages in that the husband is not the sole provider and his wife is not the sole homemaker. Rather, financial and child care responsibilities are shared. Pepper Schwartz, in her essay, "Peer Marriage" notes that when women are working at high-powered jobs, the rate of divorce increases. "In a society in which divorce is prevalent and the economic independence of both spouses is the rule, marital stability is a crucial ingredient of this form of intimacy," writes Schwartz, who also stresses how important the "emotional satisfaction" of both partners is to the success of a marriage today.

"If there is anything that I wanted to convey to my stepdaughters, it was that their father and I were partners in the marriage," begins Marcia, forty-five, a stepmother for six years. "At first my stepdaughters, Shelby and Romy, resisted my overtures to them. They were only eleven and thirteen at the time. I think that they viewed my marriage to their father as negating their mother's marriage to their father. And I understood, because I had a stepmother myself. Without that experience in my past, I would not have known what to do. She and my father had a great life together and that made me know that I could have that with Harry.

"My marriage to Harry is about being equal partners in all that we do. Our decisions are based on both our thoughts and needs. We both have careers that we love and we make joint decisions. I usually defer to my husband when it comes to the girls, but I also feel that after six years of having Shelby and Romy living with us on weekends that I do have some say. In the past year I think that my stepdaughters have begun to appreciate how their father and I interact. They see that we are very close and that the marriage has many layers."

The optimal situation for a stepmother is one in which she has bonded with her stepdaughters and yet her marriage remains a separate entity. Although a stepfamily struggles to maintain an equilibrium and there is competition between family members, a rocky road can be followed by a peaceful coexistence for family members. It is beneficial for the daughters to be exposed to their mother's or stepmother's peer marriage. If a mother and stepmother alike have embarked on their new marriages with an improved self knowledge and sense of what they require in a partner and in marriage, they set the stage for the daughter to follow suit.

Although Nanette's second marriage did not succeed, she believes that her stepdaughter recognized the redeeming qualities of the marriage and the reasons why it ultimately failed. "I'd like to think that my stepdaughter, who was twelve when I married her father and twenty-four when I divorced him, learned something from me," Nanette, fifty-two, muses. "The marriage would have worked if there had been more equality and I suspect that this was the problem in his first marriage as well. I thought, naively, that he had learned from his past, but it wasn't so. All of his promises about a marriage based on two equal partners went down the tubes in a matter of months. I felt humiliated in front of my stepdaughters and disappointed in the marriage. I always believed that my stepdaughters knew how much Troy and I loved each other, but they also saw a repeat of how he had treated their mother. My situation was a bit unusual because to this day I am in touch with Troy's first ex-wife, and I am close with my stepdaughters. We all have the same problem and that's Troy."

Once again, figures from the United States Census Bureau show the rate of divorce for first marriages to be over fifty percent. For second marriages, the figure is over sixty percent. While on average, most first marriages fail after eleven years, second marriages fail after only seven years. Issues involving stepchildren are the primary cause according to the Census; another main reason is finances. I have found in my research that if either the husband or the wife has not grown and learned from the mistakes made in the first failed marriage, they cannot apply any newfound wisdom to the second marriage. Despite any intentions to make the second marriage into a peer marriage, old patterns often prevail. As in Nanette's case, often the mother, daughter and stepmother are aligned when they all see that the father/husband has failed each woman in different ways.

When a daughter realizes that her father treats both her mother and stepmother similarly and that both women are ultimately disappointed, it colors her view of men and, as I found in my interviews, can also create a bond between the women. In these cases, the three women become joined in their flawed vision of the father/husband. If the daughter was not already skeptical of marriage after having endured her parents' divorce, her stepmother's failed marriage to her father sometimes takes her over the top. This is when the negative stance of daughters of divorce comes to the fore. Critics of divorce contend that the lingering deleterious effects remain with daughters for the rest of their lives. This argument is supported by Judith Wallerstein's twenty-five year follow-up study which reveals that only sixty percent of adult children of divorce marry while eighty percent of children from nuclear families marry. On a positive note, I found in many cases when peer marriages exist within stepfamilies, the daughters are better able to evaluate their own needs in relationships and, ultimately, in marriages. The necessity to build a strong foundation has been shown to them.

"I doubt that my stepmother would have tolerated my father if he had treated her the way he treated my mother," begins Carolyn, twenty-eight, whose father has been remarried for six years. "My dad always shows respect to Shirley and he rarely raises his voice. He always yelled at our mother and I think she finally couldn't stand it anymore. My sisters and I wonder what might have happened if he had been this decent to our mother.

"I have come to understand myself better through my father's remarriage and through my mother's, too. Both my father and my mother married better partners the second time around. And both marriages are about equality. I take the best of both their marriages to heart for my own future."

Some mothers/stepmothers told me that they divorced because equality was nonexistent in their marriages and that they remarried because they had found it at last. Thus an egalitarian relationship between their husbands and themselves becomes not only their new reality but a new reality for the daughter of divorce as keen observers.

The Future for Daughters of Divorce
No matter the paths they take, daughters of divorce are forever influenced by their past experiences. "I believe that my parents' divorce

has affected my entire life and every decision I've made," Celeste, forty-four, reveals. "My father left before I was born and he remarried when I was twelve. I never really got to know his wife and I was raised by my mother and stepfather. My mother was so strong while she was single and then she became this perfect wife and stopped working once she married my stepfather. Our lives improved financially, but it was confusing. Then my mother and stepfather had my baby sister. I loved her but that was the end of my relationship with my mother. She became totally wrapped up in her new baby. It was like I didn't exist anymore. Today, my mother and I do not even talk.

"The divorce taught my mother nothing. She made mistakes with us because she did not bother to learn anything—she didn't want to. My mother forgot how hard it had been when my father left her and that we'd been abandoned. She did not encourage me to have a relationship with my father or his wife, and now that I don't have that in my life, I regret it. I refused to make the same mistakes my mother did, so I married a man who is solid as a rock, and we have three daughters. I needed this kind of stability after my mother and my stepmother were like ghosts to me."

Some mature daughters of divorce take hard looks at the choices their mothers or stepmothers have made and evaluate what they can and cannot tolerate in their own lives. Their choices in adulthood, positive and negative, are reflections of their understanding of their parents' divorce and the events that follow these divorces. "As women going into adult relationships, the divorce becomes the model for them," comments Claire Owen, psychologist. "It may be difficult for these women to enter in a healthy relationship with men." For those daughters who are determined to make it work, there is the belief that their adult lives must be departures from their childhoods and pasts. As Claire Owen warns, "Women who refuse to repeat their mother's and stepmother's mistakes might think they know everything. This is not always the case and they might find themselves divorced, even with the best of intentions."

One of the daughters of divorce with whom I spoke, Monica, at thirty-seven, has contemplated divorce for years and it is her experience as a daughter of divorce that has kept her in a less-than-happy marriage. "I know how I suffered and how my little sisters suffered," recalls Monica. "I do not want to do to my daughters, who are eight and eleven, what my mother did to us. My mother constantly made bad decisions that pushed her children further away from her. I kept waiting for her to be the good mother, but she couldn't be. No only did she have a drug addiction, but the men she married had the same problem. My sisters and I were starved for a mother throughout our whole childhoods. Though my father married a wonderful woman who gave us the only stability we had in our lives, she was my step-mother, not my mother.

"My husband and daughters are the only real safety net I have. Not only would I never leave because my mother left us, but I could never do that to my girls. I have decided on my future based on my past. Whatever I do, I encourage my girls to be brave and fearless, something I could not pull off. My mother wasn't strong and inde-pendent but serially dependent. Her legacy is my fear."

If her mother has disappointed her tremendously and repeat-edly, the daughter of divorce is greatly affected. If a mother abandons her daughters by divorce and subsequent remarriages, the daughter can have serious abandonment issues. Author Joan Borysenko writes in her book, *A Woman's Book of Life*, that "the potential for abandon-ment, which to our paleomammalian brain is equivalent to death, mobilizes a potent fear response." When the daughter operates out of fear based on an unhappy history with her mother, she cannot actual-ize her own life nor set the example for her daughter. Joan Borysenko writes of a mother's obligation to her daughter: "...perhaps the great-est danger overall is the failure to nurture courage and initiative in our daughters."

The divorce rate in the United States and other places indicates that the concept of remaining in a poor marriage for the "sake of the children" is no longer a first choice for many people. Stepfamilies offer daughters hope, because they offer second chances. As Carol, a twenty-eight-year-old daughter, representative of eighty percent of my pool of daughter interviewees, explained, "I have seen what both my mother and stepmother have done and I don't intend to make their mistakes. I have learned from their mistakes and I have learned from their suc-cesses. I plan to be married once and I will not put my daughters through a divorce and a second marriage. I will be more careful and I will know who I am when I marry. Still, I do respect my mother and stepmother and I admire that they have tried again."

The complexities of remarriage for mothers, stepmothers and daughters are many. Yet it is striking to note that the majority of daughters of divorce, like their mothers and stepmothers, continue to believe in the institution of marriage. In his 1996 study, "Values, Attitudes and the State of American Marriage," Norval Glenn found that seventy-eight percent of high school students aspired to a good marriage and family. Suzanna, one daughter of divorce I interviewed, is among those who value marriage, yet is realistic in her view of the institution.

"I am engaged to be married and it feels very right, but I also know that if this fails, and I have to, I will marry again," remarks Suzanna, twenty-six, who became a stepdaughter at the age of eleven. "My dream is to marry just once and I want Derek, my fiancé, to be everything to me—best friend and confidante, someone I trust, and someone who is my equal and will not expect me to do more and to be less. If Derek and I grow apart, if he and I do not always have the same goals, I have the option of divorce. It isn't my first choice, but I would not wait years, like my mother did. She not only wasted precious years of her life, but she found a better life after the divorce—so she stayed trapped without any real reason. I respect that she finally left, even though it was hard for me.

"I'm very lucky that my father chose such a strong woman for his second wife. I not only love Cordelia, but I see that she and my mother fill in different parts of my life. I feel blessed to have them both and to know that I can count on each one. I know that they want similar things in their lives and that they had to leave their first husbands to get them. Their present marriages show me what qualities to look for in my own marriage. In the end, I recognize that there is care and love for me in both stepfamilies."

Though most daughters are closer to the mothers, the strong female identification which the stepdaughter can develop with her stepmother has a merit all its own. Ultimately most women, whether mothers, daughters or stepmothers, are drawn to the nurturing of life and in this common goal, they will realize the value in having each other. The hope here, as seen in the myriad of true life experiences of these women in all three roles with whom I spoke, is that their common bond will overcome the historical, societal and cultural biases that keep them apart and pits the three members of the new triangle against each other. It is the new family construct (different from its nuclear antecedent but still protective and nurturing) that offers the promise of a future in which new and lasting bonds can be formed by the three women of the triangle: mother, daughter and stepmother.

Afterword

It has been eight years since I first began my research on relationships of mothers, stepmothers and daughters who because of divorce and remarriage find themselves in a triangle. At the time I began I was seeking my own divorce and entering an unknown and frightening world. Although I had read many books on divorce and children, it was more difficult to acquire information on the women who were impacted by divorce and remarriage. I had a sense, even before I began my own journey, that divorce, like most parts of life, is delineated by gender and that a woman's experience would be different from a man's. After extensive research, this intuition proved right: divorce is not the same for women. And this is especially true for daughters of divorce who are impacted in different ways than sons. I remember looking into my daughters' eyes and seeing their pain. My failure at marriage and the complexity of the world we were about to enter was reflected in their actions and their feelings. I remember wondering how it would be if their father remarried and what their place in his new family would be. I understood how profound it would be for all of us, for every female who has been thrown into the turbulent waters of divorce. As I journeyed on, I found the threesome of mother, daughter and stepmother is one where each of us carry our own wounds and our own secrets. Each of us is in search of a perfect world through imperfect actions.

The intricacies of divorce are significant as exhibited in this book and the repercussions in lives of mothers, stepmothers and especially daughters can be devastating and enduring. If the divorced parents are

mutually respectful to each other and avoid allowing in ugly histories
and bitterness, the daughters are relieved and less encumbered. If the
battles of the past are ongoing and manifest themselves in terms of
money and power plays, the daughters suffer. My interviews with hundreds of daughters indicate that, even in the best of circumstances,
daughters are torn over their parents' break up—this is the nature of
divorce for daughters. Although it is common sense on parents' parts to
avoid conflict, parents often engage in destructive scenarios nonetheless,
further harming daughters who are already quite vulnerable. Long
before the stepmother comes into their lives, daughters struggle to
remain loyal to both parents, or in some cases, to the parent who did not
initiate the divorce but is instead the injured party. When a stepmother
enters the scene, the waters are often already turbulent.

Thus each female in the triangle has her own issues to content
with and her own needs and requirements. Patricia Papernow's concept
of the seven stages of becoming a stepfamily shows us that, during
these imperative stages, each member struggles to get to a healthy place
and in time, a stepfamily establishes itself and creates its own set of
standards and values. Of course the grieving that begins at the outbreak
of a divorce is also a necessary step to the eventual health and new life
which awaits all three females of divorce.

The Daughters' Paths

The scars are there and the myth that the parents were an ideal couple
dies hard for the daughters. As readers of this book and as survivors of
divorce, we are well aware of how far-reaching the consequences are.
The daughters' identification with her mother and the gender bonds that
bind them might be shaken and questioned, depending upon the circumstances of the divorce. While most research indicates that daughters
in single-sex homes fare better with their mothers, they are not exempt
from the stresses and stigma of divorce, which include emotional, financial and physical repercussions. As Andrew Cherlin and his colleagues
found, girls fare more poorly than boys due to their parents' divorce,
academically and behaviorally. Navigating a new world in which her
mother and father live in separate homes and may be carrying leftover
anger for each is the next phase the daughter must face. The arrival of
the stepmother, as we have seen, further changes the daughter's world.
Whatever drama plays out, whether it is a daughter who adores her

stepmother, a mother who encourages her daughter to reject her step-mother or a father who cannot handle his new wife and his daughter at the same time, it is apparent that the three women have a heightened awareness of each other. For the daughters of divorce, their mothers and stepmothers, there is an ongoing sense of the other's existence and influ-ence. Some daughters carry the legacy of their parents' marriage and divorce into their adult relationships with men—some feel that they can never trust men because of their father's actions, others become promis-cuous and avoid stable, long-term relationships with men. Then there are those daughters who get along with their fathers and understand why her parent's divorce was necessary. This kind of acceptance is pos-itive and these daughters not only have higher self-esteem but usually do better in their adult relationships with men. I found there are daugh-ters who use divorce as a learning device and resolve to do better, to not repeat their parents' mistakes. There are others who decide that they are allowed to make their own mistakes and that second chances do exist, as evidenced in their parents' remarriages. In these heartfelt tales shared by daughters, I recognize ambivalence, strength of character and forti-tude to get their lives right. Finally, and most importantly, I have talked to daughters of divorce who realize the benefit of having two mothers.

Mothers' Choices

For mothers, there are opportunities to have second chances and to put the past to rest. They have the opportunity to grow personally and to apply self knowledge to new marriages, new careers or single life that represents freedom and choice. Their personal odysseys require that they welcome the stepmothers and allow the stepmothers and the daughters to establish their own relationships. Yet mothers' reactions to stepmothers are often limited by where they are in their own lives. Mothers who resist stepmothers' involvement might also resist their own enlightenment. The residual anger from divorces may influence mothers to a great degree. They often feel rejected and some may not have healed from the rejection. In cases where stepmothers were the fathers' lovers before the divorce, mothers are typically more hostile and unwilling to interact with the stepmothers. Unfortunately, daughters see this and, since they often take cues from their mothers on how to treat stepmothers, in these cases daughters will likely reject any overtures from the stepmothers. Though it's difficult to move past hurt, anger and bitterness for some mothers, the ideal scenario is one in which the mother puts aside her own emotions and not only works with the step-mother to co-parent the daughter, but also encourages her daughter to embrace the stepmother and welcome her into the daughter's life.

The Stepmother's Place

Stepmothers' roles often begin after a succession of negative events. In many cases, they too are divorced mothers with daughters of their own. In cases where stepmothers do not have their own children, they might be more motivated to build relationships with their stepdaughters so it is easier to unite future half siblings. In any stepmother situation, her efforts may be thwarted by the constant mantra of stepdaughters: "You are not my mother." There are those stepmothers who want the mar-riage and not the stepdaughters, yet some sort of connection between these stepmothers and their stepdaughters exists anyway. In time the reality of the situation sets in and an attachment may form despite resis-tance from either stepmothers or stepdaughters, or from both.

Even after a tenuous beginning, enough good may generate allowing stepmothers and mothers to get along and stepmothers and stepdaughters to bond. As Dr. Margorie Engel, President and CEO of the Stepfamily Association of America, remarks, "Stepfamilies don't have a [family] tree: they have a forest—and that is bound to effect us. Fortunately for children and adults, most exes eventually realize that animosity is destructive and prevents them from moving on to healthy relationships in their lives. The reality is that years ago, parents had a lot of children. Today children have a lot of parents." It is imperative that everyone get along, and for the stepmothers who came forward to share their feelings with me, there is the awareness of the consequences of a successful triumvirate of women of divorce. A stepmother who respects the bonds between her stepdaughter and her mother, and between her stepdaughter and her father, and appreciates a civility between her husband and his ex-wife, ensures a successful future after divorce and a positive stepfamily life.

The Stepfamily

The great balancing act required to put and keep a stepfamily on the right path cannot be underestimated. The number of ongoing family crises which exists in the stepfamily is monumental. Despite the amount of discord that occurs in a stepfamily, few adults, let alone daughters, are prepared for this, nor are they informed. As Patricia Papernow explains in *Becoming a Stepfamily*, "For stepparents, the process of becoming a parent takes place in front of and in supposed cooperation with [the biological] parent, [who has] a more direct claim on the title, a more intense and often more cooperative relationship with the child." If only mothers and stepmothers could be told that their issues are not unusual but are part and parcel of the evolution of divorce and remarriage—then their isolation would be lessened and the promise of a better future would appear more likely.

Out of the acceptance of mothers and stepmothers, successful triangles between mothers, stepmothers and daughters emerge. My belief, which is substantiated by the personal experiences of many of these three females with whom I spoke, is that the best of all worlds is possible for them—if they shed their preconceived notions, work as a team and dispel the myth of the disadvantaged, divorced, single mother, the damaged daughter of divorce, and the wicked stepmother. Granted, the terrain is rough, the challenges are there, but for mothers, daughters and stepmothers who band together to face these obstacles, to create new lives and to work together for the greater good, success can be theirs.

The Future

Many of these women attest, as living proof, to the prospering of such relationships. The late Emily Vischer, divorce expert, presented the ideal stepfamily situation in which the mother, the father, the stepmother, the stepfather, the children from former marriages and the new children born into the second marriages share happily in the "trust between two houses." For daughters of divorce, there is the opportunity for double love, double protection and double mothering with two homes to live in. Yet developing a "trust between two houses" is not an easy feat and requires communication between mother and stepmother, father and mother.

Since so little research has been conducted on daughters of divorce and their interactions with both their mothers and stepmothers, the conflicting or confluent aspects of their interwoven lives has been little known until now. This book provides a definitive exploration, based on the voices of all three women. By understanding who these women are, their dreams and their hopes, we can be guided in the complicted universe of divorce and mothering.

As I complete this project, the Sunday *New York Times* has arrived at my door. The lead article in the Style section by Alex Kuczynski, "Guess Who's Coming to Dinner Now?" validates the extended, blended family of today and tomorrow. "Around the holiday table," writes Kuczynski, "is a new tolerance for exes: Dad and wife number two sit down with Mom and her new beau." According to Kuczynski, who notes there are no statistics on divorced families spending time with their exes, "experts who study marriage and advise couples note that stepfamilies where ex-spouses are on good terms to the point that they celebrate holidays together are becoming more frequent." Photographs of mothers, daughters, stepmothers and fathers accompany the article, validating the possibility of daughters of divorce finding love and support in their new extended family structures.

If only the mother, daughter and stepmother enter the arena slowly, with time, constant efforts at open communication, appreciation and maturity, then mothers, daughters and stepmothers would be able to relate and bond. What the daughters require is a sense that they are anchored, that their families, with mothers and stepmothers involved, provide them with a basic core of protection and the qualities to successfully interact with others.

I project a scene: that my daughters will become engaged one day in the not so distant future. For each occasion, their stepmother and I shall sit down to tea to plan the wedding together. The notion of the mother, daughter and stepmother as an impossible trio will be dissolved. She and I will be adult, communicative and pragmatic. The fact that she is married to my ex-husband will be irrelevant. Our daughters' best interests will be at the heart of each meeting. We will both share not only the happiness of the day but the satisfaction of our joint cooperation in raising strong, independent women who are capable of love and will make effective contributions to the complex world in which we all live.

References

Abelsohn, David and Graham S. Saayman. "Adolescent Adjustment to Parental Divorce." *Family Process* 30, no. 2 (June 1991): 177-192.

Ahrons and Wallisch. "Parenting in the Binuclear Family: Relationships Between Biological and Stepparents." In *Remarriage and Stepparenting: Current Research and Theory*, edited by Kay Pasley and Marilyn Ihinger-Tallman. New York: Guilford Press, 1987.

Allison and Furstenberg. "How Marital Dissolution Affects Children, Variations by Age and Sex." *Developmental Psychology* 25, no. 4 (1989): 540-549.

Amato, Paul. "Children's Adjustment to Divorce Theories, Hypothesis and Empirical Support." *Journal of Marriage and the Family* 55, no. 1 (February 1991): 23-28.

Amato, Paul and Alan Booth. "The Consequences of Divorce for Attitudes Toward Divorce & Gender Roles." *American Psychologist* 44, no. 2 (February 1989): 303-312.

Amato, Paul and Bruce Keith. "Parental Divorce and Adult Well-Being: A Meta-Analysis." *Journal of Marriage and the Family* 55 (1991): 23-28.

Ashton-Jones, Olson and Perry, eds. *The Gender Reader*. Needham Heights, MA: Allyn and Bacon, 2000.

Barash, Susan Shapiro. *A Passion for More: Wives Reveal the Affairs that Make or Break their Marriages*. Berkeley, CA: Berkeley Hills Books, 2001.

Barash, Susan Shapiro. *Mothers-in-Law and Daughters-In-Law: Love, Hate, Rivalry and Reconciliation*. Far Hills, NJ: New Horizon Press, 2001.

Barash, Susan Shapiro. *Second Wives: The Pitfalls and Rewards of Marrying Widowers and Divorced Men*. Far Hills, NJ: New Horizon Press, 2000.

Barash, Susan Shapiro. *Sisters: Devoted or Divided*. Bridgewater, NJ: Replica Books, 2001.

Berry, Dawn Bradley. *The Divorce Recovery Sourcebook*. Los Angeles, CA: Lowell House, 1998.

Bernstein, Anne C. "Women in Stepfamilies: The Fairy Godmother, the Wicked Witch, and Cinderella Reconstructed." In *Family in Transition*, edited by Skolnick and Skolnick. Boston: Allyn and Bacon, 2001.

Bourduin and Henggeller. "Post-divorce Mother-Son Relations of Delinquent and Well-adjusted Adolescents." *Journal of Applied Psychology* 8 (1987): 273-288.

Borysenko, Joan. *A Woman's Book of Life: the Biology, Psychology and Spirituality of the Feminine Life Cycle*. New York: Berkeley Publishing Group, 1996.

Bray and Hetherington. "Families in Transition: Introduction and Overview." *Journal of Family Psychology* 7, no. 1 (1993): 3-8.

Brinig, Margaret and Douglas Allen. "These Boots Were Made For Walking: Why Most Divorce Filers Are Women." *American Journal of Law and Economics* 2, no. 1 (2000): 126-169.

Buchannan, Maccoby and Bornbusch. "Caught Between Parents: Adolescents Experience in Divided Homes." *Child Development* 62 (1991): 1008-1029.

Bumpass, Martin and Sweet. "The Impact of Family Background and Early Marital Factors on Marital Disruption." *Journal of Family Issues* 12, no. 1 (1989): 22-42.

Bumpass, Larry. "The Changing Character of Stepfamilies: Complications of Cohabitation and Non-marital Childbearing." *Demography* 32 (1995): 425-436.

Burns, Cherie. *Stepmotherhood: How to Survive Without Feeling Frustrated*. New York: Times Books, 1985

Cherlin, Andrew, et al. *Science* 252, no. 5011 (June 7 1991): 86-89.

Chopin, Kate. *The Awakening*. New York: Avon Books, 1994.

Chodorow, Nancy. "Family Structure and Feminine Personality." In *Women, Culture and Society*, edited by Rosalda and Lamphere. Palo Alto, CA: Stanford University Press, 1974.

Clapp, Genevieve. *Divorce and New Beginnings*. New York: John Wiley & Sons, 1992.

Clay, Carolyn. "From a Child of Tradition, a New Approach to Ibsen," *New York Times*, 30 September 2001.

Compton, Karen. "I Never Thought I'd be a Stepmother." *Self* (December 2000).

Coontz, Stephanie. "Divorcing Reality." *Children's Advocate News Magazine* (Jan/Feb 1998).

Crawford, Mary and Rhoda Unger. *Women and Gender a Feminist Psychology*, 3rd Edition. New York, McGraw-Hill: 2000.

Crittenden, Ann. *The Price of Motherhood*. New York: Henry Holt & Company, 2001.

Cyr, Barbara. "Divorce and Its Effects on Children." Internet, http://www.umm.maine.edu/BSED/students/BarbaraCyr/bc310.html, 2001.

Day, Randal, et. al. "Social Fatherhood and Paternal Involvement: Conceptual, Data and Policymaking Issues." In *Nurturing Fatherhood: Improving Data and Research on Male Fertility, Family Formation and Fatherhood*. Federal Interagency Forum on Child and Family Statistics, 1998.

Drucker, Pam. "The One Thing I Got From My Mother." *Marie Claire* (September 2001).

Duncan and Hoffman. "A Reconsideration of the Economic Consequences of Marital Dissolution" *Demography* 22 (1991): 485.

Edelman, Hope. *Motherless Daughters*. New York: Addison-Wesley Publishing Co., 1994.

Ellison, Sheila. "My Life Didn't End After Divorce." *O, The Oprah Magazine* (July 2000).

Erikson, Erik. *Childhood and Society*. New York: W.W. Norton, 1993.

Fassell, Diane. *Growing Up Divorced: A Road to Healing for Adult Children of Divorced Parents*. Newbury Park, CA: Haynes Publications, 1993.

Fine, McHenry, Donnell and Voydanoof. "Perceived Adjustments of Parents and Children: Variations by Family Structure, Race, and Gender." *Journal of Marriage and the Family* 54 (1992): 118-127.

Fingerman, Karen. "Aging Mothers and their Daughters: A Study of Mixed Emotions." *Focus on Women* (January 2001).

Fisher, Helen. *Anatomy of Love: A Natural History of Mating, Marriage, and Why We Stray*. New York: Fawcett Books, 1995.

Friday, Nancy. *My Mother My Self: The Daughter's Search for Identity*. New York: Delacorte, 1977.

Furstenberg, F. "Childcare After Divorce and Remarriage" In *Impact of Divorce, Single-Parenting on Children*. Edited by Hetherington and Arasteh. Hillsdale, NJ: Erbaum Publishers, 1988.

Furstenberg, Nord, Peterson and Zill. "The Life Course of Children of Divorce: Marital Disruption and Parental Contact, *American Sociological Review*, 48 (1983) 656-668.

Furstenberg, Furstenberg and Spanier. *Recycling the Family: Remarriage After Divorce*. Beverly Hills, CA: Sage Publications, 1984.

Gardner, Richard. *The Parents' Book about Divorce*. New York: Doubleday, 1992.

Gaskell, Elizabeth and Pam Morris. *Wives and Daughters*. New York: Penguin USA, 2001.

Gerhardt, Pam. "When Parents Remarry Kids May Need Time to Feel at Home in the New Family." *Washington Post*, 23 February 2000.

Gerhardt, Pam. "Remarried...with Children." *Washington Post*, 7 December 1999

Gilligan, Carol. *In a Different Voice*. Cambridge, MA: Harvard University Press, 1982.

Gilman, Charlotte Perkins. *Women and Economics: A Study of the Economic Relations Between Men and Women as a Factor in Social Evolution*. Los Angeles: University of California Press, 1988.

Glenn, Norval D. "Values, Attitudes and the State of American Marriage" In *Promises to Keep: The Decline and Renewal of Marriage in America*. Edited by Popenoe, Elshtain and Blankenhorn. Lanham, MD: Rowman and Littlefield, 1996.

Goldberg, Herb. "In Harness: The Male Condition." In *The Norton Reader*, 9th Edition. Edited by Peterson, Brereton and Hartman. New York: Norton, 1996.

Grimm Brothers. *Grimm's Fairy Tales*. Commentary by Joseph Campbell. New York: Random House, 1992.

Grimm, Jacob. Editor. *Snow White*. Boston, MA: Little Brown, 2000.

Hackstaff, Karla B. "Divorce Culture: A Quest for Relational Equality." In *Marriage, Family in Transition*, edited by Skolnick and Skolnick. Boston: Allyn and Bacon, 2001.

Hales, Dianne. *Just Like a Woman: How Gender Science Is Redefining What Makes Us Female*. New York: Bantam Books, 1993.

Harrison, Kathryn, "Pity the Poor Stepmom." *New York Times*, 25 August 2000.

Heilbrun, Carolyn G. *Reinventing Womanhood*. New York: W.W. Norton, 1979.

Hetherington, E. Mavis. "Marital Transitions: A Child's Perspective." *American Psychologist* 44, no. 2 (1989): 303-312.

Hetherington, E. Mavis, et al. "An Overview of the Virginia Longitudinal Study of Divorce and Remarraige with a Focus on Early Adolescence." *Journal of Family Psychology* 7, no. 2 (1993): 39-56.

Hetherington, E. Mavis and W.G. Clingempeel. "Coping with Marital Transitions: A Family Systems Perspective." *Monographs of the Society for Research in Child Development* (1992).

Hetherington, Cox and Cox. "Long-term Effects of Divorce and Remarriage on the Adjustment of Children." *Journal of American Academy of Psychiatry* 24 (1985): 518-530.

Hetherington, Cox and Cox. "Effects of Divorce on Parents and Children." *Non-Traditional Families*. Hillsdale, NJ: Erlbaum, 1982.

Hetherington, Stanley-Hagan and Anderson. "Marital Transitions: A Child's Perspective." *American Psychologist* 44, no. 2 (February 1989) 303-312.

Hetherington, Law and O'Connor. "Divorce Challenges, Changes and New Chances." In *Normal Family Processes*, edited by Froma Walsh. New York: Guilford Press, 1993.

Hetherington, E. Mavis, and Josephine Arasteh, Eds. *Impact of Divorce, Single Parenting and Stepparenting on Children*. Hillside, NJ: Erlbaum Publishers, 1988.

Hite, Shere. *The Hite Report on the Family*. New York: Grove Press, 1994.

Hite, Shere. *Women and Love: A Cultural Revolution*. New York: Alfred Knopf, 1987.

Hrdy, Sarah Blaffer. *Mother Nature: Maternal Instincts and How They Shape the Human Species*. New York: Ballantine Books, 1999.

Hughes, Robert, Jr. "The Effect of Divorce on Children." Internet, http://www.hec.osu.edu/famlife/divorce/childins/effects.htm, 1996.

Hughes, Robert J. "Demographics of Divorce." Internet, http://www.hec.osu.edu/famlife/divorce/childins/demo.htm, 1996.

Johnson, Miriam M. *Strong Mothers, Weak Wives*. Los Angeles: University of California Press, 1988.

Kelly, J. B. "Long Term Adjustment in Children of Divorce." *Journal of Family Psychology* 2, no. 10 (1988): 19.

Kimmel, Michael. *Manhood in America: A Cultural History*. New York: Free Press, 1996.

Klein, Melanie. *Love, Hate and Reparation*. New York: W.W. Norton, 1964.

Kleinman, Gerald L. and Myrna M. Weissman. "Depressions Among Women." In *The Mental Health of Women*. London: Academic Press, Ltd. 1980.

Kuczynski, Alex. "Guess Who's Coming To Dinner Now?" *New York Times*, 23 December 2001.

LaManna, Mary A. and Agnes Riedmann. *Marriages and Families*. Belmont, CA: Wadsworth Publishing Co, 1999.

Lemonick, Michael D. "Teens Before Their Time." *Time* (October 30, 2000).

Levin, Irene and Marvin B. Sussman, Eds. *Stepfamilies: History, Research and Policy*. New York: Haworth Press, 1997.

Maccoby, Buchannan, Mnookin and Dornbusch. "Post-Divorce Roles of Mothers and Fathers in the Lives of Their Children," *Journal of Family Psychology* 7, no. 1 (June 1993): 24-38.

Mason, Mary Ann. "The Modern American Stepfamily: Problems and Possibilities." In *All Our Families: New Policies for a New Century*, edited by Mason, Skolnick and Sugarman. New York: Oxford University Press, 1998.

Moseley, Douglas and Naomi. *Making Your Second Marriage a First Class Success*. Rocklin, CA: Prima Publishing, 1998.

Norwood, Perdita Kirkness with Teri Wingender. *The Enlightened Stepmother*. New York: Avon Books, 1999.

Papernow, Patricia. *Becoming a Stepfamily: Patterns of Development in Remarried Families*, Gestalt Institute of Cleveland Book Series. Hillsdale, NY: Analytic Press, 1998.

Paterson, Wendy A. *Unbroken Homes*. New York: Haworth Press, 2001.

Poponoe, David. "Scholars Should Worry about the Disintegration of the American Family." *Constellations*. (1995): 206.

Poponoe, David. *Life Without Father: Compelling New Evidence that Fatherhood and Marriage are Indispensible for the Good of Children and Society*. Cambridge, MA: Harvard University Press, 1999.

Porter and O'Leary. "Marital Discord and Childhood Behavior Problems." *Journal of Abnormal Psychology* 8 (1980): 387-295.

Price, Sharon and Patrick McKenry. *Divorce*, Family Studies Text Series, Volume 9. Beverly Hills, CA: Sage Publications, 1988.

Roberts, Cokie. *We Are Our Mother's Daughters*. New York: William Morrow, 1998.

Russo, N.F. "Overview: Sex Roles, Fertility and the Mother Mandate." *Psychology of Women Quarterly* 4 (1979): 7-15.

Sales, Nancy Jo. "Ben and Dara are in Love." *Vanity Fair* (September 2001).

Santock, John and Karen A. Sitterle. "Parent-Child Relationships in Stepmother Families." In *Remarriage and Stepparenting: Current Research and Theory*, edited by Kay Pasley and Marilyn Ihinger-Tallman. New York: Guilford Press, 1987.

Schwartz, Pepper. "Peer Marriage." *The Responsive Community* 8, no. 3 (Summer 1998).

Seltzer, Judith A. "Relationships Between Fathers and Children Who Live Apart." *Journal of Marriage and the Family* 53 (1991): 79-102.

Simon, Ann W. *Stepchild in the Family: A View of Children in Remarriage*. New York: The Odyssey Press, 1964.

Simpson, Mona. *Anywhere But Here*. New York: Vintage Books, 1988.

Stahl, Stephanie. *The Love They Lost: Living with the Legacy of Our Parents' Divorce*. New York: Dell Publishing, 2000.

Stepfamily Association of America Newsletter. New York (Spring 2000).

Steinem, Gloria. "Sisterhood." In *The Gender Reader*, edited by Ashton-Jones, Olson and Perry. Boston: Allyn and Bacon, 2000.

Swigart, Jane. *The Myth of the Bad Mother*. New York: Doubleday, 1991.

Tavris, Carol. *The Mismeasure of Women*. New York: Touchstone Books, 1992.

Teyber, Edward. Helping Children Cope with Divorce. New York: John Wiley & Sons, 2001.

Thoele, Sue Patton. *The Courage to be a Stepmom*. Wildcat Canyon Press, Berkeley, CA. 1999.

Tierney, John. "A New Look at Realities of Divorce." *New York Times*, 25 August 2000.

Tolstoy, Leo. *Anna Karenina*. New York: Modern Library, 2000.

Trollope, Joanna. *Other People's Children*. New York: Berkeley Books, 1999.

Twaite, James, Daniel Silitisky and Anya K. Luchow. *Children of Divorce: Adjustment, Parental Conflict, Custody, Remarriage and Recommendations for Clinicians*. North Bergen, NJ: Jason Aronson, 1998.

Vischer, Emily. "Love Under Siege." Speech presented at the Stepfamily Association of America Conference, New Orleans (February 2001).

Waite, Linda and Maggie Gallagher. *The Case for Marriage*. New York: Broadway Books, 2001.

Wallenstein, Judith S., Kelly, Joan B. *California Children of Divorced Study*.

Wallerstein, Blakeslee and Lewis. *The Unexpected Legacy of Divorce: A 25 Year Landmark Study*. New York: Hyperion, 2001.

Wallerstein, Judith S. and Sandra Blakeslee. *Second Chances: Women and Children a Decade After Divorce*, New York: Ticknor & Fields, 1989.

Walsh, Froma, editor. *Normal Family Processes*. New York: Guilford Press, 1993.

Walters, Marianne. "Single parent, Female-Headed Households." In *The Invisible Web: Gender Patterns in Family Relationships*, edited by Walters, Carter, Papp and Silverstein. New York: Guilford Press, 1988

Weitzman, Lenore. *The Divorce Revolution: Unexpected Social and Economic Consequences for Women and Children in America*. New York: The Free Press, 1985.

Zaslow, M. J. "Sex Differences in Children's Response to Parental Divorce: Research and Methodology and Post Divorce Family Forms." *American Journal of Orthopsychiatry* 58, no. 3 (1994): 355-378.

Zill, Morrison and Coiro. "Long Term Effects of Parental Divorce on Parent-Child Relationships." *Journal of Family Psychology* 7, no. 1 (1993): 91-103.